Essential
Bulgaria

by

DAVID ASH

David Ash has toured Bulgaria extensively on visits since 1962, when he was one of the first Western travel writers to cover the country's emergent tourism.

Following 13 years as travel editor of the Daily Express, he has written freelance for a variety of national publications, including Country Life and the Daily Telegraph.

D1428550

AA

Produced by the Publishing Division of
The Automobile Association

Written by David Ash
Peace and Quiet section by Paul
Sterry
Consultant: Frank Dawes

Edited, designed and produced by
the Publishing Division of The
Automobile Association. Maps ©
The Automobile Association 1990.

Distributed in the United Kingdom
by the Publishing Division of The
Automobile Association, Fanum
House, Basingstoke, Hampshire,
RG21 2EA

The contents of this publication are
believed correct at the time of
printing. Nevertheless, the
publishers cannot accept
responsibility for errors or
omissions, nor for changes in details
given.

© The Automobile Association 1990

First published 1990
Reprinted 1990

A CIP catalogue record for this book
is available from the British Library.

ISBN 0 86145 867 2

Published by The Automobile
Association

Typesetting: Microset Graphics Ltd,
Basingstoke
Colour separation: L C Repro,
Aldermaston
Printing: Printers S.R.L., Trento, Italy

Front cover picture: Shipka Pass

This book employs a
simple rating system to
help choose which
places to visit:

◆◆◆   do not miss

◆◆   see if you can

◆   worth seeing if
      you have time

Near Cape Kaliakra,
on the Black Sea coast

INTRODUCTION

Bulgaria is still largely one of Europe's best-kept touristic secrets, despite its claim to be its oldest nation state. Just north of Greece and Turkey, east of Yugoslavia and south of Romania, it contains a great variety of attractions in addition to the sunny Black Sea beaches and the ski resorts best known to holiday-makers.

About four-fifths the size of England, but with a population of only nine millions, scenically it boasts several mountain ranges for wintersports and summer recreation, fertile plains, the Valley of Roses, the Danube and lesser rivers, ancient cities and hill villages, monasteries and churches with painted icons, mosques, Roman and Thracian antiquities, modern and long-established health spa resorts, the parks and metropolitan features of Sofia, and much more.

These have virtually all been open to foreign visitors for years. But *Preustroistvo*, Bulgaria's *Perestroika*, may more actively encourage a greater diversity and ease of travel arrangements.

Since 1957, Bulgaria has planned mass tourism amenities more whole-heartedly − more professionally, some might say − than have most other Soviet bloc countries.

Achievements

Being the satellite which traditionally has the closest links with the Russians (through language and culture, and the Russians' liberation of Bulgaria from 500 years of Ottoman domination), it is thought to have had a freer hand to 'do its own thing' in tourism − and with remarkable achievements for a nation whose troubled history had reduced it to little more than a backward peasant economy not many years ago.

Bulgaria's location in For inclusive tours or individually arranged
southeast Europe holidays, the Black Sea's large or small resorts − with reliable sun from April through October,

clean golden-sand beaches and safe bathing —
variously cater for families with children, the
youth market, the over-55s, those seeking extra
comforts or reasonable luxury in hotels,
self-catering villa clients, guests in village
rooms, or 'basic' campers.

Holiday atmosphere is boisterous, especially in
ski resorts where, incidentally, instructors
speak *and* understand English well after
intensive courses in more than one language.
There is plenty of varied nightlife including
discos and folk-style restaurants, but not the
'wild' scene of some Mediterranean areas.

The Bulgarian coast is 235 miles (378km) long,
with vast sand beaches, large bays and rocky
shores. The sea is clean, without tides,
predatory fish or dangerous animals. The sand
bottom slopes gently, making it suitable for
small children.

Together with the requirements of many tour
operators, Bulgaria's economic costings — with
its 80 per cent currency bonus and flexible
meal-vouchers system (see Tight Budget, page
109) — have perhaps led to a superficial and
unfair view of Bulgaria as just another
cheap-and-cheerful sun/sand/sea destination for
the packaged masses (though not, so far,
drunken and rowdy elements).

Culture and Heritage

Culturally, Bulgaria has an importance
disproportionate to its size, and especially in
music and ballet. Where else can a *world-class*
opera performance be attended at rock bottom
prices? Its choirs are among the very best
anywhere, and Sofia's May/June Music Weeks
attract the cream of international orchestras and
soloists.

Musicality has been strong from earliest times.
The southern Rhodope mountains gave rise to
the legends of Orpheus, his lute and his poems.
And today a haunting song from that region
(see Shiroka Luka, pages 63-64) is travelling
beyond our planet aboard *Voyager*.

'Peasant' traditions, kept very much alive and
kicking in regional varieties, give package
tourists folklore performances that can be more
vividly authentic than commercially contrived
efforts elsewhere. And there are unique

Bulgaria's turbulent history is frequently commemorated by monuments. Above, near Aitos

displays by troupes of fire-walkers.
It may surprise some to learn how much Bulgarians venerate their monasteries — there are at least 120 — and churches. Whether or not they are believers, they acknowledge the role of the Christian religion in the early founding of their State and its culture, and its often-active support in campaigns against oppression by (for instance) Ottoman occupiers. Many religious buildings, their art treasures and devotional symbols, are carefully preserved.

Wining and Dining
Bulgaria's fresh salads and fruits are memorable, as are the stews with multiple vegetables and herbs, slowly casseroled in earthenware dishes. Its name is virtually synonymous with ewesmilk yoghurt that is the best in the world. Its wines now enjoy an international reputation for quality and value. Anyone who has regarded them as outlandish novelties did not know, presumably, that the Thracians were enjoying local wine hereabouts 2,400 years ago and more — as evidenced in the amazingly preserved murals of a tomb near Kazanluk.

People and Politics
Socially, most Bulgarians have a friendly disposition — it seems even jollier and more

ebullient as one travels southwards — and they are now even less likely to be inhibited about talking to foreign visitors since *Preustroistvo*. Whether all their police are likely to be smilingly indulgent is another matter, though they are helpful as far as language permits. They can certainly keep Good Order: hooliganism and crime are rarely seen. Cars at border points may be searched for drugs, especially if occupants have what officials perceive to be a 'hippie' appearance. 'Wild camping', on unscheduled sites, is not allowed, and it is absolutely forbidden to drive with any alcohol in the bloodstream (heavily penalties!) or without being able to produce your driving licence.

Photographing airports, military installations, railways, bridges and tunnels is not permitted, as is unofficial currency exchange, and certain border zones (*grannitzenzonne*) are kept out of bounds to those without a special pass. (Please also see How to be a Local, pages 105-106). However, harassment or sinister presentiment should not be a worry even when unaccompanied by any 'official' person.

Balkantourist guides are usually efficient, helpful and knowledgeable. They do *not* drone on about record productivity in tractor plants and collective farms. Just a little extra patience, and sense of respect, may be needed by a tour itinerant who may feel he or she is visiting *one more* monument to heroic national achievement than is ideal for holiday relaxation.

There will be a great variety of other attractions and diversions — sometimes in places which seem unpromising at first sight.

Archaeology
The Thracians, the Hellenes, the Romans and the Byzantines contributed to Bulgaria's archaeological monuments. There are many remnants of monumental buildings, public baths, tombstones, sculptures, fortification walls and coins.

Among the masterpieces of ancient art in the country are the murals of the Thracian Tomb (4th century BC), the Gold Treasure of Panagyurishte, the Gold Treasure of Vulchitrun, and the Silver Treasure of Lukovit.

Bulgaria also has numerous monuments from
the period of the Bulgarian Khans and kings.

Architecture
The greatest medieval buildings are in Pliska,
Veliki Preslav, Turnovgrad and Boyana.
National Revival buildings of interest are in Rila,
Bachkova, Troyan, Plovdiv, Kotel, Tryavna,
Koprivshtitsa, Zheravna. More recent
architecture can be seen in the buildings of the
National Assembly, Ivan Vazov National
Theatre, the mineral baths building, market hall
and the National Museum in Sofia, theatres in
Ruse and Varna, etc.

Organised Holidays
For those who prefer an organised holiday with
a theme, Balkantourist offer about 40 special
interest holidays, from agricultural or
architectural tours to wild fruit gathering or
ornithology.
For the active tourist there are walking

*Veliko Turnovo, a
picturesque town in a
picturesque setting,
has carefully
preserved its older
buildings*

holidays, high mountain tours, donkey trekking, hunting, fishing, horse riding, sports camps, tennis courses and folk dancing.

For the artistic there are courses in handicrafts, pottery, sculpture, woodcarving, poker-work, Bulgarian rug making, painting, drawing, icon painting and photography.

For the gourmet there is herb gathering, mushroom picking, wild fruit gathering, cookery courses, canning of fruit, wine making and tastings.

There are trips by narrow gauge railway, and by cart along the mountain roads.

Festivals include the June Rose Festival in Karlovo, the Trifon Zarezan Vine Growers Festival in February: the March Music Days in Ruse, the Sofia Music Weeks in May and June, Lilac Music Celebrations in Lovech, the Festival of Humour and Satire in Gabrovo, folklore festivals in Burgas and Rozhen, the 'Pirin Sings' folklore festival, etc.

HISTORICAL BACKGROUND

The first people that the historian can name as living in the lands that became Bulgaria were the Thracians, who, with their highly developed culture, founded colonies on the Black Sea coast. The Thracians were fine horsemen and these, and other animals, are depicted on the magnificent tomb finds made in Bulgaria. Eventually the Romans stretched their yoke as far as the Black Sea by subduing the Thracian tribes. Christianity first arrived when the Roman Emperor Constantine made it the official cult of his realms. Even when the northern barbarians finally demolished the remnants of administration flowing from Rome at the beginning of the 5th century AD, the land remained part of the Greek-speaking Roman world under emperors ruling from Constantinople.

But waves upon waves of heathen tribes were pouring down from the north and east: Avars, Slavs — and the Bulgars, who were to give the land the name it still bears.

The Bulgars crossed the Danube towards the end of the 7th century AD and in 681 Khan Asparoukh founded the first Bulgarian State, with a blending of Slavs. Early in the 8th century this was independent of the Byzantines

Relics from the ancient civilisations of the area may be seen in Sofia's Archaeology Museum

and controlled the land between the Balkan Range and the Carpathian Mountains.

Violent Acts

It was at its most powerful at the beginning of the 9th century when a Bulgarian Tsar captured a Byzantine Emperor, had his head chopped off and ordered a drinking cup to be made from the skull.

The Bulgars and Slavs became Christian later in the century when their prince, Boris I, was converted by the brothers Cyril and Methodius — also renowned for devising the Cyrillic alphabet still used in Slav languages.

The Bulgars' power was destroyed in a battle in 1014 which culminated in more outrageous violence. The Byzantine victor Basil II took more than 15,000 prisoners, blinding all but 150 whom he left with one eye each, to guide the defeated blind army back to the Bulgarian Tsar. The point was taken, and Bulgaria became a province of the Byzantine Empire shortly afterwards. But the Byzantine Empire had its problems — attacks not only from the former barbarians from the north but from the ever-present Arabs.

Turbulence and conflict: the war between the Serbians and the Bulgarians, 1885

So the Bulgarians, after a series of unsuccessful uprisings, were able to break away again in 1187. This Second Bulgarian Empire was to last for more than 200 years and become the strongest state in the southeast Europe; stretching from the Black Sea to the Mediterranean and taking in modern-day Hungary and Yugoslavia.

The Tatars plundered from the north and the Arabs pressed from the south, but it was internal strife that divided this Empire into three separate kingdoms which finally fell, one by one, to the Ottoman Turks. Muslim domination was to last for five centuries, yet the individual culture, customs and religion of the Bulgarians survived.

The Eastern Question

It was this strong cultural identity that sustained the Bulgarians through the long, slow decline of the Ottoman Empire from the end of the 17th century. The Great Powers bolstered up the Sultans for their various reasons — Britain because her diplomats were obsessed with protecting her trade routes to India. All were suspicious of Russia, the rising star of the Slav nations, who might take the spoils of rotting Turkish rule.

Slav nationalism, inspired by the publication in 1762 of Father Paissi's Slav-Bulgarian History, grew — but only slowly among the illiterate peasants of Bulgaria.

Many Russians supported Pan-Slavism — and the idea that it was natural for the oppressed Slav peoples to come under the protection of Russia. Bulgarian volunteers fought for Russia in several successful wars against the Turks.

But when the Turks refused the Russian demand to protect Christians within the Turkish Empire, the 'Eastern Question' lurched into the Crimea War, with Britain, France and Austria coming to the aid of Turkey, the 'Sick Man of Europe'.

Russian Action

After Russia's retreat, the Bulgarian national liberation movement grew. In April of 1876 they rose against their oppressors. This uprising was suppressed with such ferocity that the whole of Europe was shocked. The Turks armed irregular Muslim troops who fought for loot and slashed their way through 60 villages killing everyone in sight.

In Britain, Gladstone spoke in Parliament of the Bulgarian horrors and the public began to wonder just why its government supported a nation capable of the massacre of 30,000 men, women and children.

A conference was called in Constantinople but nothing was decided. The Turks refused to accept reforms.

So Tsar Alexander II of Russia declared war on Turkey in April 1877 'to preserve the dignity and honour of Europe'. Eventually, helped by Bulgarian volunteers and other oppressed Slavs, the Turks were defeated.

The San Stefano Peace Treaty, signed on 3 March 1878, set up (among other things) a Bulgarian independent state. But the Great Powers had plans to divide the Turkish Balkans more to their advantage.

A new peace conference was called resulting in the Treaty of Berlin. This divided Bulgaria into three, restoring the southern part to Turkish

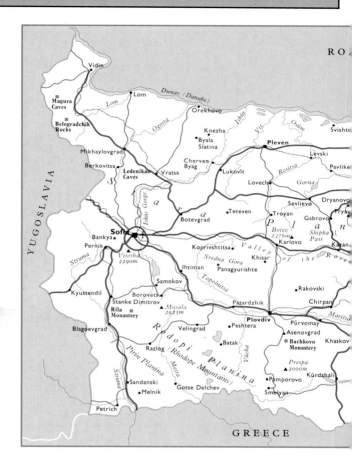

rule. The Bulgarians were angry but set about looking for a constitutional ruler and imported a German prince, Alexander of Battenburg.

The Smouldering Balkan Fuse

Western diplomats knew that the unsettled state of the Balkans was an issue that threatened the delicate balance of power in Europe. Bulgarians, unhappy with the Berlin treaty, realised that friendly big brother Russia did not favour her eventual union with Roumelia, the former Ottoman possession which had incorporated Thrace together with Macedonia and Albania. Moreover, their new prince was forced to accept Russian generals as ministers.

In the south the Roumelians revolted in September 1885, and in spite of Turkish protests even Britain would soon recognise the new union. Bulgaria appeared to have reached a precarious independence.

Then the Serbs declared war on Bulgaria in November, were defeated smartly, but were rescued when the Austrians threatened to intervene. The Russians added to the heated situation by supporting an army kidnap of Prince Alexander, forcing him to abdicate. He came back, but the Tsar refused to accept him and the Bulgarians had to look for another prince. They found Prince Ferdinand of Coburg and in the teeth of opposition from the Russians voted him in in 1887.

Relations with Russia only became amiable again after the death of Alexander III. When the baby heir of Ferdinand was baptised into the Orthodox Church in 1896 Tsar Nicholas II stood as godfather. In 1897 both the neighbouring big powers, Austria-Hungary and Russia, had accepted the status quo.

Rise of Socialism

Bulgaria was to remain a monarchy until the end of World War II, but the economic developments that came with independence brought industrialisation and the foundation of a politically active proletariat.

In 1891 the Bulgarian Social Democratic Party,

which later became the Communist Party, appeared, and the Bulgarian Agrarian Union was set up in 1899.

An independent Bulgaria was able to make its own alliances and in 1912 agreed with Serbia that Macedonia should become Bulgarian. Later in the year it was also allied with Greece and Montenegro in fighting the Turks in the first Balkan War.

In the second Balkan War she fought both

The National Liberation Movement finds itself under attack

Le Petit Journal

SUPPLÉMENT ILLUSTRÉ
Huit pages : CINQ centimes

TOUS LES VENDREDIS
Le Supplément Illustré
5 Centimes

TOUS LES JOURS
Le Petit Journal
5 Centimes

Deuxième Année   SAMEDI 18 AVRIL 1891   Numéro 21

LES ÉVÉNEMENTS DE BULGARIE
(Assassinat de M. Beltchef en présence de M. Stamboulott)

Serbia and Greece, was attacked by Romania
and lost most of what she had gained.

World Wars Role

Bulgaria declared itself neutral when World
War I broke out. Britain offered her
Macedonian territory to join the Allied side but
in 1915 she allied herself with Germany and
attacked Serbia. In the fighting that followed
Bulgaria defeated a British and French army
who were then bottled up in Salonica.
Greece declared war on Bulgaria.
When the Allies' offensive began in Macedonia
the Bulgarians were themselves defeated. In
the peace of Neuilly they lost valuable territory
and had to pay heavy indemnities.

A Peoples' Republic

After a period of Agrarian government, a
right-wing *coup d'état* in May 1923 brought a
Fascist dictatorship which retained a king to
keep the peasants happy.
In September of 1923 the first Communist
rising, led by Georgi Dimitrov and Vassil
Kolarov, was brutally suppressed. Between the
wars Bulgaria suffered severely from economic
depression and support for the Communists
gradually increased.
When World War II started Bulgaria again
declared neutrality but in 1940, with German
help, regained some land it had lost to Romania
during the Balkan Wars. In March 1941 it
associated itself with the Axis, and in a few
days was occupied by German troops. Bulgaria
declared war on Britain and the USA in
December of the same year.
In 1942 Dimitrov, the Communist leader, set up
the Fatherland Front, an organisation of pro-
gressive and democratic forces against Fascism.
A mass anti-Fascist uprising started, that ended
in the overthrow of the monarcho-fascist government on 9 September 1944. The government of
the Fatherland Front was formed. In 1946
Bulgaria became a People's Republic.
The People's Republic has remained a member
of the socialist community ever since,
concerned in mutual economic assistance with
other Warsaw Pact countries, but also involved
in increasing trade and cultural relations with
the West.

SOFIA

Sofia today would surprise anyone who may still vaguely visualise Bulgaria as an insular peasant state. Its population was only 20,000 in 1878, the year before it was declared capital of the country newly liberated from the Turks. Just over a century later, however, its populace has increased 60-fold to 1,200,000, it has hosted sessions of UNESCO and the World Tourism Organisation in its vast Palace of Culture, and has been bidding for the Winter Olympics.

Thus it can claim to have stuck to its motto: 'To grow but not to age'.

Its outer suburbs extend to the

The Ivan Vasov National Theatre in Sofia, a city whose cultural life is held in high regard

foothills of Mount Vitosha, whose peaks rise to a maximum 7,500 feet (2,290m). It builds and refurbishes hotels in partnership with Western and Japanese corporations. But it carefully preserves its native trees, its antiquities, and musical traditions — ranging from folkloric to operatic and symphonic in the annual International Sofia Music Weeks from 24 May to 20 June.

Culture comes with a formal capital C in at least 20 museums and galleries, 14 dramatic and opera stages, eight concert halls, five permanent exhibitions, 57 cinemas, and scores of historical, architectural and commemorative monuments. Graffiti is not a noticeable alternative art form along its litter-free boulevards and parks, where sturdy women

SOFIA

Gara Zaharna Fabrika
Centralna Gara
GEORGI DIMITRO
GABROVO SKOPIE
GENERAL N.G.STOLETOV
VALCO IVANOV
OPALCENSKA
HRISTO BOTEV
SLIVNICA
KIRIL
SLIVNICA
I
METODIJ
CAR SIMEON
OPALCENSKA
BOTEV
GEORGI KIRKO
Park Kiril i Metodij
VELICKOV
SLIVNICA
CAR SIMEON
ANDREJ ZDANOV
HRISTO
ANDREJ ZDANOV
ROMAN
KONSTANTIN
NAJCO CANOV
NAJCO CANG
ALEXANDAR STAMBOLIJSKI
ALEXANDAR STAMBOLIJSKI
OPALCENSKA
Cathedral o Holy Sunda
Park Aleksandar Borimeckov
Vladajska Reka
HRISTO
ALABIN
STOJAN LEPOEV
STEFAN STAMBOLOV
DIMITRI BLAGOEV
BOTEV
VA
GENERAL M.D.SKOBELEV
GENERAL TOTLEBEN
PATRIA
PENCO
PRAGA
SLAVEJKOV
VITA
9 SEPTEMVRI
GEORGI SOFIJSKI
ERNST TELMAN

0   200   400 metres

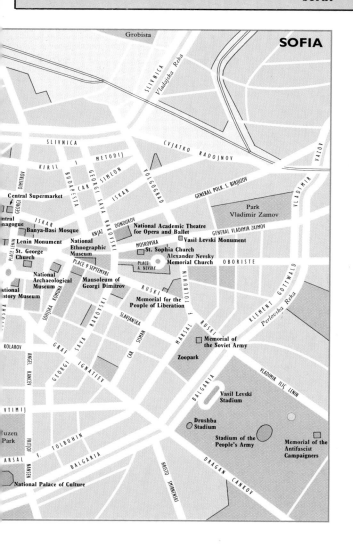

SOFIA

Grobista

SLIVNICA

Vladajska Reka

SLIVNICA

CVJATKO RADOJNOV

KIRIL I METODIJ

DIMITROV

BUDAPESTA

GEORGI SAVA SIMEON

CAR

ISKAR

VOLGOGRAD

GENERAL POLK. S. BIRJUZOV

VLADIMIR

VAZOV

Central Supermarket

Park
Vladimir Zamov

ntral
nagogue

ISKAR

Banya-Basi Mosque

KNJAZ

DONDUKOV

RAKOVSKI

**National Academic Theatre
for Opera and Ballet**

GENERAL VLADIMIR ZAIMOV

Lenin Monument

GEORGI

PLACE LENIN

**National
Ethnographic
Museum**

MOSKOVSKA

St. Sophia Church

Vasil Levski Monument

**St. George
Church**

PLACE 9 SEPTEMVRI

PLACE
A. NEVSKY

**Alexander Nevsky
Memorial Church**

OBORISTE

KLEMENT GOTTWALD

**National
Archaeological
Museum**

**Mausoleum of
Georgi Dimitrov**

RUSKI

**ational
story Museum**

SOFIJSKA KOMUNA

**Memorial for the
People of Liberation**

F. TOLBUHIN

Perlovska Reka

SLAVJANSKA

RAKOVSKI

MARSAL

RUSKI

KOLAROV

GEORGI SAVA

GRAF

CAR

SUMAN

IGNATIEV

**Memorial of
the Soviet Army**

ANGEL KANCEV

Zoopark

BALGARIA

VLADIMIR ILIŠ LENIN

VTIMIJ

**Vasil Levski
Stadium**

FRITJOF

F. TOLBUHIN

**Drushba
Stadium**

uzen
Park

NANSEN

**Stadium of the
People's Army**

**Memorial of the
Antifascist
Campaigners**

ARSAL

BALGARIA

HAJTO SMIRNENSKI

DRAGAN

CANKOV

National Palace of Culture

sweep up autumn leaves with besoms.

There is no notional equivalent in the city of London's Soho, New York's Greenwich Village, the Paris Left Bank, or the Croisette in Cannes (with which Sofia shares roughly the same southerly latitude) — or, visibly, any really wild youth scene. Discos offer fairly standard Western/international rock/pop, but most of them are in hotels where staff sometimes seem rather busy keeping local people out of them because of the demand.

Après-ski in the Vitosha resorts, however, is likely to be as lively as in almost any wintersports area. And there is quite an animated atmosphere at numerous bars and restaurants — some national and folkloric, some with overseas cuisines — in Sofia and surrounding summer resorts.

History

From ancient times the Sofia plain was a crossroads for east-west and north-south migrations, as indicated by its early name: Sredets (centre). Archaeological excavations locally have yielded traces of civilisation from 7,000 years ago. In the 8th century BC the Thracian tribe of Serdi settled here, giving way to the Romans and their town Serdica. After standard demolition work by Attila the Hun's hordes, this was rebuilt in the 6th century by the Byzantine Emperor Justinian. In 811 it was conquered by the incoming Bulgarian Khan Krum (whose name now graces labels on bottles of sensationally good,

cheap Bulgarian Chardonnay) and incorporated into the First Bulgarian State. Following re-occupation by the Byzantines, as Triaditsa, it was annexed into the Second Bulgarian Kingdom by Tsar Ivan Shishman in a 14th-century deed which had the first known reference to the name Sofia.

The Ottomans captured it in 1382 after a long siege, and did not finally leave hold until the Russian General Gurko entered Sofia with his troops in January 1878.

Heavily bombarded in 1944, it was a centre of Communist resistance to the Fascist regime, which ultimately capitulated on the Ninth of September — a date which has become a ubiquitous memorial name.

What to See in Sofia

ROMAN FORTRESS WALLS have been found by archaeologists and are now on view in a city-centre pedestrian underpass at the lower ground floor of the Sofia department store, and at Exarch Yossif Street.

The **Western Gate of ancient Serdica** is behind the Lenin monument, and the **Northern Gate** is under the Central Supermarket in Georgi Dimitrov Boulevard.

ROTUNDA OF ST GEORGE
Stamboliiski Boulevard
In a courtyard behind the Hotel Balkan, finely preserved, 4th-century. Also remains of a 2nd-century street and other antiquities.

The Alexander Nevsky Memorial Church, as resplendent inside as out

◆
ST SOPHIA CHURCH
Parizh Street
The 4th–6th-century church has survived intact, down to 1,600-year-old mosaic details of trees, flowers and birds.

◆◆◆
ALEXANDER NEVSKY MEMORIAL CHURCH
Alexander Nevsky Square
Between Moskovska Street and the handsome Ruski Boulevard that is lined with several rows of horse chestnut trees.

Completed in 1912 in tribute to the Russian liberators from Ottoman rule, golden-domed and the most splendid of many notable buildings from around the turn of the century. Craftsmen and artists from six countries worked for 30 years, in all, on the five-aisle church, which can accommodate 5,000. The glow from huge chandeliers and candelabra illuminates 82 icons, 273 mural paintings, and the finishes of marble, onyx, alabaster, gold, copper and bronze.
Services, especially at Eastertide, offer a magnificence of singing and spectacle.

◆◆◆
THE NATIONAL HISTORY MUSEUM

2 Vitosha Boulevard

The world's oldest known gold artefacts were found in Bulgaria, as were the Thracian gold treasures of Vulchitrun and Panagyurishte. Items of these can be seen in this important

A display of souvenirs of Sofia which reflects the country's traditional crafts

museum, sometimes in reproduction if the originals are 'on tour' for exhibition elsewhere. Its ground floor houses a wealth of rare objects ranging from the Palaeolithic Age to the 14th century AD, which may account for an hour before the visitor contemplates the next floor and its detailed illustration of the centuries of the Turkish Yoke — subject matter which will not be lacking elsewhere.

Open: 10.30 to 17.30; Friday
14.30 to 17.30
Closed: Monday

◆
THE NATIONAL ARCHAEOLOGICAL MUSEUM
2 Alexander Stamboliiski Boulevard
In the Buyuk Mosque dating from Ottoman days. Culture of the tribes and peoples of Bulgaria from antiquity to the 19th century.
Open: 10.00 to 12.00; 14.00 to 18.00
Closed: Monday

◆
THE NATIONAL ETHNOGRAPHIC MUSEUM
Ninth September Square
Housed in the former royal palace. 30,000 items illustrate Bulgarian life and culture from the 18th to the 20th century.
Open: 10.00 to 12.00; 13.30 to 18.30
Closed: Monday, Tuesday

◆◆
MAUSOLEUM OF GEORGI DIMITROV
Ninth September Square
Guarded by sentries in old-style dress uniform, roughly the symbolic equivalent of Lenin's Tomb in Moscow's Red Square. Dimitrov took charge of Bulgaria after the war.
Open: Wednesday, Thursday, Sunday 15.00 to 18.00

Entertainment

THE NATIONAL PALACE OF CULTURE
Vitosha Boulevard (south end)
Built to mark the 13th centenary of the creation of the Bulgarian State, this modern complex is an ambitious building. It is an established congress centre. Set in new public gardens with fountained ornamental ponds, it could notionally accommodate 16,844 people participating simultaneously in some kind of activity, it has been claimed. Its central hall has several thousand seats, and there are a dozen other halls attached, with hi-tech facilities and infrastructure, 160,000 sq ft (15,000 sq m) exhibition space, restaurants, café, and shops.

It can rise quite efficiently to the big occasion. But massive congresses of world bodies like UNESCO do not happen every week, and it might seem that there is scope here for Western incentive-conference organisers to negotiate extra-competitive rates.

At theatres, performances are naturally most likely to be in Bulgarian. There may occasionally be Shakespeare in the vernacular.

Shopping
Shopping Centres: TSUM (the Central Department Store), Lenin Square (credit cards accepted). **Halite** (the Markets), Georgi Dimitrov Boulevard. **Zornitsa,** Vitosha Boulevard. **Valentina,** in the triangle between Graf Ignatiev, Sofiiska Kamouna and Alabin Streets, and on Vitosha Boulevard. **Denitsa,** in the underpass of the Central Railway Station.

Speciality Stores: Bulgarski Houdozhnik (applied art works), 6 Ruski Boulevard (credit cards accepted). **Bulgartabac,** 2 Ruski Boulevard. **Vitex** (fabrics), 29 F Nansen Boulevard; 28 Tolbukhin

Boulevard. **Quartz** (crystal, glass and china ware), 35 F. Nansen Boulevard; 8 Vitosha Boulevard (credit cards accepted). **Mineralsouvenir** (articles and gifts made of marble and semi-precious stones, jewellery), 10 Ruski Boulevard. **Mladost** (sports articles), 1 Positano Street and 18 Ivan Assen II Street. **Pamoukotex** (cotton fabrics and ready-to-wear), 33 F. Nansen Boulevard. **Peroun** (fashions), 42 Dondukov Boulevard. **Pirin** (footwear and leather wear), 4 Slavyanska Street; 19 Vitosha Boulevard; 86 Vitosha Boulevard; Stamboliiski

Typical cuisine – simple, natural and healthy

Boulevard. **Rila** (ready-wear), 63 Vitosha Boulevard; 35 Vitosha Boulevard and 52 Vitosha Boulevard. **Rouen** (knitwear), 50 Alabin Street; 34 Tolbukhin Boulevard (credit cards accepted).

Corecom shops, usually in hotels, sell cigarettes, spirits, watches, radios, perfumes, etc., at prices below those of duty-free shops at West European points of departure. These are strictly for hard currency, not leva, and with receipts can be exported duty free.

Food and Drink
Bulgarian Folk-Style
Restaurants: Goroublyansko

Hanche, Goroublyane suburb; *Mehani* (taverns) in the larger city hotels; **Koprivshtitsa,** in the Trade Centre on Vitosha Boulevard; **Zheravna,** 26 Tolbukhin Boulevard; **Rozhen,** 74 Vitosha Boulevard, serves specialities from the southern, Rhodope region, e.g.: *cheverme* (tender spit-roasted lamb), *drob-sarma* (rice with mutton, liver, spices and egg), large white Smolyan beans (can produce a 'Blazing Saddles' wind effect), *Katchamak* (fried maize-flour cakes with cheese). The less folksy **Ropotamo,** facing Liberation Park on Lenin Boulevard, just east of the junction with Sitnyakovo Street,

The Viennese café, one of the restaurants in the 1930s-style Sheraton Hotel, Sofia

is fashionable if sedate. Potted plants lurk everywhere, and the cocktail pianist gradually updates from 'It's a Sin to Tell a Lie' and 'Somewhere Over the Rainbow' to 'Stardust' and 'Too Young'. Menu suggestions: *Kotleti po Moskovski* (pork fillet stuffed with ham, cheese and peppers), Baklava dessert.

Other National Cuisines: Havana (Cuban), 27 Vitosha Boulevard; **Budapest** (Hungarian), 145 Rakovski Street; **Berlin** (German), 2 General Zaimov Boulevard; **Warszawa** (Polish), 15 General Zaimov Boulevard; **Vietnam** (Vietnamese), 1 Georgi Kirkov Boulevard; **Forum** (French), 64 Vitosha Boulevard;

Pyeong Jang (Korean), 24 A. Zlatarov Street.

Restaurant Complexes: Rubin, Lenin Square; **Kristal**, 10 Aksakov Street; **Coop**, Vitosha Boulevard; **Forum**, 64 Vitosha Boulevard; **Havana**, 27 Vitosha Boulevard, and at the National Palace of Culture.

Cafés: Prolet, 21 Ruski Boulevard; **Kristal**, 10 Aksakov Street; **Magoura**, 80 Vitosha Boulevard; **Sportna Sreshta**, 17 Tolbukhin Boulevard.

Accommodation
Hotels:

Sheraton Sofia Hotel Balkan, 5-star, Lenin Square (tel: 87-65-41; telex 23030). A characterful thirties-style establishment carefully refurbished to Sheraton standards; chandeliered conference rooms, Bulgarian-style restaurants, Viennese café, tavern, coffee lounge, nightclub, fitness centre.

Vitosha New Otani, 5-star, Anton Ivanov Boulevard (tel: 62-1-51; telex 22797). Spacious, high-rise, hilltop, calmly modern international-style luxury with plenty of daylight; Sakura Japanese restaurant, Lozenets Bulgarian restaurant, day and night bars, variety bar and casino, fitness centre, indoor swimming pool and sauna, bowling, tennis court, shops.

Rodina, 4-star, 8 General Totleben Boulevard (tel: 5-16-31; telex 22200). High-rise, with de-luxe features but possibly depressing taste in dark-brown modern ceilings. Good restaurants and banquet halls, snack bar, night club, Russian restaurant/floor show, conference halls, coffee lounge, bars, shops, bowling, swimming pool, sauna.

Novotel Europe, 4-star, 131 Georgi Dimitrov Boulevard (tel: 3-12-61). High-rise, modern/functional style; restaurants, lounge bars, night clubs, conference halls, shops.

Grand Hotel Sofia, 3-star, 3 National Assembly Square (tel: 87-88-21; telex 23405). Opposite the Parliament and other august buildings, giving a feeling of where it's all at, modern and not highly stylised; lofty, airy main restaurant, night club with floor show, tavern, coffee lounge, bars, Triaditsa hall for business meetings.

Park Hotel Moskva, 3-star, 25 Nezabravka Street (tel: 7-12-61; telex 22411). Restaurants and banquet halls. Panorama restaurant, snack bar, night club, coffee lounge, day bars, Russian restaurant with floor show, conference halls, shops.

Bulgaria, 3-star, 4 Ruski Boulevard (tel: 87-19-77).

Hemus, 3-star, 31 Georgi Traikov Boulevard (tel: 66-14-15).

Slavia, 2-star, 2 Sofiiski Geroi Street (tel: 52-55-51).

Slavyanska Besseda, 2-star, 127 Rakovski Street (tel: 88-36-91).

Serdika, 2-star, 2 General Zaimov Boulevard (tel: 44-34-11).

Pliska, 2-star, 87 Lenin Boulevard (tel: 712-81). Intended for Balkanair passengers; restaurant diners serenaded by piano/violin/cello/flute quartet, then more contemporary keyboard/vocal items; bar, snack-bar.

Tourist Offices
See page 119

Hotel Shtastlivetza in Vitosha, Bulgaria's highest ski resort, just half an hour from Sofia

THE WEST

VITOSHA MOUNTAIN DRAGALEVTSI, BOYANA

The No. 66 bus from the Hladilnika tram stop on Sofia's Cherni Vruh Boulevard, bound for the Shtastlivetsa Hotel in Vitosha, reaches **Dragalevtsi**, in the wooded foothills, within 15 minutes.

At lunchtime, alight at the Vodenicharski Mehani — preferably on a weekday, when there is not such heavy booking at this folk-style restaurant, converted from three 200-year-old water mills. Specialities here include *katchamak* (fried maize dough) with meat, and a *shish-kebab*, skewered meat and onion grilled and flamed with vodka. There is often folk music.

◆
DRAGALEVTSI MONASTERY

Frescoes date back to the 14th century when it was founded by King Ivan Alexander. About 2 miles (3 km) further near a No. 66 bus stop.

Boyana and its celebrated church, nestling at the foot of Mt Vitosha, can be reached by bus from Sofia. The Balkantourist office, 1 Vitosha Boulevard will give details.

◆◆
BOYANA CHURCH

Begun in the 11th century, it contains frescoes from 1259

which are claimed to be among the best-preserved and most interesting examples of Eastern European medieval art.

Some of the 90 scenes are painted from life rather than stylised. The picture of the Last Supper contains typical early Bulgarian detail, including the people's everyday fare of garlic, radishes and bread.

At a stop 20 minutes' drive further from the **Zlatni Mostove** area (3,900 ft/1,200 m) is reached. Surrounded by forests, it has a restaurant quite near the curious 'stone river' of boulders strewn by early flood torrents.

ALEKO VITOSHA

The highest of Bulgaria's ski resorts, Aleko on Mount Vitosha lies at 6,129 ft (1,868 m) with skiing up to 7,415 ft (2,260 m), so the season lasts reliably from early December until late spring. The mountain forms a backdrop to Sofia, just half an hour's bus ride from the slopes. Vitosha's lifts rise high above the treeline and the slopes are long and steep enough for the resort to make an almost successful bid for the Olympics. Only last-minute protests about the ecology — and the difficulty of putting up extra lifts, an Olympic village and helicopter pads which would be pulled down again after the Games — stopped the bid going through. Japan and Calgary had no such problems.

The slopes are mainly north-facing and can be windy (except where they descend into the protecting treeline) but they are never icy. Cherni Vruh at the highest point gives wonderful views over the whole region. Vitoshko Lale, the run down from Cherni Vruh, is the blackest and most difficult in Bulgaria. There is also a steep wall, Stenata, which is particularly challenging, and the whole area is good for training. A four-person chairlift, a triple, a double and several draglifts give a total uplift of 7,000 skiers an hour.

This means that queues, even when a proportion of the million inhabitants of Sofia decide to ski, are kept to a minimum. Of course, those in ski-school have priority on the lifts and so do not suffer queues. The Bulgarian ski-school was founded on Mount Vitosha 30 years ago. At least 20 of its instructors speak English (and understand it).

Classes are grouped according to language, for Vitosha is very international. Skiers come from West and East Germany (German and Russian are commonly spoken in Bulgaria); from Greece, Holland, Belgium and Hungary.

The village of Aleko is small and purpose-built. You can ski from the door of the Hotel Shtastlivetsa and back again to it at the end of the day. It has a big sun terrace, from which to watch skiers returning after the challenge of the day. Prostor is more luxurious with a small swimming pool, nightclub, sauna and solarium.

Prices are reasonable in all the Bulgarian resorts and Vitosha has a special flavour for those who have only skied in Western resorts. The proximity of Sofia offers sightseeing and shopping possibilities and the ski area will keep all the enthusiasts in the party happy.

SAMOKOV

Samokov may look somewhat prosaic in general now, but it fostered famous 19th-century schools of master craftsmen and artists — and it has a singular mosque and a decorated 17th-century Turkish drinking fountain, both just opposite a functional plate-glass bus station.

Six miles (10 km) north of Borovets winter resort, it is roughly half way along the road linking Stanke Dimitrov on E79

The exquisite Turkish drinking fountain in Samokov, dating from the 17th century

and Ihtiman on E80. It can be reached in a 38 mile (62 km) drive south from Sofia along the road via Pancharevo which follows the Iskur valley through wooded mountain-and-lake country which is particularly colourful in autumn.

The **museum** in the main square traces histories of iron founding, printing, etc. The **Belyova Church** contains many murals by painters from Samokov, whose sons included leading icon painters like Zahari Zograph.

◆

THE BAIRAKLI MOSQUE

Designed and internally decorated by Bulgarian artists who presumably also painted

house and monastery interiors, and who here managed to reach a friendly compromise with Muslim worshippers about the use of various motifs which did not strictly accord with Koranic tradition. Madgalina Yaprakove, its usual custodian, is deeply informative in fluent English about the mosque and the town – which, for instance, had the first workers' commune in the Balkans.

◆
ISKUR GORGE

Northwards from Sofia, the road from Novi Iskur to Lyntibrod follows the winding Iskur Gorge, carved out by the fast-flowing River Iskur over countless aeons.

The walls of the gorge are spectacular rock formations, sometimes so steep and close that – from the passenger seat of a car or train (on the Sofia-Mezdra line) you have to look up vertically at their summits, looming up to 800ft (250m) or so.

Eroded by weather and water, some resemble canyons in the North American Rockies. Others, with symmetrical terracing and cloud-piercing pinnacles, would make a theatrical backdrop for some Wagnerian epic.

The sheer Ritlite rocks in the Iskur Gorge, a winding canyon sculpted by the River Iskur

Partially grey limestone, their strata are seamed at intervals with 'stripes' of other rock — a· diagonal band of yellowish colour, then a parallel one above it of dusky pink hue, and so on.

About half-way between Novi Iskur and Svoge (a town with coal mining and other industry) a right turn leads off 2½ miles (4 km) to the village of Batuliya, whose railway halt is named **Tompsan**. This commemorates Major William Frank Thompson, member of a British mission aiding Bulgarian partisans who died in a 1944 battle with the gendarmerie.

Beyond Lakatnik, where the canyon rocks are particularly impressive and popular with climbers, is the village of Cherepish, near whose railway halt is the **Cherepish Monastery**. This is a 14th-century foundation restored in the 16th century after being ravaged several times during the Ottoman occupation.

◆
RITLITE ROCKS
Just left of the small town of Lyutibrod. Three parallel walls of outcrop rock ranging down over hill contours into the valley. Though known locally as 'Cart Rails', from a distance they also look strikingly like man-made fortified ramparts whose watchtowers and turrets have been knocked about a bit.

VRATSA and LEDENIKA CAVE
Vratsa stands near the foot of Kamarata mountain, where Hristo Botev, Bulgarian guerilla leader, hero and poet, was killed by Turkish troops after a hard battle in the early uprisings of 1876. It has a theatre, history museum and art gallery.

From April to October the Balkantourist Office at 21 Georgi Dimitrov Street can direct sightseers to The Lift (so called locally) — a funicular whose chairs will carry them above wooded hillsides to the 2,700 ft (830 m) high pastures in which is the entrance to the Ledenika (Icicle) Cave. A 20-minute, 1½ mile (2½ km) ride; low-season alternative is a 10 mile (16 km) taxi or car ride up a southwesterly road signposted to Ledenika.

◆
LEDENIKA CAVE
Limestone complex formed 2½ million years ago by water action. Its floodlit caverns include the 'Concert Hall', 197 ft (60 m) by 148 ft (45 m) and 75 ft (23 m) high, whose excellent acoustics encourage the Vratsa Philharmonic Orchestra and/or famous choirs to perform programmes in it on special occasions. Normally, the only sounds in the caverns are the echoes of visitors' voices, the slow drips of stalagmite-forming water and the occasional hissing of (harmless) bats hanging from the cave roof.

Electric lighting shows up stalagmite formations perceived fancifully as giants, Jack Frost, the Madonna, Santa Claus, elephant, octopus, and the Hut of the Slav witch Baba Yaga. Cave temperatures drop from a summer 40°F (4°C) to something well below freezing in winter,

when water penetrating the roof causes opaque ice formations which brilliantly reflect the spotlighting. In pre-refrigeration days, silk worms were stored in an upper, moderately cold cavern. Warm clothing is an obvious necessity, as are non-slip shoes for the damp walkways. There is a basic café near the entrance.
Open: Virtually year round, 08.30 to 16.00; 45-minute tour.

Food and Drink/
Accommodation
Hotel Hemus, 2-star (tel: 235-80/1), with restaurant, pastry-shop, bar and 'beer-pub'; **Hotel Balkan**, 1-star (tel: 244-69), with restaurant. **Hotel Hashore,** 2-star (tel: 21287), with restaurant. Accommodation at the **Hotel Tourist** is intended mainly for members of the Bulgarian Hikers' Union (BTC) but its restaurant is apparently open to all. Comfortably furnished, it offers good value for money.

BERKOVITSA
Berkovitsa is an old-established town producing wines from locally grown strawberries, raspberries and blackcurrants. It has a warren of narrow streets and several museums. On the northern slopes of the Balkan range, 12 miles (20 km) west of the spa resort of Vurshets (or Varsec) and 15 miles (24 km) southwest of industrial Mikhaylovgrad, Berkovitsa boasts a mild climate and is being developed as a mountain resort.
Among local sights are **The Clock Tower** of 1762, the **Virgin Mary (Sveta Bogoroditsa)**

Church and its artistic contents, the **Kaleto hill fortress** and early Christian basilica remains, and the **Gramada**, 2 miles (3 km) out by the road to Mikhaylovgrad — a pile of stones which grew over many years as a symbol of anti-Turkish sentiment; each one was thrown there with a hearty curse.

The Belogradchik fortress, built into a fairy-tale world of rock formations resembling animals, people and castles

♦
HOUSE OF IVAN VAZOV
Home of the revered writer of *Under the Yoke* and other chronicles of struggles against the occupying Turks.

Food and Drink/ Accommodation
Hotel Mramor, 2-star (tel: 22-12), with restaurant.

Balkantourist office, 1 Berkovska Komuna Square (tel: 30-44).

♦♦♦
BELOGRADCHIK ROCKS
Some of the strangest natural sights in Europe are the rocks and gorges in an 18 mile (30 km) by 2 mile (3 km) area around Belogradchik, a small town a short distance along a left turn off the E79 road northwest from Mikhaylovgrad. Often more massive than the most grandiose of Bulgaria's man-made monuments, they are sometimes over 500 feet (150 m) high and have reminded travellers of solitary obelisks, many-towered castles, giant representations of historical figures, or mythical beasts sculpted by nature in red or vari-coloured sandstone.
Set amongst winding gullies or leafy wilderness, they led a 19th-century traveller to enthuse: 'The famous Oliul gorges in Provence, the Pancorbo defile in Spain, the Pyrenees, the Alps . . . all these are incomparable with what I saw near Belogradchik in Bulgaria!'
An asphalt road now enables motorists to drive up to a fortress, built high in the rocks, with various accretions from the 1st century to the 19th century.

Accommodation
Hotel Belogradchik Rocks, 2-star.
Madonna campsite with bungalows.

◆◆
MAGURA (MAGOURA) CAVE

Magura Cave, 7 miles (11 km)
west off the E79 road at Dimovo,
is one of the most interesting of
Bulgaria's many natural caverns
because of its evidence of
prehistoric human habitation
and its mysterious rock
'paintings'.

These latter, depicting
cartoon-like animal and human
figures, are daubings with bat
guano, a dark brown substance
so durable that it has preserved
the area of rock covered by the
'paintings' — which thus stand
out in relief.

Some archaeologists have dated
them back merely to the
beginning of the Bronze Age
(2,700 BC). But another school of
thought suggests they are as
much as 17,000 years old —
which may be nearer the mark
if the animal pictures were
anything like authentic
reproductions. They seem to
include creatures somewhat like
giraffes, ostriches and even
kangaroos, which might only
have existed in this region at an
early time when its climate was
much hotter.

Human figures include hunters
with bow and arrow, dancing
women (in grass skirts?) and
men (presented in a way which
may have suggested fertility
rather than palaeolithic
pornography).

One of the 'halls' nearer the
cave entrance contains remains
of a fireplace, clay pots, and
other items from almost 3,000 BC,
while another cavern has been
variously used by Bulgarian
freedom fighters since the 19th
century.

The most massive of the
stalagmite formations may be
nearly three million years old.
As in other caves, they are
taken to resemble buildings,
trees, and human or animal
figures when floodlit. Live
resident bats still drop guano.
The cave is very extensive, and
a tour can take 1½ hours. A
short walk down the hillside
from its entrance, which gives
views over the large Rabisha

Lake, is a simply furnished *mehana* (tavern). This serves excellent minced meat balls (*kyufte*) plus inexpensive house wines or the pink Magura champanska which is fermented by *methode champenoise* in a bottle and stored in the cave. The town base for visiting Magura, and Belogradchik Rocks, might well be Vidin.

Vidin, a major centre

VIDIN

Vidin is a major port on the Danube, at the northernmost point of the E79 highway. Linked by ferries to the factory town of Calafat on the Romanian bank, and to a wooded river island, it appears from southern approaches to be more mundanely industrial than touristic until you reach the area around the medieval Baba Vida fortress, built on riverside

foundations of a Roman fort from the 3rd-4th century BC.

However, there are aspirations to make Vidin a Duty Free area – presumably with some upgrading of its amenities, though its hotels currently meet demand as unpretentious bases for local sightseeing and jaunts out to Magura Cave and Belogradchik Rocks.

A new theatre under construction in Vidin is intended to be 'the most modern in Bulgaria'. And a Vidin District product which can hardly be bettered anywhere for zestful value is the famous red Gamza wine of Novo Selo, a village in its northwest corner between the borders of Romania and Yugoslavia.

◆◆
THE BABA VIDA FORTRESS

Impressively preserved towers, ramparts and (since the occupying Turks sometimes met a lot of resistance here) former prisons, death cells and a scaffold. In park-like surroundings. Some of its vintage cannons were made in England. It contains a museum, and in summer provides an outdoor theatre for its 'Shakespeariad' (though its historical plays are not always Shakespeare's). Periodically it is used as a film set, and it often attracts archaeologists.

Rila Monastery's wealth of frescoes make it the country's most important monument from the National Revival period

◆
THE DISTRICT HISTORY MUSEUM

A short walk away from the Baba Vida Fortress, in the 18th-century Krustata (Cross-shaped) Barracks, it features items from the agricultural past to the acrylic-fibre and water-pump producing present.

◆
TURKISH KONAK

Displays earlier arts and crafts. The remaining mosques tend to be closed, perhaps for restoration work.

Accommodation

The **Hotel Rovno**, 2-star (tel: 244-02), in the town centre, is apparently due for refurbishment (and perhaps this will stop its windows rattling when late-autumn winds blow along the Danube). It has a reasonable restaurant, a bar with music, and a friendly enough welcome.
The **Bononia**, 2-star, 4 Bdin Street (tel: 230-31), has restaurant, bar, and snack-bar.
The **Nora Pizanti Campsite**, 1-star, run by the Union of Bulgarian Motorists, is out on the road south to Sofia.

Balkantourist Office, 4a, Dondukov Street (tel: 249-76).

◆◆◆
RILA MONASTERY

Rila Monastery is the most famous of Bulgaria's seven major monasteries (there are quite a number more), and a prime example of work from the National Revival Period, with 1,200 beautifully preserved wall paintings.

The stern stone building is 3,500 feet (1,100m) up in a leafy valley of the Rila Mountains, 74 miles (119 km) from Sofia on an east turn off the E79 from Kocherinovo. Its central fortified Tower of Hrelyo (1335) is the only surviving medieval portion. The monastic community was founded in the 10th century, and continues its devotions today. A full-bearded priest glides around its colonnaded courtyard, hammering out summonses to prayer on a wooden sounding-board. Visitors light prayer candles in its Holy Virgin Church, which glows with murals by Zahari Zograph and other National Revival artists.

The museum has a vast collection of ancient documents, painted icons, fabrics, jewellery, carvings, carpets and metalwork from all over the country, a cross sculpted by the monk Raphael with a needle contains 140 biblical scenes, with 1,500 tiny human figures, which he completed in 1802, after 12 years — at the cost of his eyesight. The library contains 20,000 old books. One of the nine Bulgarian landmarks on UNESCO's protection list, Rila Monastery was awarded the International Federation of Travel Journalists Golden Apple Prize in 1980.

Accommodation

The **Hotel Rilets**, 3-star, just west of the Monastery, has 14 single rooms, 64 doubles and five suites.

◆◆
BANSKO

Bansko is a museum town with

period houses, native place of famous Bulgarians, and year-round mountain resort in the 87-peak Pirin range with lakes in the vicinity. It is 25 miles (40 km) east of Simitli on E79, and may be reached by buses from there or from Blagoevgrad.

In spring and early summer its slopes can be iridescent with wild flowers such as tiger lilies, globe flowers, alpine poppies and (high up towards the 9,560 ft [2,914 m] Vihren peak) Pirin edelweiss.

Though not greatly developed for wintersports, it has good snow from early December until March, and there has even been talk of local skiing in August. There is a 1,500 m long ski run, with two 330 m beginners' courses, ski drags

Melnik's houses nestle in a deep valley against a backdrop of sandstone pyramids

and a semi-stationary electric drag.

Sons of Bansko include Paissi of Hilendar, the 18th-century monk whose important *Bulgarian History* helped to buoy up nationalist spirits, and Nikola Vaptsarov, the anti-Fascist poet who was executed in 1942 and whose house is now a museum. In cobbled streets are National Revival houses with fascinating façades, windows and eaves.

Food and Drink/ Accommodation

The **Pirin Hotel** (tel: 2295 or 2536) has a restaurant, plus a tavern serving national dishes, bar, discothèque, and tourist office. There are restaurants and other facilities on the main Georgi Dimitrov Boulevard.

◆◆◆
MELNIK

The smallest town in Bulgaria, but rich in interest, Melnik is scattered along a gorge flanked by tall and very neatly eroded canyon rocks, in pale gold sandstone, which variously resemble pyramids, obelisks, or cathedral architecture by Gaudi. Apart from its topography, it is famous for its dark red wine of dense gravity (it was reputedly once so thick that 'you could take it away in a cloth').

Melnik is best visited from Sadanski, along an east turning 5 miles (8 km) south down the E79. Some other approaches, especially to the east, are through areas designated by road signs in German to be *Grannitzenzonne* − out of bounds for security reasons to those without a special pass. Founded by the Thracians and Slavs, in ancient times it was a crossroads for travellers between the eastern Mediterranean and lands to the east and north. The Romans and Byzantines left their marks. Around the turn of the 12th century, Melnik was the capital of the despot Alexii Slav, who ruled much of the Rhodopes and Struma region. In the 17th-18th centuries Melnik flourished and grew with its wine and tobacco trade, eventually to a population of 14,000 with 74 churches. It declined in the late 19th century, and much of it was destroyed in the later Balkan

war. But it retains the shell of its 10th–11th-century **'Boyar's House'** and numerous well-preserved houses of the National Revival Period, their jettied upper storeys supported by fine beams. Especially notable is the 1754 **Kordopulov House**, atop a steep cobbled path towards the village's inner-gorge extremity. It is now a museum, with intriguing furnishings and extensive wine cellars tunnelled into bedrock.

In the street below, opposite an ancient bath house, are impressive houses including one whose owner may invite you in to his cellar, where his own red wine is an alternative to that sold at the cosy bar by the huge plane trees in what is roughly the town centre.

Food and Drink

The **Chinarite Mehana**, just opposite, serves good chicken soup, meatballs and salad, with Melnik red wine.

Accommodation

On the same side of the gorge, built almost against a cliff, is the **Melnik Hotel**, 2-star (tel: 272), newish but in architecture meant to be sympathetic, for visitors who would savour local atmosphere longer − and perhaps before the regular coach parties arrive.

SADANSKI SPA

Spartacus was said to have come from what is now Sadanski, and he was a healthy enough Thracian to have overpowered a gladiator or two while leading the slaves' revolt against the Romans in the 1st century BC. Whether or not he looked like Kirk Douglas in the Hollywood epic you can check at his statue by the entrance to the town, 36 miles (58km) south of Sofia on E79.

Sadanski is a leading health centre, with a mild Mediterranean-type micro-climate, mean annual temperature of 58°F (14°C), and the purest of air, claimed to be the best in Europe for bronchial and respiratory problems (a counter-blast, perhaps, to the effects of tobacco, of which Bulgaria is a major and high-quality producer).

Its slightly mineralised hot springs, ranging from 100 to 160°F (37 to 72°C) at source, are used in the hydro of the ultra-modern 4-star Sadanski Hotel for treatment of kidney conditions, gastritis, colitis, and inflammations of the skin – as well as in the hotel's swimming pools.

Also dealing with arthritic, muscular, gynaecological and nervous complaints, the hydro additionally offers electric treatment, paraffin wraps, electric ionotherapy, acupuncture, light treatment, inhalations, herbal medicine, massages, mechanotherapy, and remedial exercises in gymnasia.

Thus it attracts quite a clientele of West Europeans who find the treatments and holiday cost of living much less expensive than in their own countries. However, even travellers with less receptive national attitudes to hydrotherapy could find Sadanski, with its walks through wooded parkland, a pleasant base for excursions into the scenic Pirin mountains and to such fascinating villages as Melnik (see page 41) and Rozhen (see below).

Accommodation
There is a bowling alley plus billiards and slot machines in the **Hotel Sadanski** (tel: 50-00), whose versatile band can cater for the music/dance tastes of numerous nationalities over dinner. But those wanting another brandy after 22.00 hours when the main bar may close, should either stay in the restaurant or join the scrum waiting to be let in to the downstairs disco. (300 rooms)

The **Spartak Hotel**, 2-star (tel: 24-25), has 27 single and 50 double rooms, seven suites, restaurant, bar, night club and coffee shop.

Balkantourist Office 28 Georgi Dimitrov Street (tel: 20-98).

◆◆
ROZHEN VILLAGE, MONASTERY

Cockerel crow and donkey bray greet the visitor to Rozhen. It is a village more truly rural and less self-consciously touristic than is Melnik (see page 41), though it is in a similar sandstone gorge just to the north and has been used as a film set.

Its houses have a sometimes rickety charm. Their wooden balconies are festooned with red peppers, gourds, pumpkins, and geraniums, their unruly kitchen gardens shaded by vines and murmuring with the lazy drawl of hens. Rozhen village may not be a prime

cultural monument of the
National Revival Period, with
UNESCO recognition. But it has
memorable atmosphere.

Food and Drink
The **Rozhen Mehana** does
inexpensive meat balls (there is
a choice: with or without onion)
and local wine in an
earthenware jug and mugs.
Lively southern badinage may
compete with the outlandish
pop music on the bar's video
television.

◆◆
ROZHEN MONASTERY
Just beyond Rozhen church,
reached about a mile (1½ km)
up and along a track which

Walking in the scenic Rila
mountains, a popular area for hikers
as well as skiers

gives views of the gorge. Built
in the 12–13th centuries, it is
noted for its carved altar and
lecterns, for paintings of monks
and hermits apparently unknown
anywhere else, and for its very
early calligraphy school.
Externally, it looks rather like an
outsize version of a Rozhen
farmhouse. A shopping bag,
hung in a tree just outside its
walls, may contain a large
earthenware pot full of lunch for
the remaining monks.

BOROVETS
Borovets is set in the Rila
Mountains about an hour and a
half's drive from Sofia. The old
kings of Bulgaria — deposed
after the last world war — had a
hunting lodge here. Several
mansions, built by the

aristocracy, still lie back from the village road, now turned to hotels and hostels. As a ski resort it provides a fair challenge to intermediate skiers and opportunities for slalom training on the steep slopes. The village is attractive and facilities for families with young children are good.

The pine trees grow tall and broad (*Bor* is Bulgarian for pine) in these southern climes, and those slopes which are south-facing can get a bit patchy late in the skiing season, but the snow is usually reliable between December and the end of March because the lifts rise so high.

The Musala range of the Rila Mountains has hosted many world cup ski races and a local hero is the now retired Peter Popangelov, who has inspired all the small boys of the area to become ski-racers.

The ski-school offers four hours' instruction a day, six days a week and caters especially for beginners but also up to advanced and race-training standard. Classes are videoed and once a week there is a video evening, with predictably hilarious audience reaction. There is a long green 'road' which any beginner can tackle successfully, a sheltered bowl under Mount Musala and the longest run in Bulgaria. The recent addition of a four-man chairlift to the existing 3-mile (5km) gondola, chairlift and many draglifts, gives plenty of uplift between 4,340 ft (1,323 m) and 8,399 ft (2,560 m) and opens up three separate small areas. Evening entertainment includes wine-tasting evenings, and folklore with traditional music and dancing. The **Rila Monastery** is a fascinating relic of the past and well worth a day's visit (see page 39).

Food and Drink/ Accommodation

A few years ago experts from the French resort of Les Arcs were called in to design a new hotel called the **Rila**. This provides all the comfort and convenience usually only found in more Western resorts. There are three restaurants, including a taverna for traditional Bulgarian food and a two-storey, fast-food café. The nursery for children up to four years of age operates 24 hours a day. From the age of three, children can join the kindergarten and learn to ski. The Rila has two- and three-bedded rooms, each with private bathroom. There is a gym, a sauna and an electronic games room. Each week there is a fancy dress party.

There are, of course, other hotels, including the **Club Hotel Breza** reserved for Balkan Holiday clients, and the new **Hotel Ela** which is close to the slopes. As Borovets is partly a historic rather than a purpose-built resort, there are some hotels set a short bus-ride from the slopes.

A **chalet village**, Malina, has also been built about a mile (2 km) from Borovets, linked by a shuttle bus. The chalets have two twin rooms and space for a fifth person in the living room. There is also a **cottage village,** Jagoda, 40 Finnish houses, some with saunas.

THE BALKAN AND CENTRAL REGION

◆◆◆
KOPRIVSHTITSA

This tongue-twisting hill town presents a serene picture of Bulgarian National Revival architecture. It is fortuitous that it is so well-preserved, since it was here that the 1876 April Uprising got under way prematurely.

A local patriot shot dead the Turk who came to arrest him on discovering insurrection plans — which included production of cannon from lead-lined cherry trees — then wrote a letter of urgent exhortation to rebels elsewhere, in the blood of the Turk.

Khisar: people have been taking the waters of its thermal springs for some 7,000 years

The town straddles gentle hills around the Topolnitsa river and its hump-backed bridges. It is on a turning south, towards Strelcha, from the Sofia-Kazanluk-Burgas motorway 6 miles (10 km) beyond Srednogorie.

Its houses attract photographic interest with their flowery courtyards, wooden balconies, bay windows and (sometimes) heavy studded gates. Several of them are museum houses, often linked with people and events in the April Uprising, which can be visited at various times.

The town is on the itinerary of Balkan Holidays' 'Discover Bulgaria' Tour.

Every five years, Koprivshtitsa is the setting for a major folklore festival — something the Bulgarians do exceptionally well.

TROYAN, TROYAN MONASTERY

Troyan, on the road to Kurnare and Sopot from Lovech, is a friendly town where folk enjoy telling you all about themselves, and are perhaps more interesting than the topography. At Oreshak, nearly 4 miles (6 km) east, is a folklore school which teaches wood-carving and pottery, and sells craftsware when open to the public in summer.

◆◆◆
TROYAN MONASTERY

Founded around 1600, but much of it dates from 1835. The master Zahari Zograph painted the murals inside and outside. Those illustrating Doomsday and Hell are perhaps more suitable for sensitive family viewing than Devilish practices depicted in some ecclesiastical interpretations elsewhere. The church's icons and carvings are by several leading masters.
In 1872, Vassil Levski set up a revolutionary committee joined by all the monks and headed by the Father Superior here, making the monastery an early citadel for the 1876 April Uprising.

Accommodation
Hotel Troyan (tel: 43-23, 23-96), unpretentious, overlooking the quaint area by the bridge over the River Osum.

◆◆
KHISAR (HISSARYA)

Khisar and its hot mineral water springs had attracted long-stay visitors for at least 5,000 years before the Romans came and installed baths, other mod. cons, and thick brick-and-mortar **defensive walls**. Much of the latter still remain, despite being knocked about by later tourists, including the Crusaders. Their Kamilite Gate is supposed to resemble a camel.
Reached via a turning west after Banya, on the Karlovo-Plovdiv road, the spa provides treatments for digestive, intestinal, gynaecological and arthritic conditions. It also bottles mineral water which is bought all over Bulgaria, recent testimonials having claimed (for instance) total dispersal of kidney stones after drinking it regularly for some months. Visitors drink one of the 22 different waters, at source, from the spouts of teapot-like containers. Roman and later remains offer quite some sightseeing interest.

Accommodation
Balneohotel Augusta, 540 beds (a new hotel)
The enthusiast wishing to stay cheaply might try the shabbily quaint **Hotel Republika**, roughly opposite the stone arcade with mineral water fountains.

PLOVDIV

Plovdiv is Bulgaria's second city, but perhaps the one with the most character and variety within itself — even if this is not the first impression from some approaches, or in the commercial centre.
Its history is many-layered. And it has a lively present, with its university, big trade fairs and its food, tobacco, textile, metallurgical, machinery, truck-building, and typewriter-making industries. Its genuine period restaurants

Plovdiv, its old town rich in fine examples of the National Revival period houses

are better than most elsewhere in the country, but its rather expensive 3-star hotels do not all provide the sophisticated level of service and facilities expected by the international business community.

◆◆◆
THE OLD TOWN

Cliché descriptions like quaint or picturesque hardly do justice to the elaborately painted façades, jutting oriel windows, columns, beams, curving eaves, and intimate courtyards of the National Revival Period houses which rise in serene ceremony above its cobbled streets.

Mellow and other-wordly as they are, these 18th- to 19th-century preserves are comparatively recent structures on the three hills of ancient *Trimontium*. Here the Romans built a great acropolis with a theatre, whose semi-circle of tiered stone seats, stage and backdrop of classical columns remain sufficiently undamaged by time and tumult to accommodate ambitious drama and music events today. (On the nearby hilltop is a musical academy, and passers-by may hear the voices of vibrant young sopranos or rich-toned basses – perhaps future operatic successors to Bulgaria's Nikolai Ghiaurov or Boris Christov.) Before the Romans, came the Macedonians – in 343 BC, when their King Philip II (father of Alexander the Great) seized this hill citadel and called it Philippopolis. But the place had known other names and foundations from the Thracians and early folk for nearly 6,000 years before him. And in various centuries AD the Goths, Byzantines, Bulgarians and Ottomans left their marks – sometimes in more than one period of occupation.

The modern town attracts more peaceable influxes from many nations, with its international trade fairs – for consumer goods in May, and technical equipment in September. Discerning business visitors (especially those who benefit from incentive travel schemes) might well find time for the displays at some of Plovdiv's museums (the **Archaeological Museum** has examples of the Panagyurishte 'Thracian Hoard'), and for dining in the genuine period ambience of the Puldin, Alafrangite or Trakiiski Stan restaurants (at the latter International Food and Wine Society members praised the wholesomeness of the food and exceptional quality of vintage

The Roman theatre, Plovdiv, dating from the 2nd century, where festivals are staged during the summer months

and ordinary wines).

In Freedom Park 'Dancing Fountains' are accompanied by music and coloured light effects. Plovdiv Old Town's appeal to artists and writers is obvious. An ochre-tinted edifice on the corner of T. Samodumov and K. Tsertelov Streets was home in 1833 to the French poet, Lamartine, and contains a small museum.

The Georgiadi House has remarkable bay windows and yoke-shaped eaves. At 1, Starinna Street, it houses the **Museum of the National Liberation Struggles** (in which a titled British lady is warmly remembered as a sort of Florence Nightingale). The **Ethnographic Museum** has ornate gilt wreaths and scrollwork on its bluish-grey façade under a roof which rolls like a sea swell. Its cosily decorated rooms have displays of period furniture, folk items and paintings. In these domestic interiors the atmosphere can perhaps be best appreciated outside the summer tourist season, when you may be sharing it with polyglot guided tour groups on each echoing floor. There are mosques dating from the mid-15th century — the **Djoumaya** and the **Imaret**. Decorations in the **St Marina Church** on Taxim Tepe Hill include scenes from the life of St George, whose dragon deterrence was well-known in these parts. One of Europe's oldest clocktowers is on Sahat Tepe Hill.

In Suedinenie (Union) Square is the gleaming modernistic monument to commemorate the 1878 Union of the two Bulgarias. Monument-building remains a great and respected growth industry in Bulgaria, as in Russia. Squads of men and women were seen applying hasty finishing touches to the Union monument and its surrounds on the day before it was to be unveiled by President Zhivkov. Would they complete in time? — 'They shall work all the night', said an official.

Food and Drink

Trakiiskistan, 35 Puldin Street.
Alafrangite, 17 Kiril Nektariev Street.
Puldin, 3 Knyaz Tseretelev Street.
Ribkata, a rare fish tavern (fried carp, trout) in a street parallel with the Central Square as viewed from the front of the Trimontium.

Accommodation

Hotel Novotel Plovdiv, 5-star, 2 Zlatyu Boyadjiev Street (tel: 5-58-92), has international-style modernity in its seven floors, eight suites and 314 double rooms, restaurant, day bar and night club, national restaurant, coffee shop, free shop, indoor and outdoor swimming pools, sauna, bowling alley, hairdressers, post office, covered parking lot, air-conditioning.
Trimontium, 3-star, 2 Kapitan Raicho (tel: 22-55-61). Facing the Central Square, portentously porticoed and vaulted. The Garden Restaurant has Palm Court overtones. It has four floors with four suites and 260 beds, restaurant, night club, national restaurant, coffee shop, hairdressers, post office,

information and rent-car bureau.
The Leningrad Park Hotel,
3-star, 97 Moskva Boulevard (tel:
5-58-03), is modern — except in
attitudes, which have been
known to be dourly
disciplinarian, especially
towards guests attempting to
enter its 'fully booked' nightclub
as its violin and piano duet play
for a one third-full house. It has
21 floors with 26 suites and 675
beds, restaurant, night club, day
bar, indoor swimming pool, free
shop, hairdressers, post office,
coffee shop, information bureau.
Maritsa, 3-star, 5 G. Dimitrov
Street (tel: 55-27-35). 11 floors
with four suites, 47 single and
120 double rooms, restaurants,
day bar, coffee shop,
hairdressers, rent-a-car office.
Leipzig, 2-star, 70 Ruski
Boulevard (tel: 23-27-70). 11
floors, two suites and 250 beds,
restaurant, night club,
information bureau.

KAZANLUK

Kazanluk may be most noted
amongst modern Bulgarians for
its production of milling
machines and musical
instruments, but its touristic
appeal stems from the fragrant
harvest of its **Valley of Roses** —
yielding 80 per cent of the
world's supply of rose attar for
perfumes — and the vivid
folklore which follows this.

◆◆
THE THRACIAN TOMB

A unique attraction in Tyulbeto
park on the town's northeastern
outskirts. Commemorating a
chieftain who was called to
higher things around the 4th
century BC, it features in
UNESCO's list of outstanding
cultural sites. But its murals,
whose 2,300-year-old dyes
depict elegant women, soldiers
and horses ready for banquet or
battle, are more worryingly
sensitive to sunlight and
changing air conditions than are
the annual roses. Thus the
average visitor sees a perfect,
detailed replica built near the
original tomb, which is opened
up only occasionally for the right
kind of archaeologist or VIP.

◆
MUSEUM OF THE ROSE INDUSTRY

Illustrates the history of this
business since its first blooming
150 or more years ago, with
ancient sepia photographs,
huge distilling kettles, and
examples of the rose oil's use in
'Green' medicines, rose liqueur,
and various confections. And
the Rose Institute has collected
more than 1,500 rose species
from all over the world.

◆◆◆
FESTIVAL OF THE VALLEY OF THE ROSES

This takes place over several
days in late May or early June
between a nearby Balkan Valley
and the main square of
otherwise ordinary-looking
Kazanluk (best to check exact
dates with the Bulgarian
National Tourist Office or
Balkantourist; coach tours take
in Kazanluk and the Valley).
For some time, pickers in
prettily embroidered folk garb
will daily have been gathering
rosebuds while they may —
from pre-dawn until 08.00, or
whenever the morning sun
becomes so hot as to steam
away the precious aroma from

THE BALKAN AND CENTRAL REGION

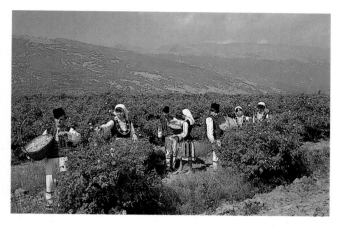

Gathering rosebuds during May (and June): rose-pickers in folk costume celebrate the annual Festival of Roses

the dewy petals of pink *rosa damascena* or white *rose alba*. Visitors re-load cameras with colour film as the 'rose maidens' empty basketfuls of blossoms into quaint mule-carts for despatch, in procession, to town and distillery. They are welcomed with a confetti of rose petals and a liberal spraying with rosewater (presumably a dilution of the attar, which is literally worth its weight in gold).

Tape recorders pick up fluttering cadences from rustic flute, oriental fiddle and Balkan bagpipe, and great cowbells strike an awesome, pagan note when hung around the torsos of evil-spirit-scaring 'demons' wearing head-masks.

The annual Rose Festival's folk extravaganza has been known to enchant even tourists who would normally switch off at the threat of folklore. Gorgeously costumed, the dancers and singers are the proudly competitive best from each of their regions.

At other times of year, Kazanluk is not so lively and colourful, but provides a convenient stopover on tours which feature also (for instance) Veliko Turnovo, Gabrovo, Shipka Pass and Plovdiv.

Accommodation
Hotel Kazanluk, 3-star (tel: 272-10), with amenities including indoor swimming pool, restaurants, bars and a *Mehana* tavern selling snacks and excellent draught beer.
Hotel Roza, 2-star (tel: 247-03).
Hotel Zornitsa, 2-star (tel: 223-84).
These are all in the centre of town, and there is a **campsite** about three miles along the Shipka road, reached very cheaply by bus.

Balkantourist Office 1 Dolina Street (tel: 210-87).

Etura, an open-air museum park where craftsmen work in traditional workshops making individual souvenirs

◆◆
ETURA

Etura Ethnographical Museum, 5 miles (8 km) from Gabrovo, is much cosier than its name may suggest. It is an artistic reproduction, with authentic atmosphere, of a village street with traditional workshops, in a lovely wooded valley by a stream which drives a watermill. The houses, workrooms and shops are simply but attractively built, sometimes of stone with weather-boarding and a little wooden balcony; carved shutters, under overhanging eaves of heavy shingled roofs, add homely touches.

Their interiors tend to smell of wood and whatever material is being hand-worked by the resident craftspeople — leather for old-style wine containers or harnesses, sheep's wool for spinning and weaving into rugs, cloth for items of folkwear, the paraphernalia of metalworkers, potters, painters, and musical instrument makers. (Craft courses can be arranged for visitors, by arrangement through Balkantourist.)

Here you can buy souvenirs, including silver, gold and copperware, all with more individual character than the mass-produced offerings of the *Corecom* hard-currency shops in resort areas. You may also be tempted by the aroma of fresh 'organic' bread and buns from the bakery, or the sizzle of meaty sausages at a folksy tavern.

Some of the crafts shops may be closed on certain days, perhaps with a frustrating lack of information as to when they will open. But the place also lacks the commercial hassle and marketing gimmickry of the 'theme parks' in some countries.

SHIPKA PASS

This is one of the places where Bulgaria's friendship with Russia can be seen to be deeply forged. It saw one of the most decisive battles of the three-prong Russian military incursion to drive out the cruelly dominant Turks in the hard winter of 1877.

Here 7,000 besieged Russian soldiers and Bulgarian volunteers kept at bay 27,000 élite troops of Suleiman Pasha, finally beating them off — and advancing rapidly southwards towards the Turkish border when the Russians sent reinforcements after taking Pleven in another key struggle. When their ammunition ran out after days of stubborn defence, they had hurled mountain rocks, tree boughs and corpses at the Turks.

◆◆
THE ONION-DOMED CHURCH

On the wooded hillside above Shipka village, which commemorates the battle. Has 17 bells 12 of which were cast entirely from melted-down shell-cases and shrapnel found on the battlefield. Today, visiting Bulgarians and Russians of all ages place flowers and wreaths by the memorial tablets in the church's crypt.

◆◆
FREEDOM MONUMENT

On nearby Stoletov Peak. Having climbed the steps to the monument, visitors can descend to slake thirsts or eat at cafés in a parking area below — cafés whose facilities do *not* share the epic quality of the monuments.

Shipka Pass, on E85 between Gabrovo and Kazanluk, is visited by coach tours.

GABROVO
◆◆◆
THE HOUSE OF HUMOUR AND SATIRE

Gabrovo overturns stereotype preconceptions about stone-faced or unimaginative bureaucracy in this part of the world — the town's House of Humour and Satire is the headquarters for local, national and overseas jokes. (These are not all state-controlled Glorious Jokes of the People's Republics, with a Marxist-Leninist precept in every punchline.)

The House itself has cool white marble interiors with the rather clinical look, as it were, of a modern art gallery.

Gabrovo's occasional Experimental Satirical Theatre

performances are apparently broadly based programmes of comedy, music and carnivalia at its Biennial Festival of Humour and Satire, staged in May of each odd-numbered year.

A description of Gabrovo as 'one of Bulgaria's prettiest towns' seems somewhat prone to poetic licence or local humour, since it does not have such obvious eye-appeal as have Plovdiv Old Town, Koprivshtitsa, Nesebur, Sozopol and numerous other places.
Its more tangible and serious products come from textile

The golden-domed church in Shipka, built in memory of those who fell in the fiercest battle of the Russo-Turkish war

mills, machine shops, and 'the world's biggest combine for building electric hoists'. It has many technical colleges.
There are atmospheric, older enclaves flanking the River Yantra, in which a rock supports the statue of the town's 14th-century founder, Racho the Blacksmith. And tradition is handed down in crafts shops, some of them along Opulchenska Street.

The **National Museum of Education** is housed in the Aprilov School, set up in 1835 as the first school to provide secular teaching in the Bulgarian language, and to many prominent pupils.
In the Liliana Dimitrova main square, the memorial to Mitko Palaouzov — a 14-year-old partisan who died fighting Fascists in 1944 — may well be guarded by Young Pioneers, who periodically 'present arms'.

Food and Drink
The Inn, 15 Opulchenska Street, a fairly folksy national taverna — as is the **Mogilyov** on Plaza Parvi Mai.

Accommodation
Hotel Balkan, 3-star, 14 Emanouil Manolov Street (tel: 2-19-11), with three banqueting halls, coffee shop, day bar.
Yantra, 2-star, Railway Station Square (tel: 2-48-12), with restaurant and bar.
Campsite 'Gabrovo', 2-star, run by the Union of Bulgarian Motorists, on the road out to Stoletov Peak.

Balkantourist Office 2 Opulchenska Street (tel: 2-48-31).

◆◆
BOZHENTSI

Bozhentsi, a village which rambles around its rural valley as randomly as do the roses in its sometimes overgrown gardens, is a special architectural and historic preserve.

Charming, indeed, are the woodcarvings on the entrance gates and verandahs of its whitewashed houses along cobblestone streets. But they do not now echo with the sounds of old-fashioned artisan labour. Often empty, they are used as holiday rest homes for Bulgarian writers and artists.

One or two former dwellings are museum-houses which can be visited by coach tour parties, their interiors having 19th-century folk-furnishings. For the average visitor, Bozhentsi offers pleasant and very peaceful sightseeing walks — but no tourist accommodation and not much indigenous life.

◆◆◆
VELIKO TURNOVO

More wholly picturesque and preserved than some ancient cities, Veliko Turnovo presents a splendid theatrical backdrop to its history since (and before) it was fortress capital of the Second Bulgarian State from 1187 to 1396.

It seems to grow naturally out of the rock of three hills above several loops of the River Yantra. In almost Disneyesque (but dignified) jumbles, its older dwellings — sturdily beamed and tiled, sometimes balconied, hung with creepers and roses — terrace its contours or cling to cliff-edges like elaborate nests of martins under house-eaves.

It was on Tsarevets Hill that, in 1185, the brothers Assen and Peter seized the fortress and led an uprising which eventually freed Bulgaria from Byzantine rule. Its ramparts, gates and battle towers are often spotlit at night; within the walls archaeologists have for years excavated the remains of the royal palace, religious and mercantile buildings.

On Tsarevets and Trapezitsa Hills, antiquities include surviving churches that are rich in murals and monuments — notably those of St Dimiter of Salonika (12th-century), the Holy Forty Martyrs (13th-century) and St Peter and Paul (14th-century). On Sveta Gora Hill was a medieval monastery with schools of literature and painting which produced masterpieces like Tsar Ivan Alexander's *Four Gospels* (in the British Museum, London) and the Manasses' *Chronicle* (in the Vatican Library, Rome). Now it supports the city's Cyril and Methodius University — named after the 9th-century monks who devised the original Cyrillic script of Slav languages. Many of the buildings which give the city its distinctive character today date from the National Revival Period of the 18th/19th centuries. Numerous examples are by self-taught architect Nikola Fichev, 'founder' of the Bulgarian national style of architecture, which conforms with the landscape and combines new features with medieval traditions. Especially worth seeing are the

House with the Monkey, at 14
Vustanicheska Street, the Hadji
Nikoli Inn, 17 Rakovski Street,
the Town Hall in Suedinenie
Square, and the Samovodene
Market Place, with its restored
workshops, café and exhibition
section.

The **archaeological museum**,
dealing with Veliko Turnovo's
12th-14th-century period as
capital of Bulgaria, is at 21
Boteva Street.

Four miles (7 km) northwest of
the city, on a secluded hillside,
is **Preobrazhenski Monastery**
(open to the public), safe former
refuge of the revolutionary
Vassil Levski.

*Veliko Turnovo: memorial to the
brothers Assen and Peter who led
the 1185 uprising against
Byzantine rule*

Food and Drink
Slavyanka restaurant, café and
night club, 35 Levski Street.
Stadion restaurant, 2 T. Balina
Street.
Vladishki Most tavern, Assenovo
suburb.
Poltava café, 1 Hristo Botov
Street.
Oriental café, 32 D. Blagoev
Street.

Accommodation
Interhotel Veliko Turnovo,
3-star, 2 E. Popov Street

(tel: 3-05-71). Amenities include disco.

Yantra Hotel, 2-star, 1 Velchova Zavera Square (tel: 3-03-91/92).
Etur Hotel, 2-star, 1 Ivailo Street (tel: 2-68-61).
Sveta Gora Motel and **campsite**, 2-star, 1¼ miles (2 km) from Veliko Turnovo on the E771 international motorway.

Balkantourist office, 1 V. Levski Street, (tel: 21836).

◆◆
ARBANASSI

Secluded on high ground just north of Veliko Turnovo, with connecting bus services, Arbanassi is one of Bulgaria's most attractive and unusual villages. Its stone-built houses are decorated externally with floral and geometrical figures carved or figured with large-headed nails in wood panelling, doors and shutters. Carved wooden ceilings are popular (especially in Konstantsiliev's, Kandilarov's, and Hadjiiliev's houses), and often feature 'sunburst' designs. In the 17th and 18th centuries, craftsmen in copper, gold and silverware flourished here. In early spring they would set off on merchant venturer trips, their caravans stocked with hides, dried meat, sausage, wool, furs and wine. They travelled to Hungary, Italy, Poland, Russia, even Persia and India, returning with silks, velvet and spices. There are two monasteries, the **St Nikola**, whose chapel's filigree work is particularly beautiful and intricate — and the **Holy Virgin**. Each of the five village churches has an eastern section traditionally intended for men and a western (rear) section for women. The stark-looking exterior of the **Holy Nativity (Rozhdestvo Hristovo) Church** belies the exceptional wealth of painted murals within.

◆
PRESLAV

Preslav was the second capital (succeeding Pliska) of the First Bulgarian Kingdom under Tsar Simeon around the turn of the 9th/10th century, and it was from its famous academic institutions that the Slav alphabet was spread to other countries. Unfortunately, various medieval occupiers were less culturally inclined than Simeon, having tendencies to raze the city to the ground or burn it down. Thus, much that remains of the original site of Veliki (Great) Preslav is marked out by ruined columns. However, there has been considerable restoration of the castle walls, palace buildings — and the Round Church, which is a unique example of Old Bulgarian architecture.

In recent years, excavators have unearthed sections of the archbishop's building, the basilica, the city wall and a decorated pool. And the Veliki Preslav Museum in the archaeological reserve contains rare antiquities from the 10th century.

Just east of Preslav is the **Patleina Monastery**.

SHUMEN (SHOUMEN)

Shumen is one of the Bulgarian names seen on bottles of its district's exported white wine,

In the traditional style: heavy tiled roof, broad eaves, wide balcony, white-washed walls

as well as of beer locally. An industrially important town, roughly half-way between Veliko Turnovo and Varna, it has character, culture — and vintage history.

The **Vassil Kolarov Museum**, 11 T. Ikonomow Street, and the **Lajos Kossuth Museum**, 35 Tsar Osvoboditel Street, are significant.

The town's older quarters are down by the river. Its symphony orchestra is Bulgaria's oldest. There is opera and theatre. During the First and Second Bulgarian States, and later, it was a key fortress. The fort's foundations are Roman and Thracian.

◆◆
1,300 YEARS OF BULGARIA MEMORIAL

A massive concatenation of concrete figures on Ilchov Bair Hill.

◆
THE TOMBUL MOSQUE

Built in 1745 with materials from ancient local towns, the largest in the country. A former Turkish primary school in its courtyard contains an ethnographic exhibition.

Accommodation

Hotel Madara, 3-star (tel: 5-75-98), in town centre, with restaurant, coffee-shop, tavern, tourist information and car rental offices.

Hotel Sofia (moderately priced), 37 Tsar Osboditel Street. Bookings through Balkantourist office (see below).

Balkantourist office tel: (054) 5-70-29.

Car repairs: 14 Gagarin Street. **Union of Bulgarian Motorists office**: 1 Tsvetan Zangov Street.

THE BALKAN AND CENTRAL REGION

◆◆◆
MADARA

The Madara National Historical and Archaeological Reserve, near the village of Mutnitsa 6 miles (10 km) east of Shumen, contains the famous bas-relief of the **Madara Horseman** cut into the rock of an ancient cliff fortress.

Who was he? — A Bulgarian Khan, say the majority. Inscriptions below him, though in Greek, date from the reign of Khan Omurtag (816-31) and refer to 8th- and 9th-century events in Bulgaria. Others have suggested he may have appeared much earlier than that, and with a religious significance.

Holding a goblet in one hand, he sits astride a proud-stepping steed, with a hound pursuivant and speared lion couchant on the ground below him.

On a terrace below are remains of a 9th-century pagan shrine and ecclesiastical buildings from the late Middle Ages. To the southwest are ruins of Roman houses and farm buildings.

PLISKA

Pliska is more than the name of a popular Bulgarian brandy. It was the first capital of Bulgaria, from the 7th century until Preslav supplanted it in 893.

◆
FORTIFICATION RUINS

Ruins of three concentric fortifications, covering nine square miles (23 sq km), one mile from the town which is on a turning north from Kaspichan on E70 (east of Shumen).

The best-preserved remains are of the Great Palace, but other remnants include those of a small palace with water mains that were previously unknown, and of the Great Basilica from the 9th century. The nearby museum contains pottery, weapons and other items from a site which may engage archaeologists for some time to come.

Accommodation

The **Pliska Hotel** is open to visitors year round.

◆◆
KOTEL

A characterful town with traditional carpet, rug and blanket-making industries, Kotel lies in a hollow of hill country on a road north towards Omurtag from E772, 19 miles (31 km) east of Sliven.

It was the home of several Bulgarian National Revival Period revolutionaries and writers including Georgi Rakovski and Sophronius. There are schools for folk-instrument making and for arts and crafts, at which Balkantourist may arrange courses for visitors (with advance notice).

Kotel carpets have geometric patterns in strong colours. Both they and the tufted or fleecy rugs find a ready export market. Along narrow cobblestone streets of the **old part of the town**, which survived a great fire of 1894, are wood-clad houses with good carvings and broad eaves. An **Ethnographic Museum** is in one of them, and not far away (these things are not done by halves!) is the **History Museum** in an old school building.

Accommodation

The **Hotel Kotel**, 2-star (tel: 28-65), has restaurant and discothèque.

◆◆
ZHERAVNA

This is a pretty 'living museum' village, 9 miles (14 km) along a turning to the west, south of Kotel. Houses of the 18th and 19th centuries have been restored to their original appearance, with their rounded roof tops, jutting eaves and oriel windows, and wood carvings. Mod. cons have been installed without disturbing the character of their interiors — furnished with divans, traditional carpets, rugs, curtains and runners. A bakery and church café have also been resurrected and put back into business. Craftsmen's shops and a tavern with restaurant have been added, in architecture which is intended to harmonise.

Monument to National Revival notable, Sophronius, in Kotel, his native town

The former houses of Russi Chorbadzhi, Sava Filaretov, and Dimcho Kehaya are said to be museum pieces especially worth seeing.

SLIVEN

This is an important industrial town on the southeast edge of the Balkan range, at the foot of the **Sinite Kamani ('Blue Rocks') mountain**. Several museums have memorabilia of revolutionary action against the Turks and others, but textiles are mainly what the town turns out today.

Accommodation

The Hotel Sliven, 2-star (tel: 69-11), in the centre of town, has a restaurant, bar, discothèque, café, and Balkantourist Office.
The Zora, 1-star, 1 Mitropolit Seraphim Street.
Bookings may be made through the Balkantourist office (see below).

Balkantourist office, 7 Georgi Kirkov Street, tel: 2-22-55.
Union of Bulgarian Motorists, 1 Bratya Miladinovi Street, Block 'Olympus'.

THE RHODOPES AND THE SOUTH

Pamporovo, an international ski centre, is also a popular mountain resort in summer

THE RHODOPES AND THE SOUTH

PAMPOROVO

For the skier Pamporovo starts with two great advantages. The Rhodope mountains in which it lies stretch along the Greek border about 53 miles (85 km) from Plovdiv and catch the moisture in the winds as they blow up from the Aegean. In winter this falls as snow and gives a long and quite snow-sure season. The second advantage is the sun. At a latitude further south than that of Rome, Pamporovo enjoys hot sunshine.

Another Greek connection is Orpheus, who according to legend was born near Pamporovo and now has a hotel named after him. There is still plenty of music in the restaurants and discos — often live groups playing ancient-looking instruments — and dancing and singing to traditional airs forms part of the entertainment.

The skiing is of good intermediate standard with six main lifts covering an area between the village at 5,250 feet (1,600 m) and the top of Snezhanka at 6,319 feet (1,962m). (At this point there is a radio

THE RHODOPES AND THE SOUTH

beacon with a revolving restaurant, which gives spectacular views over the surrounding countryside.) As the skiing is mostly on north-facing slopes, the snow escapes the sun and remains powdery. The runs are cut through quite dense forest and provide variety. There are easy blues, some longish reds and short sharp black slopes so that beginners, intermediates and experts can all enjoy the challenge. It is not too big an area — about right for an intermediate skier over a week's holiday.

It is also an excellent resort for beginners. The 60-man Bulgarian ski school is well organised; classes rarely exceed 12 and the instructors are competent in foreign languages.

A great many schools organise

The Rhodope Mountains and southern Bulgaria

skiing trips to Pamporovo and much of the accommodation, therefore, is economical, consisting of bunks in rooms with showers, in hotels serving nourishing but basic food. There are, however, good three-star hotels and the fact that the school operators send large numbers to the resort means that they get excellent rates for adults too, even when the accommodation and food is of a much higher standard. The **Perelik Hotel**, for example, has an indoor swimming pool, sauna, gymnasium, bowling alley and a good selection of shops including **Corecom**, where you can buy only with foreign currency. Its rates for halfboard in a twin-bedded room are about half those for a comparable Swiss hotel.

In the evening there are the usual entertainments — sleighrides, barbecues with

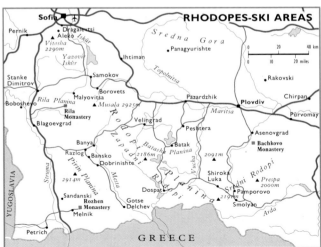

Picturesque Shiroka Luka:
traditional houses perch on the
mountain slopes above the main
village street

whole lambs spitroasted on
open fires, taverns and discos to
use up any energy left after a
day on the slopes. All the
incidentals to a holiday — ski
hire, the odd meal, a cup of
coffee — are less expensive in
Bulgaria than in the Alps. It is
also a good place to buy
presents. Bulgarians make good
carved wooden toys and
ornaments in the mountains and
their Pliska brandy is cheap and
potent. With the added benefits
of currency concessions,
presents are worth buying in the
ski resorts.

In some Eastern bloc countries
equipment hire can be a
gamble but Bulgaria imports
good quality skis, bindings and
boots. The hire shop takes care
that the bindings suit the weight
and ability of the skier and
boots are fitted carefully so that
no sore heels or squashed feet
take the pleasure out of skiing.
Altogether Pamporovo is a good
place to start skiing — the
patient ski-school, easy slopes
and low prices combine with
the southern sunshine to
provide an excellent holiday.

◆◆◆
SHIROKA LUKA
President Todor Zhivkov has
said he is as fond of this village
as he is of Pravets, his

birthplace, far away to the northeast of Sofia. Shiroka Luka has a much more wholly traditional look than the latter. It is on the road down from Pamporovo (or Smolyan) to Devin, at a point where tall mountain pines begin to merge with varieties of broad-leaved trees and there are clearings with tiny cow pastures.

The main street is as quaint as the steep little lanes where weatherboarded houses and barns cling to the mountain rock. And here the keen photographer may regret not having brought in more film — hard to find, even in Pamporovo.

On the terraces of a tavern or two, you can sit on a half-log bench at a half-tree-trunk table and listen to birdsong.

◆◆
SCHOOL OF FOLK MUSIC

If you arrive with a tour group, there may be a pre-arranged concert by pupils, aged 13-19, who will have competed nationwide for places at the School of Folk Music on the southern side of this village. With a variety of plucked or bowed instruments, or a kaval flute, or a bagpipe, they can play or sing in numerous widely differing regional styles and cadences.

Perhaps they may intone 'The Haidouk Came Out . . .', the typical Rhodopean song taped by Valia Balkanska. (This was chosen to accompany tapes of Beethoven's 'Ode to Joy' and other Earth-representative themes aboard the American spacecraft *Voyager*, in case it is

Bachkovo Monastery, artistically one of the country's most significant sites

ever intercepted by some Intelligence beyond our Solar System.)

They learn to make instruments, including bagpipes. And there are special days when Shiroka Luka shrills with the sound of a hundred pipers gathered from the Bulgar highlands far and wide — though perhaps only every other year.

SMOLYAN

Smolyan, 62 miles (100 km) south of Plovdiv and 3,310 ft

villages, which also has some striking National Revival houses. There are buses to **Smolyan Lakes** amidst high pastures north of the town, which offer trout fishing and craggy scenery with forests that may contain deer and bears minding their own business.

◆◆
MUSEUM and ART GALLERY
Two of the town's special amenities worth a visit.

Accommodation
Hotels include the **Smolyan**, 3-star (tel: 71-76), whose extensive main restaurant overlooks the Cherna river's wooded valley. The hotel has Balkantourist and car rental offices. In the skiing season (particularly), bus services connect it daily with Pamporovo.
Panorama campsite, 2-star.

Union of Bulgarian Motorists
Deveti Septemvri Street, Raikovo section.

(1,010 m) up in the Rhodopes, has 'a climate that is particularly beneficial for the vocalist'. It has organised summer opera singing courses in a newly built local theatre, and singing is an activity in which Bulgarian experts are in a super-class of their own.

It has flourished remarkably since 1960, when it was rebuilt and combined with two other villages which had once been ruined by the Turks because their people would not convert to Islam under pain of death. To the east is the Oustovo section, one of the original

◆◆◆
BACHKOVO MONASTERY
The oldest monastery in Bulgaria, this is about 43 miles (70 km) north of Smolyan towards Plovdiv, and 5 miles (9 km) south of Asenovgrad — which produces the famous full-bodied red Mavrud wine for home and overseas consumption.

Just above Bachkovo village, with chickens pecking amongst its courtyard cobbles, the monastery has a more 'domestic' atmosphere than some others. Some of its murals, however, do depict nasty things happening to sinners in Hell, who happen to resemble 19th-century notables of Plovdiv who refused to open a Bulgarian school in the city. The artist is Zahari Zograph, the most famous National Revival artist, who permits himself a self-portrait in better company.

There are other notable paintings in the refectory. The monastery was founded in 1083, originally for Georgian monks. The architecture of the one remaining building of this period contains elements of Armenian, Georgian and Syrian building styles in rows of stone and brick.

BATAK

This is the place where Turkish atrocities became so barbaric in 1876 as finally to shock the world into recognition that something must be done, thanks to the uncensored reporting of a brave American journalist.

◆◆
ST NEDELYA'S CHURCH

To suppress local activities following the April Uprising, the Turks and their Pomak henchmen besieged 3,000 citizens in the church and then — after promising immunity for surrender — proceeded mercilessly to behead and butcher virtually every man, woman and child in the church and its yard. Blood-stained palm-prints remain on the church walls.

European reaction to these atrocities was not entirely decisive.In Britain, for instance, Disraeli wanted a continued alliance with the Turks against the Russians, although this met with strong opposition from others more moved by the brutality — and still helped them to retain a portion of Bulgaria after the Congress of Berlin, in 1878.

Despite this history, detailed in the church and a local museum, Batak and its surroundings — with beech and pine forests, and carp-fishing in the dam — are regarded as a peaceful recreation area. It is 27 miles (37 km) south of the E80 from Pazardzhik.

Accommodation

The youth tourist organisation **Orbita** (tel: 23-27) has local hostel accommodation.

VELINGRAD

Named after a partisan heroine, Vela Peeva, and developed from three merged villages in 1948, Velingrad is a leafy spa with parkland, 77 warm mineral water springs and 40 balneo-therapy establishments treating various conditions from rheumatoid arthritis to hypertension and nervous fatigue.

There is a 'Holiday Palace' of the trade unions.

Velingrad is 10 miles (16 km) east of Yundola resort, which is 16 miles (26 km) south of Belovo (E80).

Food and Drink

The **Kleptouza Restaurant** overlooks the Kleptouza karst lake, in the Chepino Quarter, which sometimes has rowing boats.

Accommodation

The **Zradvets Hotel**, 2-star (tel: 99-41), caters inexpensively for Westerners, as may local campsites and chalets.

THE BLACK SEA

VARNA

This is Bulgaria's third city and a major seaport, with a long history and a multi-cultural present. It retains Roman and other remains, exudes a friendly atmosphere in ornamented late 19th-century avenues and public buildings, and has added modern developments in human scale and leafy settings.

It is popular with package tourists who fly into its airport to stay in surrounding resorts, visitors on ferries from Russian Black Sea ports, sports champions, and world professional bodies attending congresses (sociologists and architects have been among them).

It has serious everyday business in shipbuilding, power generation, the food and light industries, its major university institutes of Economics, Electrical Engineering and Medicine, and its Naval Academy. Early evening seems to bring out a relaxed, Mediterranean-style 'promenading' custom in summer.

The Varna Summer Festival in June presents theatre performances in the former Roman thermal baths, chamber music amidst the icons of the old St Atanas Church, the ballet contest on the open air stage, and symphony concerts at the Festival Complex. This latter, between Lenin Boulevard and Vassil Drumer Street has a circular hall with 5,000 seats and a revolving stage. Other

The Stone Forest, a weird natural phenomenon near Varna

conference halls also have simultaneous translation facilities.

Attached to the complex is a sports ground which stages a variety of international events.

◆◆
SEASIDE PARK

Beaches (including one for nudists) with warm mineral water shower facilities fringe this extensive park, with its Black Sea and Mediterranean varieties of flora and shrubs, its fountains, its Dolphinarium, Zoo, and (next to its central entrance) Copernicus Astronomy Complex. The Aquarium in Chervenoarmeiska Boulevard contains native and exotic marine and freshwater species.

◆◆
MUSEUM OF ART AND HISTORY

Forty exhibition halls, including three showing artefacts from the celebrated Varna Necropolis. In

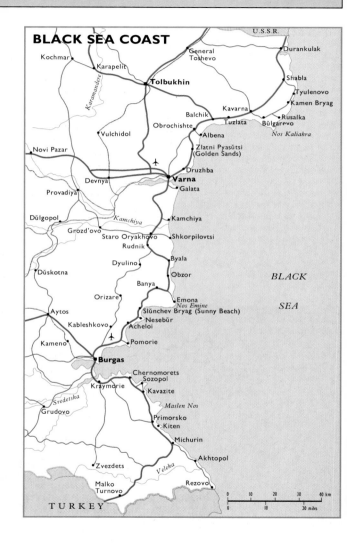

BLACK SEA COAST

U.S.S.R.

Kochmar
Karapelit
Tolbukhin
General Toshevo
Durankulak
Shabla
Tyulenovo
Kamen Bryag
Kavarna
Balchik
Rusalka
Tuzlata
Bŭlgarevo
Obrochishte
Nos Kaliakra
Vulchidol
Albena
Zlatni Pyasŭtsi
(Golden Sands)
Novi Pazar
Druzhba
Devnya
Varna
Galata
Provadiya
Dŭlgopol
Kamchiya
Kamchiya
Grozd'ovo
Staro Oryakhovo
Shkorpilovtsi
Rudnik
Byala
Dyulino
Obzor
Dŭskotna
Banya
BLACK
Orizare
Emona
Nos Emine
SEA
Aytos
Slŭnchev Bryag (Sunny Beach)
Kableshkovo
Nesebŭr
Acheloi
Kameno
Pomorie
Burgas
Chernomorets
Sozopol
Kraymorie
Kavazite
Sredetska
Maslen Nos
Grudovo
Primorsko
Kiten
Michurin
Zvezdets
Akhtopol
Veleka
Malko Turnovo
Rezovo

0 10 20 30 40 km
0 10 20 miles

TURKEY

1972 more than a thousand gold objects dating from about 4,000 BC were found in one of the Necropolis tombs, among them finely worked bracelets and necklets around the skeletal bones of a tribal chieftain. (Some of these unique items are periodically on tour to other museums.)

Inhabited from the Stone Age, Varna area became the Greek colony of Odessos in the 6th century BC and was named Varna by the Slavs 12 centuries later. Traces of early Christian churches remain in Tsar Krum Street and elsewhere. Ottoman dominance was challenged by Crusaders under a Polish prince in 1444, and the first Russian assault, of 1828, resulted in two years of liberation. One of the first socialist groups was set up locally in the late 19th century.

◆◆
STONE FOREST
An early natural formation, 50 million years old, apparently of stalagmite-type. Around 12 miles (20 km) west.

Food and Drink
Baikal, 9 G. Dimitrov Boulevard. **Galateya**, Cape Galata.

Kamchiya, near Varna, a resort set in the beautiful scenery of a nature reserve

Dimyat, 111 Lenin Boulevard.
Euxinograd, 2 Anton Ivanov Street.
Zlatnoto Pile, 7 G. Dimitrov Boulevard.
Kotva, 29 San Stefano Street.
Komitovo Hanche, in the city's western part, at the start of the Hemus motorway.
Morsko Casino, near the Central Beach entrance.
Morsko Konche, 7 Dimiter Kondov Street.
Morska Sirena, at the Passenger Docks.
Morska Zvezda, on the terrace of the Central Sea Baths.
Nectar, 62 Lenin Boulevard.
Ocean, San Stefano Street.
Ostrava, 54 Dubrovnik Street.
Preslav, 1 Avram Gachev Street.
Pliska, on Red Square.
Pochivka, Lenin Boulevard, Pochivka bus stop.
Rostock, 20 Karl Marx Boulevard
Sevastopol, on the corner of Lenin and G. Dimitrov Boulevards.
Starata Kushta, 14 Druzki Street.
Horizont, in the Seaside Park, Akatsiite bus stop.
Chinarite, Ninth September Square.

Accommodation

Hotel Cherno More, 3-star, 35 Georgi Dimitrov Boulevard (tel: 30-50-66 or 2-71-17), part of the Interhotels chain. Three restaurants, one panoramic, on the 22nd floor. Ground floor café with terrace, day bar, congress halls, shops and a night club.
Hotel Odessa, 2-star, 1 Georgi Dimitrov Boulevard (tel: 22-53-12), right next to the Central Beach. Ground floor restaurant with terrace and café.

Hotel Musala, 1-star, 3 Musala Street (tel: 22-39-25).
Orbita Youth Tourist Complex, 25 V. Kolarov Boulevard (tel: 22-51-62).
Private lodgings and villas
Besides hotels, Balkantourist also offers accommodation at reasonably priced private lodgings and villas in the city suburbs and coastal villa zone.

Tourist Services Offices

Tourist services provided include: information, currency exchange, hotel reservations

Sozopol, a picturesque old town with several beaches in the area

and accommodation in private lodgings, excursions inland and abroad, visits to folkstyle restaurants, night clubs, etc.
Offices working all year round:
No 1, 3 Musala Street.
No 2, 33 Avram Gachev Street.
No 3, 5 Tolbukhin Street.
No 4, 73 Lenin Boulevard.
No 5, Chaika Suburb, block 68 (Stadiona bus stop).
At Odessa Hotel - 1 G. Dimitrov Boulevard.

KAMCHIYA

About 18 miles (30 km) south of Varna, seaward of E87, is the mouth of the Kamchiya river, which flows through the

Longoza nature reserve of forest and marsh said to be rich in waterfowl.

Accommodation
The area has two hotels and six campsites.

Food and Drink
There are four restaurants (including the **Nestinarka**, with barefoot fire-walking performances).

◆◆◆
SOZOPOL
Founded in 610 BC as the Greek settlement of Apollonia, Sozopol is a picture-book museum town and fishing port 21 miles (34km) south of Burgas (which has an international airport).
It is built on a rocky peninsula fringed by small rocky islands, but there are plenty of sandy beaches in the vicinity, with comfortable bathing in the sea whose temperatures reach 75°F (25°C) in July and August.
There is a laid-back, southern atmosphere in its cobbled lanes over which the wood-beamed upper storeys of houses jut out in neighbourly proximity. Near the waterfront you can sometimes buy local-style fish (probably small mackerel) and chips in paper wrapping to eat as you walk around.
Sozopol claims to attract poets, actors and architects (who, if native, will be state-employed and probably benefiting from low-cost accommodation provided by their unions). Extra tone and colour is lent in the first half of September when the Apollonia Arts Festival stages music, drama, pictorial art, cinematic and poetry events.

Preserved through the centuries of oppression: Nesebur has a number of fine old churches

The spirit of Apollo, Greek god of music, song and poetry, lives on.

Excursions

◆◆
ROPOTAMO RIVER
From Sozopol excursions may be made to the River Ropotamo. Reaching the sea just before Cape Maslen Nos, about 11 miles (18 km) south, the Ropotamo has banks flanked with deciduous trees often linked together with creeping vines. A row-boat trip along it only gently disturbs its waterlilies, large dragonflies, and perhaps less familiar forms of water life. Details from the Balkantourist office.

Accommodation
An accommodation bureau (tel: 258) may be able to find 'Village Rooms' in one of the old weatherboarded houses with its shade of fig or peach tree. Otherwise, **Dyuni holiday village** is a handy base. **Chernomorets campsite**, about 4 miles (6 km) north of Sozopol, 2-star, 1,500 capacity, with medical centre, snack-bar, etc.

Balkantourist Office
Chervenoarmeiska Street (tel: 378).

BURGAS (BOURGAS)

Burgas is a largely industrial port, with a harbour for the country's oceanic fishing fleet, a petrochemical combine, and an international airport. It may be a staging post on some coach tours.

Its local sobriquet as 'the Chicago of Bulgaria' may be somewhat tongue-in-cheek. It has some spacious boulevards, a symphony orchestra, theatres, some low-rise apartment blocks, and traditional links with a stockbreeding and corn belt inland. But it does not look or feel like the inspiration for a Frank Sinatra song.

Accommodation

Hotel Bulgaria, 3-star, 21 Purvi Mai Street (tel: 4-53-36), with panoramic restaurant, coffee shops, bars, nightclub, disco, and conference room with four-language simultaneous translation facilities.
Hotel Briz, 3-star (tel: 4-31-90), near the railway station.
Hotel Primorets, 2-star (tel: 4-41-17), near a beach.

Balkantourist Office 2 Purvi Mai Street (tel: 4-55-53).
Union of Bulgarian Motorists 11 D. Iliev Street.

POMORIE

This is an ancient town which produces a brandy and Dimyat red dessert wine, salt from extensive local pans, and curative mud from a lagoon which sanatoria slap on to many an arthritis sufferer.
It has ancient foundations on a rocky peninsula. But a fire of 1906 destroyed much of its character, apart from a small area in the eastern part near the breakwater.

◆
AN EARLY TOMB

A mound near the town. Something between a Thracian burial 'beehive' and a Roman mausoleum, dating from the 2nd to 3rd century AD. Open to visitors.

Accommodation

The seaside **Hotel Pomorie**, 3-star (tel: 24-40), has a restaurant, pastry shop, and balneological section for the mud cure and other therapies.
The **Europa campsite** is on the road towards Burgas, which is 13 miles (22 km) west along E87.

Balkantourist Office 49 N. Luskov Street.

◆◆◆
NESEBUR (NESSEBUR)

Nesebur is an ancient museum-town and fishing port which has somehow managed to retain its parochial appeal, despite the influx of sightseers from Sunny Beach, Bulgaria's biggest seaside resort 2 miles (3 km) away. On a pretty promontory, it is reached by a narrow isthmus road, flanked by a windmill, and is easily explored.

Weatherboarded houses huddle around its cobbled streets in almost as close formation as the boats in its small harbour. New ones have been added in similar style, with overhanging eaves and small wooden balconies. Traditionally furnished, these provide accommodation, available through tour operators like Balkan Holidays, for 4-8 people who breakfast in them but otherwise eat out with the 'Dine as you please' meal vouchers (see page 109).

Nesebur was a very old-established settlement when the Greeks built up a colony here called Mesembria in the 6th century BC. The oldest of its surprisingly numerous churches (some ruined) are from the 5th and 6th centuries AD, and there are notable Byzantine examples. The well-preserved 10th-century Church of St John the Baptist, opposite the 14th-century Church of the Pantokrator, has 16th- and 17th-century frescoes — as has the 10th-century St Stefan Church, with its decorated bishop's throne and pulpit.

Food and Drink

Street aromas of fried peppers or *gyuvetch* vegetable hotpot can be appetising. A particularly atmospheric restaurant is the **Captain's Cabin (Kapitanska Shreshta)**, as genuinely old as its floorboards suggest, and one of the comparatively few establishments on the coast which use an interesting variety of seafood recipes.

Accommodation

The Hotel Messambria, 2-star (tel: 32-55), in the tiny town's 'centre', is built in a basically local style — only to two storeys — and has a restaurant, bar, and car rental service.

Balkantourist office: in the new part of town (tel: 22-95).

DRUZHBA (DROUZHBA)

Druzhba ('Friendship') is the longest-established post-war resort, from the mid-1950s, with a tranquil and intimate ambience. About 6 miles (10 km) north of Varna along E87, which gives aspects of a bosky riviera, it is graced by stately old oaks, beech, poplars, pine, cedar, cypress and lime trees. In July and August there are folk concerts.

Rest homes restore the tissues of various unions' members who can take the local mineral waters. Little rocky coves and beaches combine with an overall smallness of scale to provide contrast to the three large coastal resorts (Sunny Beach, Golden Sands and Albena). There is a frequent bus service to Varna and Golden Sands.

Food and Drink

The **Odessos Restaurant** and the folkloric **'Bulgarian Wedding'** restaurant are both near the hotels listed below. Other restaurants: **Manastirska Izba** (Monastery Cellar), **The Sedemte Odai** (The Seven Chambers) and **Taverna Chernomorets** (Black Sea) taverna with its Tourist Service Bureau.

Accommodation

The Grand Hotel Varna, 5-star (tel: 6-14-91), big, and the finest on the coast. Yet it has been in the habit of charging only average restaurant prices for *table d'hote* dishes, for which non-resident package tourists could pay with their 'Dine as you please' meal vouchers (see page 109).

Guests can enjoy health and sports facilities including an outdoor mineral-water swimming pool and an indoor sea-water pool (both heated), a nightclub with cabaret and a casino.

Of the 20 hotels, this is one of those used by European tour operators. Others include:
The Prostor, 2-star (tel: 6-11-71), 50 yards (45 m) from the beach and of 1950s vintage, its terrace having an attractive use of stone (plentiful in Bulgaria, but international-style concrete and glass is the coastal norm).

The 7-storey beach-front **Rubin** (with its Tourist Service Bureau), 2-star (tel: 6-10-20).

The low-rise **Koral**, 2-star (tel: 6-14-14).

Reservations can also be made through the Golden Sands and

The casino at the Grand Hotel Varna, Druzhba, which also offers a range of spa treatments

Druzhba Booking Office (tel: 6-56-81/2/3).

GOLDEN SANDS
(Zlatni Pyasutsi)
Whether or not it's embryonic 'Communist California', Golden Sands and its setting of lush forested hills and adjacent low cliffs 10 miles (17 km) north of Varna have attracted more cheers than sneers from foreign pundits. 'Nowhere else in Europe have I seen such a splendid architectural ensemble, blending so perfectly with nature', enthused Jean Royer, director of the School of Architecture in Paris.

Golden Sands has a *Cultural* Information Centre. And its nightlife has touches of glamour which might betoken 'High Living' expenses elsewhere. Its Hotel International, winner of the International Tourist and Hotel Industry Prize, is among several which open year-round.

THE BLACK SEA

Golden Sands, a major resort whose long, wide beaches are backed by hills and forests

Refurbishment has been visited on numerous early-1960s hotels which were fraying at the edges, and the general scene appears somewhat upmarket of bigger but otherwise largely similar Sunny Beach (see pages 80-82) (though updating has been carried out there, too). Though less extensive than Sunny Beach's, the clean golden sands are 2½ miles (4 km) long and up to 30 feet (100m) wide. Beach umbrellas, chairs, and pedalos can be cheaply hired, and in three areas there are changing rooms with mineral-water showers and first-aid booths.

Yachts can be hired through Balkantourist. Also dinghies, motorboats, water skis, wind-surfing boards, and sub-aqua gear — with expert tuition for each, as needed.

The sea is warm and normally calm, though there are efficient lifeguard precautions. Children can enjoy a wide range of diversions, and can have their own menus in most restaurants (see Children pages 107-109). The Luna Park, near the Rodina Hotel, provides gentle lunacy for most age groups. It has ways of making them laugh with distorting mirrors, shriek on the 60 ft (18 m) high slalom dry slide and its four 160 ft (50 m) chutes, shoot in the electronic shooting range, contemplate in the cosmodrome or at the giant chess board.

There's even talk of cricket near the Malina Hotel, which also offers archery and mini-golf. Bulgaria hasn't noticeably gone in for proper golf yet, although this might help increase its international conference and incentive-travel business.

Horsemanship has been quite a native skill since Thracian and Khanate times; and the riding ground 220 yards (200 m) south of the Republika bus stop) has expert instructors. Resort roads are very safe, and bicycles or rickshaw-trikes can be hired near the Malina, Liliya and Rodina hotels. The Kamchia Hotel offers pin-bowling and video games.

Entertainment

Numerous hotels provide evening accompaniment to various types of dancing. Discothèques are at the Astoria, Gdansk, Pliska and Veliko Turnovo hotels. And there are two open-air ones: the Kolibi, which probably scares the nightingales in surrounding woodland, and the hillside Koukeri.

Folklore crops up in at least 15 restaurants. Even ultra-sophisticates who wince at this word may find folklore in Bulgaria to be more exciting, and often a more genuine living tradition, than in some other holiday countries.

The menu and programme at the Kosharata aims 'to acquaint visitors with the lifestyle of the Bulgarian shepherds'. Yes, you do see such folk with their flocks out in the countryside. Shepherds do play their flutes and whittle designs on sticks; shepherdesses do spin wool with hand-spindles.

Bulgarians sometimes tend to suspect some gypsies of laziness and smuggling interests. But the silk-costumed real gypsies at the Tsiganski Tabor tented 'gypsy camp' exceed norms of virtuosity and vivacity in song and dance, while their audience can lounge in 'gypsy carts' drinking very tolerable Bulgarian 'champagne'.

Shopping

Shopping Centre, near the post office: ceramics, wood and copper, home-spun weaves, embroidery. Perfumery and cosmetics, knitwear, ready-wear, footwear, beach articles and sports gear.

Gladiola shop, at the Gladiola Hotel: ready-wear knitwear, leather wear, carpets.

Kriva Lipa bazaar, knitwear, ready-wear, perfumery, souvenirs.

Nympha bazaar, on the south beach: beach articles, ceramics, perfumery, souvenirs.

Trifon Zarezan bazaar, next to Trifon Zarezan restaurant: knitwear, haberdashery, jewellery, perfumery.

Bowling shop, souvenirs, perfumery, jewellery.

Troyan Shop, opposite the Havana pool: wood and copper souvenirs, ceramics, homespun weaves, embroidery.

Souvenir palace, opposite the Stariya Dub restaurant: beach articles, leather wear, souvenirs, drinks.

Morsko Oko bazaar, next to the Morsko Oko Hotel: perfumery, cosmetics, souvenirs, drinks.

Representative store of the Union of Bulgarian Artists, opposite the Zlatna Kotva Hotel: original applied art work, leather wear, embroidery, ceramics, wood and copper souvenirs.

Company Store of the S.I. Peev

Glass Factory, at the Rodina Hotel: glassware and ceramics.
Book and record selling pavilions, opposite the Mimoza and Rodina hotels.
For reduced-cost Western jewellery, perfumery, cosmetics, ready-wear, cigarettes and drinks, there are hard currency **Corecom** shops at the Shopping Centre in the International, Shipka, Ambassador and Astoria hotels, and in the Nympha, Kaliakra and Morsko Oko stores.

Food and Drink
The **Vodenitsata**, up in the hills, is a convincing reproduction

Meals are often accompanied by captivating displays of traditional singing and dancing

of an old water-mill, and its meaty menu includes a rich sausage-and-lentil soup. Fish and seafood fans find more limited scope locally, though the **Zlatna Ribka** at the beach's northern end specialises in this — on its sun terrace or indoors.

Accommodation
Hotel reservations may be made through the Golden Sands and Druzhba Booking Office, tel: (052) 6-56-81/2/3. See also Tourist Service Offices, below.

Tourist Service Offices
For information, currency exchange, excursions, entertainment, accommodation bookings, etc: near the Casino restaurant; at the International Hotel; at Trifon Zarezan restaurant; at the Cultural

Centre; at the Kriva Lipa bazaar; at the Ambassador, Briz, Zlatna Kotva, Kristal, Morsko Oko, Preslav and Shipka Hotels, as well as at the Panorama campsite.

ALBENA

Not to be confused with Albania (by contrast with whose attitudes to fun and frolic this might seem in spirit to be the Malibu Beach scene), Albena is named after a famous historical beauty.

'For the Young at Heart' is its promotional tag, and it is the youngest major resort chronologically. Along the 4-mile (7 km) powdery sand beach of its bay, backed by hills, its hotels are sometimes in 'pyramid' architecture not unlike that at La Grande Motte in France's Languedoc-Roussillon. It is about 6 miles (10 km) north of Golden Sands.

The seabed shelves very gradually, so that the average adult is about shoulder-deep at 165 yards (150 m) off shore. Sports and recreational facilities are similar in scope to those at Golden Sands (pages 75-79) and Sunny Beach (pages 80-82) and those for the youngest visitors (see Children, pages 107-109). At the **Kamelia Club Hotel**, children of Balkan Holiday clients enjoy special programmes of amusement, including disco.

The big **Dobruja Hotel** has an olympic-size swimming pool with mineral water, a balneo-therapy department, and conference halls with simultaneous translation facilities. It is open year-round.

The **Orehite Picnic**, up in a walnut tree forest, is a restaurant whose folklore includes something very rare and genuine — **'fire-walking'** and barefoot dancing on glowing embers amidst whiffs of woodsmoke and a strange, almost pagan atmosphere. On a cool grass surface only, there may also be dancing bears. It is insisted that the bears are very well treated.

The **Slavyanska Kut Restaurant** features dances of the various Slav peoples, though not on anything red-hot.

The Cultural Information Centre provides diversions from Happy Birthday parties with zodiacal themes to Evenings of Bulgarian Humour, which may or may not lose something in translation if it is as thorough as Bulgarians like to be in some matters.

Excursions

Balchik; Cape Kaliakra; Nesebur, by hydrofoil or by horse-and-cart (two days) through the leafy, fertile Dobruja countryside.

Accommodation

Reservations can be made through the Albena Booking Office, tel: (05722) 20-53, 29-20.

DYUNI

Dyuni (or Düni) is a new purpose-built holiday village about 3 miles (5 km) south of Sozopol, mainly on a hillside a little way landward of coastal sand dunes, a more intimate setting for families than the big resorts.

Food and Drink

There are various individual restaurants and bars for

late-night carousel. The
Moryashka Kruchma (Sailor's
Inn) features seafood, and
the **Starata Loza** (Old Vine) has
a nightly folklore show from
22.00.

Accommodation

There are five small low-rise
3-star hotels, self-catering
accommodation in 'Fishermen's
Huts' and 'Sozopol Houses', the
Port Village on the beach itself,
and the newly opened Club
Village 'built in the style of the
Bulgarian monasteries'.
Holidays here can be arranged
by some West European tour
operators.
The nearby **campsite**, a 3-star
with 1,000 capacity, has a
restaurant, café, and shops.

SUNNY BEACH
(Slunchev Bryag)

Bulgaria's big coastal holiday
resorts are purpose-built, rather
than extensions (or ruinations) of
existing native towns. Although
they have been described as
constituting 'the California of
Eastern Europe', the effect is
more of a notional Socialist
International Utopia-on-Sea. The
People's Republic has
capitalised on its sunny real
estate. But it has not had to
maximise site values with
saturation development along
the 4 miles (6 km) of wide
fine-sand beach at Sunny Beach,
for instance. And there is plenty
of space and uncut tree foliage
between its hotels, high-rise as
many are.
Holiday prices are 'democratic',
with moderately priced
packages including half-board
and return flights. Local 'extras'
are also low-cost.

*Sunny Beach, the country's largest
seaside resort, its many hotels dotted
along the miles of beach*

Sunny Beach (Slunchev Bryag
anglicised) does not radically
differ in park-like appearance
from Golden Sands (Zlatni
Pyasutsi) — except that the
latter has 45 fewer hotels, and
its wooded hills more closely
approach the beach.
'Where Families Come First' is
the motto of Sunny Beach, with
its 122 hotels on a wide bay 20
miles (33 km) north of Burgas.
With summer water
temperatures up to 75°F (24°C),
the sea is shallow enough for
bathing by small children, and
there are lifeguard look-outs.

Traffic is minimal along resort roads, and speed-limited, like the kiddie-trains. Playgrounds and kintergartens proliferate, staffed by trained personnel with foreign language competence.

Children's menus are featured in cafés and restaurants. Balkan Holidays' 'Kiddie Clubs' at the Club-Hotel Saturn and the Hotel Continental have nannies who organise fun activities and a baby patrol who check children's rooms from 19.00 to midnight each weekday (see Children, pages 107-109 for full lists of relevant resort attractions.)

Sporting amenities include sailing, boating, waterskiing, windsurfing, parascending, tennis, mini-golf, cycling, horseriding, and ten-pin bowling. The Variety Bar Slunchev Bryag has long offered the daring decadence of a casino.

Polyclinics provide any necessary first-aid, free of charge. The Hotels Globus and Burgas have mineral water treatment wards and swimming pools in operation year round. (It is not usual for a holiday hotel to have its own pool, but there are several public ones.)

Entertainment

Numerous hotels have discos or versatile bands who can turn out anything from Folk, through Golden Oldies, to Rock, Soul and near-Rap. There is disco dancing at the Rusalka, Zlatna Yabulka, Lazur and Melodia. Individual nightlife spots often offer varying degrees of folksiness or Bulgarian tradition. One can hardly imagine the average early Bulgar Khan being regaled with cocktails, psychedelic lights, Rock music through echo-mikes and leggy showgirls in skimpy sequins as in the 'Khan's Tent' (Khanska Shatra). And the 'wine butt' at the Buchvata is fantasy sized. But there is a homelier atmosphere in the Chuchura (Fountain), which welcomes you with pre-menu bread-cakes and herb salt, plus music with intricate Balkan rhythms — and at the nearby Windmill (Vyaturna Melnitsa).

The floor show at the Yuzhni Noshti (Southern Nights) features exotic gypsy/oriental music and dances.

Biennially, in June, the Golden Orpheus international pop song festival is staged in Sunny Beach. This may include soulful ballads in a sort of Slavonic *Tom Jones* genre, but more contemporary Western influences increasingly permeate.

Excursions

Through tour operators' representatives or hotel bureaux, hydrofoil trips and Balkantourist excursions can be booked to numerous destinations including Varna, but also by sea or air to Istanbul, Odessa, Moscow and Leningrad. There are buses to Nesebur, and taxis are inexpensive.

Accommodation

Reservations of hotel beds can be made through the Sunny Beach Booking Office, tel: (0554) 21-31, 24-88.
Zora Villas, fronting gentle tree-covered hills to the north of Sunny Beach, give something of the aspect of a garden suburb. There are four handy restaurants, a supermarket, bike-hire facilities and a regular mini-train service to the main parts of Sunny Beach. With basic cooking facilities, the villas are featured in tour operators' programmes — as is accommodation in the **Elenite Holiday Village**, a joint Bulgarian-Finnish development further north.

BALCHIK

Founded in the 6th century BC, Balchik, 5 miles (8 km) north of Albena, looks, in part, more like a traditional seaside resort than any.
The local mineral waters are recommended for gastro-intestinal upsets.

◆◆◆
BOTANICAL GARDEN

Straddling several cliff terraces, this contains 3,000 species of plants from numerous countries. It was the park of the small former palace of Queen Maria of Romania, built in oriental style, with minaret, in 1924. (This area was owned by Romania between 1913 and 1940.) Ancient amphorae and tombstones are amongst the park's curiosities, which also include a church transferred piecemeal from a Greek island.

Food and Drink
Restaurant Dionysopolis, with bar.

Accommodation
Hotel Balchik, 2-star (tel: 21-66), 68 beds, with restaurant.
Hotel Raketa, 1-star (tel: 21-75), 36 beds.
Campsite Bisser, 1 mile (2 km) south.

Balkantourist office 33 Georgi Dimitrov Street (tel: 34-48).

CAPE KALIAKRA

This is a scenic promontory 7 miles (12 km) east of Kavarna. Its cliffs rear up more than 200 feet (60 km), and from them 40 Bulgarian maidens are said to have thrown themselves into the sea rather than face a fate worse than death from Ottomans.
There are caves which contain an archaeological museum and a restaurant.

Pleven, a bustling administrative and industrial centre with a rich historical past dating back to the 4th century BC

THE DANUBE AND THE NORTH

PLEVEN

Pleven marked a decisive turning-point in Bulgaria's liberation from Turkish Rule when, in 1877, 40,000 Russians and Romanians were among those who died in their capture of the city from Osman Pasha.

◆◆◆
PANORAMA OF THE EPIC OF PLEVEN

Painted on a vast canvas, stretching right round the inside of the dome of a tall 1977 building on a hilltop of Skobelev Park. A wide 'shelf' around a high viewing platform gives the impression of extending the painting into the foreground, with recreated trenches, cannon, and burnt-out ammunition carts which

(electrically) give a realistic effect of glowing embers.

The panorama, illustrating with thousands of figures the various assaults all around the city in 1877, is about as large as that in Volgograd, USSR, devoted to the World War II siege of Stalingrad. Pleven's was designed by Soviet and Bulgarian artists, who had local volunteer help.

Excursions

A trolleybus from the centre of town takes visitors to **Kailuka Park.** As well as a leisure complex, this contains a memorial monument to Jews who died in 1944 in a fire at their internment camp here.

Connected by rail with Sofia, Ruse (Rousse) and Varna, Pleven is an industrial and administrative centre, and sightseeing interest is mainly in monuments and museums.

Accommodation

Hotel Pleven, 3-star, 2 Republika

Square (tel: 2-00-62), with restaurant, bar, nightclub, information bureau and car rental office.

Balkantourist office 3 San Stefano Street (tel: 2-41-19).
Car repairs 2 Industrialna Street.
Union of Bulgarian Motorists 6a Radetski Street.

◆
NIKOPOL
Today an agricultural/industrial town and Danube hydrofoil stop, Nikopol had a Roman fortress in 169 AD and Byzantine successor from 629.
The fortifications of Bash-Tabia Kale that remain, in ruins, are those erected by King Ivan, who made Nikopol his unofficial capital during the medieval Second Bulgarian Kingdom.

◆
SVISHTOV
With a harbour on a bend of the Danube, Svishtov is the birthplace of Aleko Konstantinov, who wrote of folk-life in the 19th century when Svishtov was a pre-eminent commercial centre. He was also dubbed 'founder of the Bulgarian tourist movement'. Local sightseeing includes **Aleko Konstantinov Museum,** 17th-century churches of St Dimiter and SS Peter and Paul, 19th-century churches by the self-taught master-builder Kolyo Ficheto, and the town's clocktower.

Accommodation
Hotel Dounay, 1-star (tel: 23-61), with Balkantourist office.
Hotel Aleko, 1-star (tel: 26-83), with Bulgarian-style tavern.

◆◆
RUSE (ROUSSE)
Bulgaria's fourth city, and a major port visited by Danube cruisers, Ruse is rather handsomely set on terraces above the river. The Bridge of Friendship to the northeast is an entry point to Bulgaria with offices handling passports, customs, currency exchange, petrol coupons and tourist information. The name of the bridge symbolises the kind of welcome that incoming visitors arriving from Romania may expect to receive.
The Romans built a 1st-century fortress here at Sexaginta Prista (Port of 60 vessels), which had been a fishing village for about 5,000 years. Barbarians did a routine sack-and-pillage job on it around the 6th century and a new medieval fortress was destroyed by 14th-century Turks, who built their citadel of Roustchouk. The Romanians helped the Russians in their final assaults of 1878 against the Turks in these parts.
Ruse is important industrially, with its shipyard and major manufacture of farm machinery — and culturally, with its international March Musical Weeks, opera, art gallery, and national museum of transport. (Bulgaria's first railway linked Ruse and Varna.)
There are echoes of Vienna, Budapest and Bucharest in its older streets' Baroque, Renaissance, and fin-de-siècle architecture. The parks and sports stadia (three) are vast, as are some modern memorial monuments.
Whiffs of chlorine gas and other

wind-blown fumes that the visitor to Ruse might notice are likely to be from the vast chemical plant on the Romanian bank at Giurgiu, said to be one of the major polluters of the Danube.

Food and Drink
The Leventa restaurant near the TV Tower, features the national style of a different Danubian country in each of its seven rooms.

The Lipnik park outside Ruse has a rowing lake, and the folk-style **Ovtcharska Luka** restaurant which serves lamb specialities.

Excursions

◆◆
ROCK CHURCHES AND MONASTIC CELLS
Near the village of Ivanovo, 14 miles (23km) south of Ruse, and in the scenic canyon of the Rusenski Lom river. These ruins contain biographical murals from the 12th-14th centuries, which include a portrait of the Bulgarian King Ivan Alexander. Best preserved is the Archangel Church.

Accommodation
Hotel Riga, 3-star (tel: 221-81), with restaurant, bar and pastry shop.
Hotel Dunav, 2-star (tel 265-18), with restaurant, bar, tavern in national style and pastry shop.
Hotel Bulgaria, 1-star, bookings through Balkantourist office (see below).

Balkantourist office, 1 Raiko Daskalov Street (tel: 3-36-29).
Union of Bulgarian Motorists, 45 General Skobelev Street.

SILISTRA
Danube industrial port and hydrofoil stop, Silistra was founded in the 2nd century AD by the Roman Emperor Trajan. A **Roman tomb,** with a wealth of very well preserved wall-paintings from the 4th century, is the most interesting of the town's surviving historical sites, which include Roman and Turkish fortifications.
The **District Historical Museum** is in an old local house. One of Silistra's factories produces souvenirs, some of them made of bullrushes.

Excursions
Important sightseeing attractions in the region are Lake Sreburna nature reserve and the Thracian tomb near Sveshtari (see below).

Accommodation
Hotel Zlatna Dobruja, 2-star, Georgi Dimitrov Street, with restaurant, in main street. Bookings through Balkantourist office (see below).

Balkantourist office,
7 Svoboda Square
(tel: 2-39-90).
Union of Bulgarian Motorists, 12 Docho Mikhaylov Street.

◆◆
TUTRAKAN
A port and fishing centre about halfway between Ruse and Silistra, and once a Roman fortress, Tutrakan has a unique museum devoted to Danubian fishing and boat-building.

◆◆◆
LAKE SREBURNA
This nature reserve, about 12 miles (20km) west of Silistra, is

included on a UNESCO world list of valued natural sites. 'The Eldorado of the Wading Birds' is what the 19th-century Hungarian traveller Felix Kanitz called it. The lake's reed-and-rush-covered islands are nesting grounds for 90 varieties of birds, and are visited by almost as many migrants — including pelicans, in autumn.

Sightseers' group visits can be arranged through Balkantourist.

◆◆◆
SVESHTARI THRACIAN TOMB

Discovered in 1982, this tomb near Isperih and Koubrat on the Silistra-Razgrad road has been described by a Bulgarian archaeologist as 'not just a remarkable monument of Thracian art, but . . . also . . . one of the most outstanding works of Hellenistic art in general'.

The architecture, funerary rites, murals and sculptures in the

The Thracians were keen horsemen, as depicted in their art. Below: 4th–3rd-century BC tomb mural at Kazanluk

tomb, which has an entrance passage and three chambers under a mound, convince experts that it was that of a Thracian king and queen of the 3rd century BC — although it has been looted in early times. Paintings depict a noble horseman and his armed attendants being approached by a goddess who hands him a gold wreath and is followed by four women carrying gifts such as a perfume box and a jewellery case.

Ten stone caryatids, decoratively dressed female figures supporting an architrave, are considered to be of exceptional interest. Each has an individually sculpted face, and they are expected eventually to reveal to researchers a great deal about the symbolism of female figures in Thracian religion and arts.

With no local tourist accommodation, Sveshtari might be visited from Ruse or Shumen. Further information from a Balkantourist office.

PEACE AND QUIET

Bulgaria's Wildlife and Countryside

Bulgaria is a country of contrasting landscapes. There are vast tracts of wild and inaccessible mountains which remain largely unspoiled, but in the lowlands most of the fertile land of the plains is devoted to farming. Vineyards, olive groves and orchards of fruit trees are vital elements of the Bulgarian landscape.

The Black Sea coast is a major tourist region, and in some areas this has had a devastating effect on the wildlife. Freshwater lakes at Varna and Burgas have been modified by hydro-electric schemes and by saltpans to such an extent that most of the breeding birds have disappeared. However, they still present probably the best chances in Europe of seeing

Secretive and untameable creatures, wildcats make their lairs between boulders and among tree-roots

white and Dalmatian pelicans, which stop off on migration. Mountain ranges dominate the south and the west of the country, with many peaks remaining snow-capped throughout the year. Their lower slopes are heavily wooded and have a wide variety of woodland birds and scarce and endangered mammals such as the European brown bear and wolf.

The Northern Black Sea Coast

The Black Sea coast is a popular tourist destination which has been developed considerably over the last twenty years. Nevertheless, there are still areas rich in wildlife which is often noticeably different from that further south where the influence of the Mediterranean is still felt. Here, the plants, and to some extent the animals, too, are central European in origin. Either side of the town of Balchik, the coast road passes by chalk cliffs and rolling hillsides. The grassy slopes are

PEACE AND QUIET

covered in flowers such as milk vetches, sages, brooms, pinks and the paeony *Paeonia peregrina* and the cliffs to the south of the town have good populations of alpine swift and black-headed bunting. They are also a well-known haunt of the pied wheatear, an elegant, black and white summer visitor with a mainly Asiatic distribution — this is its only regular breeding site in Europe.
Further up the coast to the north, the road passes more cliffs where rollers, rock thrushes and eagle owls breed, and eventually leads to Cape Kaliakra, 15 miles (25km) north of Balchik. The grassy fields slope towards the sea, ending in sheer cliffs, 230 feet (70 metres) high. Although a popular tourist spot and 'managed' as such, a rich variety of interesting plants, such as showy paeonies, stocks, sages and irises can be found. Cape Kaliakra is an excellent migration spot with unusual Asiatic birds turning up from March to May and in August and September. It is a good point from which to watch seabird movements in the Black Sea, and shearwaters, gulls and terns can be numerous. Because of the crumbly nature of the soil, the cliffs are riddled with caves both above and below the surface of the water. Egyptian vultures, rose-coloured starlings and eagle owls use them as nesting sites on land, whereas at sea level they provide shelter for one of the last remaining colonies of the endangered monk seal.
To the south of Balchik, at the mouth of the River Batova, lies the Forest of Baltata. Although its wildlife interest has been severely reduced by man, it still has collared flycatchers, sombre tits, hawfinches and many other woodland birds, as well as small numbers of wild boar.

The Southern Black Sea Coast

The inviting waters of the Black Sea and the almost Mediterranean climate have made the southeastern coast of Bulgaria popular with residents and tourists alike. While this has had serious impact on the wildlife of the coast itself, the land a few miles away from the resorts is relatively unspoiled. Inland from the coastal town of Burgas are three lakes, Mandra, Burgas and Atansov, now drastically altered by recent developments. Lake Atansov is used in the extraction and purification of salt and the saline conditions are greatly to the liking of birds such as avocets and black-winged stilts. Of the other two, Lake Burgas still attracts many migrants during spring and autumn but its reedbeds no longer harbour many breeding birds.
White and Dalmatian pelicans, glossy ibises and spoonbills all pass through regularly and little egrets and white storks are a familiar feature of the shallow margins of the Lake Burgas. Particularly in spring, Mediterranean and little gulls are numerous, looking smart with their neat black hoods and white eye rings. Mediterranean gulls are especially attractive with their pure white wings and are easily distinguished by their loud 'cow-cow' calls. At the right

Despite their immense size, eagle owls are difficult to see since they nest in remote forests and on high cliffs

time of year, marsh terns and waders can be abundant.

The Istranca Mountains run from the Bosphorus in Turkey into southeast Bulgaria and have woodlands which are easily reached from the coast. A mixture of oak, beech, elm, sycamore and lime create interesting forests which still harbour wolves, wildcats and pine and beech martens. The latter two species are extremely agile predators which are equally at home in the trees and on the ground. Although shy, they are sometimes seen in car headlights when crossing the road. In clearings, medlars and tree heathers tower over hellebores, sages, crocuses, tulips and other colourful flowers.

During spring and autumn migration large numbers of seabirds pass the Bulgarian coastline on their travels through the Black Sea. Shearwaters, gulls and terns are most easily seen if an onshore breeze is blowing, while cormorants and shags are always in evidence. During the winter months the Bulgarian shores harbour black-throated divers and great-crested grebes.

Lakes and Marshes

Before the growth of the population along the coast and

the development of the tourist industry, there were interesting lakes along the length of the Black Sea. Nowadays, however, man has influenced many of them to such an extent that they have lost much of their wildlife interest.

The lakes at Burgas and Lake Varna near Balchik no longer have the vast numbers of breeding birds they once did. However, during migration times they swarm with birds. Swallows and martins stop off to feed on insects, and flocks of cranes call in briefly, particularly in March. During May, hundreds of marsh terns pass through, most in full breeding plumage. Whiskered terns and distinctive black terns are a wonderful sight as they hawk for insects, but most elegant of all is the white-winged black tern, with its pure white tail and black and white wings.

The course of the mighty River Danube, flanked by riverine forest, marks the northern border of Bulgaria with Romania. The river is most famous for its delta, but the floodplain along its course is also of major importance. Near the town of Silistra in northeast Bulgaria there are several large, reed-fringed lakes which support vast colonies of breeding birds.

One of these, Lake Sreburna, 12 miles (20km) west of Silistra is now a nature reserve, mainly on account of its breeding population of Dalmatian pelicans. Despite limited access to the reserve itself, most of the wildlife can easily be seen from the surrounding countryside. Throughout its reedbeds, colonies of little egret, little bittern, purple, night grey and squacco herons breed in profusion and marsh harriers quarter the land in search of

Small flocks of white pelicans often grace the shores of Bulgaria's lakes on migration in spring and autumn

prey. Twenty eight species of mammal have been recorded on the reserve including hamster, souslik, and the bizarre subterranean mole rat.

The marshes surrounding these lakes and along the length of the Danube have different birds. Meadows are still the haunt of the corncrake, a declining bird throughout Europe, and black-headed wagtails nest in grassy tussocks. Surely the smartest of all the races of yellow wagtail, the male is resplendent with yellow plumage and black hood.

Ropotamo National Park

Lying 31 miles (50km) south of Burgas on the Black Sea coast of Bulgaria, the Ropotamo National Park protects an extensive area of riverine forest around the mouth of the River Ropotamo. Lakes and sand dunes add to its interest and although popular with tourists and fishermen alike, there is still much of interest to the wildlife enthusiast.

The riverine forest is of a type now rare in Bulgaria and contains a mosaic of deciduous trees such as oak, ash, poplar, elm and alder, most with their 'feet' in water. Climbers like ivy and clematis reach skyward and clearings become a riot of tangled undergrowth with butterflies flitting through the dappled sunlight. In swampy areas, penduline tits weave their curious, bottle-shaped nests, suspended from branches, while in areas of dense foliage red-breasted and collared flycatchers and golden orioles provide tantalisingly

brief views in the canopy. Birds of prey are often seen circling above the tree tops and nest in the cover of the leaf canopy. Hobbies and black kites both occur in small numbers and even the occasional pair of saker or white-tailed eagle can be found. The latter is unmistakable, with a wingspan of nearly eight feet (240cm), a conspicuous white tail in the adults and a silhouette in flight which resembles a barn-door.

The lake region of Arkutino is a good place for water birds and water insects, most notably mosquitoes! The introduced, pink-flowered *Nelumbo nucifera* with its lily-like leaves provide shade for the fish, frogs and other aquatic life below. Purple and night herons are common, the latter preferring to roost during the day and feed at dawn and dusk.

Around the mouth of the river a system of sand dunes is threatened by increased camping pressure. However, the wet and dry dune slacks and stabilised dunes have a remarkable array of coastal plants, some of which are widespread in Europe, while others are distinctly local. Marram grass, sea beet, sea knotgrass, sea holly and cottonweed are all common and low bushes of thorn of Christ, *Paliurus spina-christi* remind the careless stroller of their presence with their fierce spines.

Woodlands

Much of lowland Bulgaria has long-since been cleared of

PEACE AND QUIET

woodland and turned into agricultural land, leaving only the riverine forests at the mouths of a few rivers flowing into the Black Sea. However, the slopes of most of the mountain ranges are still wooded and Bulgaria takes a certain pride in its forests, many lying in national parks of forest reserves.

On the lower slopes of the hills and mountains, the woodland usually comprises deciduous trees such as beech, hazel, oak and lime, sometimes with a shrubby understorey of juniper and privet. Depending on the amount of human disturbance, they may hold interesting mammals such as red and roe deer, polecat, badger and pine and stone martens.

Woodland birds abound, with jay, turtle dove, short-toed treecreeper and golden oriole being common. Smaller numbers of sombre tits, olive-tree warblers and hawfinches also occur, but are difficult to see. High in the canopy the delightful little red-breasted flycatcher flits from leaf to leaf in search of caterpillars. Its sharp call often gives its presence away and when in view its robin-like breast is obvious as is its habit of flicking its tail. It shares this habitat with its relative, the collared flycatcher. Unfortunately for the birdwatcher, the race which occurs in Bulgaria lacks the complete white collar which distinguishes it from the pied flycatcher of northern Europe. However, the latter only occurs in Bulgaria on passage and so any black and white flycatcher

seen is likely to be collared. The heavy shade produced by many of the deciduous trees, and in particular by beech, discourages most understorey plants: there is not enough light for them to photosynthesise. Some flowers overcome this by growing before there are leaves on the trees, while others have become saprophytic, which means they feed on decaying, underground leaf litter, using a fungal partner. The ghost orchid takes this to an extreme, spending almost all its life underground and flowering for no more than a few days. Even then a plant may not flower every year and only does so when conditions are exactly right.

The Rhodope Mountains

The Rhodope Mountain chain lies along the northern side of the Bulgarian border with Greece, between two rivers, the Maritsa and the Mesta. Although the landscape comprises gently rounded hills and valleys, the peak of Great Perelik rises to nearly 7,200 feet (2,200 metres) and over 5,000 acres (2,000 hectares) of land are protected by national park status.

The lower slopes are cloaked in deciduous woodland consisting of beech, hornbeam and oak which are the haunt of many woodland birds. Chaffinches search for insects and fallen seeds, but the hawfinch, with its massive beak, is the only woodland resident able to crack the hard seeds of the hornbeam. In the spring, golden orioles, redstarts and nightingales — all loud songsters — contribute to the woodland chorus of bird song.

Higher up the slopes, the deciduous trees are replaced by pines and spruce, under whose dense canopy one-leaved wintergreen, two-leaved squill, herb paris and coralroot bittercress often flourish. Firecrests sing their high-pitched songs from the tree canopy and crossbills noisily feed on ripe pine cones. These higher woodlands harbour secretive mammals such as brown bear, wolf and wild boar. They manage to survive in these hills, not so much because they are

In the deep shade of Bulgaria's forest the extraordinary ghost orchid appears in the summer months

protected from hunting, but because the terrain is so inaccessible. Consider yourself extremely fortunate if you see even one of these animals. Rocky outcrops among the higher regions of forest are dotted with cranesbills, saxifrages and vetches and are the haunt of the elegant rock bunting. The male birds with their chestnut bodies and grey, white and black-striped heads sing a delightful buzzing song from rocks and branches, and sometimes in flight.

Some areas of forest have been cleared for timber and the resulting clearings, as well as the natural glades, are good for wild flowers and butterflies. Meadow rues, St John's worts, sages and foxgloves are a

PEACE AND QUIET

delight after the shade of the woodland.

The Vitosha Mountains

The mountains of the Vitosha National Park lie only a short distance south of Sofia and are both attractive and good for wildlife, with over 100 species of bird having been recorded. Within the 57,000 acres (23,000 hectares) of the park, two reserves at Bistrishko Branishte and Torfeno Branishte protect areas of spruce woodland and marshy moorland respectively. Because of its close proximity to Sofia and heavy snowfall in winter, Vitosha is a popular ski-resort with its centre at Aleko. Despite the disturbance, alpine choughs and alpine accentors often feed close to the buildings, seemingly indifferent to people. Other outdoor pursuits are catered for here, and there are several routemarked trails for trekkers. The park has the advantage of allowing easy access to all the zones of vegetation found in Bulgarian mountains, from deciduous forest at low altitudes to alpine meadows and the snow line. Beautiful clear lakes and rivers and dwarf mountain pine forest add to its wildlife interest.

On remote and inaccessible rocky outcrops and deep gorges in Vitosha, eagle owls still nest and rear their young. Despite their immense size, they are very difficult to spot because they remain motionless during the day and their plumage helps them blend in with the surroundings. Often the first sign of the presence of an eagle owl is its deep, far-carrying 'boo-hoo' call uttered at dusk. If you are lucky, you may see the bird take to the wing as the light fades, off in search of its prey, which includes animals the size of roe deer! They tend to return to roost in the same spot each morning, even when not nesting, which gives the persistent observer opportunities for a prolonged view. The higher slopes of the hills are covered in pines and spruce which create the dense shade much favoured by deer and wild boar. The woods also host an even more secretive animal which is occasionally surprised near its lair or at a kill. The wildcat certainly lives up to its name and has a reputation of being completely untamable. The lair is usually among an outcrop of boulders or under fallen trees and here the females rear their kittens in the early summer.

The Rila Mountains

Lying 60 miles (100km) south of Sofia in southwest Bulgaria, the Rila Mountains contain rugged and beautiful landscapes with many towering peaks above 8,000 feet (2,500 metres), the highest of which, at nearly 10,000 feet (3,000 metres), is Musala. Within the boundaries of the national park, more than 150 lakes, heavily wooded hillsides and alpine meadows also add to the scenic appeal of the area.

The well-known monastery at Rila (see page 39) is a good starting point from which to explore the area. Rushing rivers

The elegant, trumpet-shaped flowers of Gentiana pyrenaica *are found at high altitudes in the Rila Mountains*

carve deep gorges in the hillsides and grey wagtails and dippers are ever present. The latter characteristically bob up and down on rocks in the water and submerge in search of food. Hornbeam, beech, oak and mountain ash cloak the lower slopes of the mountains and merge with Scot's and Macedonian pines and spruces at higher altitudes. Among the branches and leaves, birds such as crested tit, firecrest, nutcracker and crossbill forage for food, while on the woodland floor, rare and secretive capercaillie and hazelhen keep to the darkest shade in the company of red and roe deer. In glades and clearings, flowers such as leopardsbane, cranesbills, lungworts and saxifrages appear during the summer months, while at higher altitudes grass of Parnassus,

sticky catchfly, marsh marigold and bistort are found in damp hollows.

At around 6,500 feet (2,000 metres), just below the snow line, alpine meadows are a riot of colour from June to August with the beautiful gentian *Gentiana pyrenaica*, buttercups, milk vetches, Snowdon lily, moss campion and several speedwells. Birds that might be seen include alpine accentors, searching for insects and seeds in bare, open patches. These are sometimes accompanied by rock buntings and shore larks, the latter with their yellow throats and black, feathery 'horns'.

The slopes below support open woodlands of dwarf mountain pine and underneath the light canopy crocuses, gentians, purple coltsfoot and mountain avens grow in the rocky soil.

Vikhren Park

The Vikhren National Park lies 30 miles (50km) south of Rila in

PEACE AND QUIET

southwest Bulgaria. It contains over 16,500 acres (6,700 hectares) of mountainous country in the Pirin range which itself runs down to the Greek border. Although the park holds extensive areas of woodland cloaking the lower slopes, over half its area can be considered as 'alpine' in nature. Not surprisingly, it includes some of the highest peaks in the whole of the Pirin Mountain range, the highest being Mount Vikhren at nearly 10,000 feet (3,000 metres).

The lower slopes are covered in a mixture of beech, spruce and Balkan pine and much of the woodland is completely unspoiled. The oldest tree in the park is thought to be a Balkan pine which grows at the foot of Mount Vikhren at an altitude of 6,500 feet (2,000 metres) and is estimated to be 1,280 years old. These mixed woodlands are the haunt of many species of bird as well as forest mammals such as red and roe deer, brown bear, wolf and wildcat.

The capercaillie is the largest woodland bird found in the park. Despite the fact that the males are over 30 inches (80cm) long, they are extremely wary and difficult to see and the utmost stealth is required. The best time to search for them is in early summer when the males advertise themselves with an extraordinary display. The tail is raised and fanned out, and the bird utters some amazing sounds: first a loud rattle, followed by what sounds like a cork being pulled from a bottle, and lastly a loud crashing noise.

Above the highest tracts of dwarf mountain pine are extensive alpine meadows. Many of the flowers are endemic to the Bulgarian mountains, while others are widespread in the Alps, the Pyrenees and even northern Europe. Alpine bistort,

Beautifully marked Balkan wall lizards are found in woodland clearings and in open country where they feed on insects

Large colonies of wood ants are a conspicuous feature of Bulgaria's forests and are considered beneficial insects

saxifrages, milk vetches, alpine bartsia, pyramidal bugle, purple coltsfoot and bellflowers put on a colourful display. Some areas boast rocky, limestone outcrops which harbour a different variety of flowers including species of violets, saxifrages, mountain avens and gentians.

Open Country and Agricultural Land

Much of lowland Bulgaria is devoted to agriculture and the country is justly famous for its bottled fruits and jams. Elsewhere, land has been given over to grazing by goats. While most of the plants and animals that were originally found there have declined, others have actually benefited from the changes.

Rollers, bee-eaters and lesser grey shrikes perch on overhead wires and find open agricultural land a rich and easy feeding area. Balkan wall lizards, grasshoppers and bush crickets scurry across the broken soil, frequently falling victim to these keen-eyed predators. Tawny pipits and crested, short-toed and calandra larks work the furrows in ploughed fields in search of uprooted grubs. Wherever there are orchards or trees and scrub, red-backed shrikes, olivaceous and barred warblers, scop's owls and cirl buntings nest in the cover and shade they provide. If the ground vegetation is lush and grassy, corncrakes and quail sing their respective songs, whereas barren areas are favoured by stone-curlews and little and great bustards. Although bustards still try to breed in Bulgaria in small numbers, during the winter there is usually an influx of these birds from northeast Europe and Asia.

PEACE AND QUIET

White storks frequently build their untidy nests on roofs and telegraph poles

White storks have benefited from man's buildings and structures throughout Europe and nests on top of buildings, churches and telegraph poles are a familiar sight in Bulgaria. The birds return annually to these nests in March after spending the winter in Africa and feed in fields and marshes in the surrounding country. These nests are ramshackle affairs of twigs and domestic rubbish and are often used by other birds at the same time. In some particularly large nests Spanish, tree and house sparrows can all breed side by side like tenants in the storks' cellars!

Along the coast herring gulls sometimes noisily nest on rooftops and are certainly not as welcome as would be a stork's nest. Syrian woodpeckers are regular, if rather surprising visitors to most of Bulgaria's towns. They can often be seen flying down the road from one telegraph pole to another in search of grubs.

Wood Ants

Although most of Bulgaria's forests lie on inaccessible slopes high in the mountains, the lower slopes are often exploited for timber. However, the country treats its forests as a natural asset and felling is strictly controlled and regulated.

The Bulgarians also have a healthy respect for one of the forest's smallest but most important residents, the wood ant. This industrious insect forms large colonies in huge mounds of leaf litter and pine needles, and foraging parties spread out in every direction. Although less than half an inch (a centimetre or so) long, these creatures have a formidable bite and can spray formic acid at an intruder. There are not many animals that will take them on *en masse*. Foresters consider them to be invaluable in the woodlands because they are strictly carnivorous, collecting caterpillars, bugs, sawfly larvae and anything else they can tackle (all these creatures would damage the trees in one way or another). The prey is then carried back to the nest where it is dismembered and fed to the growing larvae safely housed inside the ant hill. Not surprisingly, wood ants are protected by the law.

Ceramic vases on a market stall

SHOPPING

'Touristic' souvenirs include glazed ceramic vases, plates and ashtrays with swirling patterns around mystical 'eyes' (most usually on a brown background, but sometimes in attractive greens and blues); wrought-iron and copper articles; carved and sculpted wooden caskets, bowls, plates and spoons; folk-music instruments, decorated wooden phials containing attar of roses, and dolls in various regional costumes.

The dolls are usually demure and chocolate-boxy, but children with a taste for the bizarre may appreciate the grotesquely masked models of Koukeri — folk-dancers whose role is to scare off evil spirits. Hand or machine-embroidered blouses, tablecloths and runners, homespun fabrics and knitwear are available and there are traditional-style rugs. Costume jewellery in silver and other metals can be inexpensive. Jackets and coats in fur, sheepskin, leather or suede can be particularly good value.

The *Corecom* hard-currency shops, in the bigger hotels or self-contained in the resorts, usually sell many or all of the items above — plus imported goods, at tax-reduced prices, including radios, cameras, perfumes, spirits, liqueurs and cigarettes.

Preustroistvo seems to be having some success in encouraging *Corecom* sales assistants to be attentive and pleasant with customers.

There are plenty of other shops, including music stores selling cheap records.

Sofia is naturally one of the best cities for shopping, and facilities there are listed on pages 25-26. Be prepared: *Photographic film,* especially for colour slides and cassette cameras, is often hard to find, particularly outside Sofia and the bigger resorts on the Black Sea. The enthusiastic photographer should bring along a good supply of this.

FOOD AND DRINK

While many of the raw materials speak for themselves as to quality and exceptional budget value, food and drink in tourist Bulgaria are often presented in a sort of show-business production.

Fire-walkers, gypsy dancers and singing shepherds are just a few of the speciality accompaniments to meals or liqueurs in folklore restaurants, which are done up with a variety of rustic or 'traditional' props and trappings. 'International' cuisine is provided in most resort hotels, with menus in several languages, though Bulgarian dishes are not likely to be too spicy or strongly flavoured for most palates — and are particularly inexpensive at a *mehana* (a tavern, which may not offer a wide choice).

Tea is usually green, often Chinese, and served without milk. Expresso **coffee** is

available from some hotel bars. Otherwise, coffee may be like Turkish, with thick grounds. Many visitors bring supplies of familiar tea-bags, instant coffee and powdered milk.

Bulgaria's climate, soils and varied terrain enable her to raise superb **vegetables,** salads, peaches, strawberries, cherries, apples — and abundant grapes

Bulgarian dishes (the Shopska salad is sprinkled with grated white sheep's cheese), accompanied by Bulgarian wine

of several types.

The country produces about 500 million litres of **wine** a year, of a quality which attracts exports to 70 countries and fulsome testimonials from leading Western experts.

Among **meats,** lamb is usually the most succulent. But beef and veal may sometimes seem tough by Western standards — though it is another matter with any meat slowly cooked in an earthenware casserole. Chicken is often free range. Pork is tastily served in stews, *kebapcheta* (oblong rissoles) or *kyufteta* (meatballs).

Black Sea **fish** are nothing much to write home about — except as prepared in a few speciality restaurants along the coast. A type of mackerel and grey mullet are what normally seem available. Trout from mountain streams or lakes are good. Carp and pike-perch are available in some areas, while cod and other sea fish are brought in by Bulgaria's oceanic fleet.

Some dishes (see also language, page 124):

Shopska salad — 'Shopska' means Sofia-style, and it is usually chopped tomato, onion, cucumber and pickled pepper, seasoned with salt, sunflower oil and vinegar, and topped with flakes of ewesmilk cheese and parsley.

Kypolou — a puree of aubergines with peppers, tomatoes and garlic.

Tarator — cold soup of sliced cucumber, walnuts, garlic and dill in yoghurt (which is reckoned to prevent 'garlic breath').

FOOD AND DRINK

ESTATE BOTTLED · ℮ 75cl
Bulgarian
Chardonnay

PRESLAV REGION
A fine white wine
11.5% vol
Produced and bottled in Bulgaria by Vinimpex, Sofia
Sole importer in the UK BULGARIAN VINTNERS Co. Ltd. London N1 9RD.

The country's wines are increasingly exported and enjoyed. In Bulgaria itself the labels may well be in Cyrillic script

Kebap — meat cut in small portions and simmered in a rich sauce (whereas *kebapcheta* are grilled mincemeat portions).

Gyuvech — usually a stew with vegetables, herbs and meats. (Gyuvech is also the name of the earthenware casserole.)

Drob Sarma — a lamb pilaff prepared with eggs, onions and yoghurt.

Sarmi — vine or cabbage leaves stuffed with minced veal, pork, onions, paprika, herbs and rice.

Banitsa — hot cheese pastry (sometimes with spinach).

Mekitsas — batter fried in oil; can be flavoured with cheese, jam or honey and walnuts.

Wines

Bottled wines sold in Bulgarian restaurants are often labelled with fanciful local names which, furthermore, are in Cyrillic script. But (in seaside resorts and big cities especially) waiters can usually advise as to their grape types.

These can be the wines now enjoying popularity in the West: the full-bodied red *Cabernet* (winner of nearly 150 gold medals in international competitions), the lighter, smooth *Merlot*, the outstanding dry white *Chardonnay* (especially Khan Krum), and various Rieslings.

But there are also distinctly Bulgarian varieties, notably: *Mavrud*, deep and fruity, ageing well; *Gamza*, with a slightly resinous flavour when young, a fine bouquet with age; *Pamid*, a light red rather like a young Rhone wine; *Melnik*, dark red and velvety, and the *Misket* medium white from Karlovo or Sungulare.

Dessert wines include *Slavianka* and *Vratsa Misket*. 'Champanska' sparklers are *Iskra*, and the pink *Magura*. Reasonable brandies are *Pliska*, *Preslav*, and *Pomorie*. The plum-brandy, *slivova*, can in quantity produce a thundering hangover for which a local prescription is yoghurt (kisselo mlyako) night and morning. This may also be needed after indulgence in anise-flavoured *mastika* and *raki*.

Bulgarian bottled beers are cheap, and taste so, though some *mehani* and seafront bars sell quite a wholesome lager type on draught. Pricey German and Dutch beers, Scotch and London gin are available in the hard-currency bars of many hotels.

Bottled fruit juices are plentiful and inexpensive.

The Bulgarian for 'Cheers' is *Naz drave* (drah-vay).

Druzhba, one of the smaller Black Sea resorts, where the wide range of hotels includes the large and luxurious Grand Varna

ACCOMMODATION

Bulgaria progressively updates its hotels, restaurants and other facilities. However, within nationally graded categories, hotel standards are not yet as uniform and predictable as those of major international hotel chains.

In other countries, self-catering accommodation is often in atmospheric touring areas inland (and is not all conveniently owned by the State). In Bulgaria, it is concentrated near the Black Sea — admittedly in places like quaintest Nesebur and Sozopol, but also in purpose-built developments which may be attractive but lack historical 'roots' and traditional local identity.

CULTURE AND ENTERTAINMENT

Bulgaria's cultural traditions date back to the legends of Orpheus with his lute and the amazing artistry of the Thracians who fashioned some of the world's earliest gold ornaments. Archaeology is very professionally pursued, incidentally. Exciting finds of artefacts in recent decades have achieved fame in touring exhibitions. A recent discovery, in 1986, was the Treasure of Rogozen, its ornate Thracian militaria now being distributed to big-city museums.

There are obviously impressive budgets for the conservation of architecture and art works from early medieval times, of monasteries and their icons, of whole villages and town centres with their National Revival buildings.

On the 'live' scene, there are about a million drama and opera performances annually in Bulgaria, and the nation's leading singers star in the world's greatest opera houses. All the larger Bulgarian cities have symphony orchestras, opera houses, theatres, cultural centres, museums and amateur art companies.

Folk music and dance traditions flourish probably more than in any other European country. But national and international Rock and Pop have a more contemporary sound than many may expect, and bands in hotels and restaurants are very versatile. The same radio channel may broadcast Pop and 'serious' music, and its producers (rightly, it seems) do not presume that young people are not capable of appreciating both.

WEATHER AND WHEN TO GO

The climate is temperate continental with a Mediter-ranean influence in the southern regions. Mountain climate prevails in highland regions with altitudes of more than 3,000ft (900m). In the east of Bulgaria the climate is milder because of the influence of the Black Sea, and winter tempera-tures may be as high as 58°F

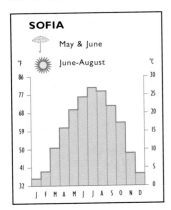

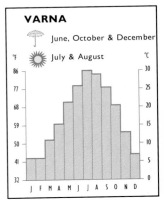

Keeping the tradition alive: thousands of singers and dancers at a folk festival in Sofia

(15°C), while the summer temperatures rarely exceed 77-78°F (25-26°C). Water temperature in summer is between 65 and 77°F (17-25°C).

HOW TO BE A LOCAL

While many Bulgarians are friendly and helpful, it seems a shame when some who are not happen to be among staff of some hotel desks and *Corecom* duty-free shops — or even (occasionally) waiters. Extra smiles and patience from the visitor may help matters along.

Confusion can still be caused by traditional body-language which reverses our own. Shaking the head from side to side may well mean 'Yes', and a downward nod 'No'! Holidaymakers on pre-booked inclusive tours can, of course, refer problems to their tour operator's resort representative or tour guide.

Tourists with very unconventional or 'hippie' clothes, or hairstyles, may receive disapproving looks in some areas — or unwittingly invite police searches for drugs. In the big cities and resorts, however, very few visitors meet with xenophobic animosity

HOW TO BE A LOCAL

unless they deserve it! Southern Bulgarians often tend to be the jolliest, though there are many friendly small towns in all regions — Troyan being a particularly good example.

Do's and Don'ts

Do bring in with you camera film and other chemist-shop items not easily found, eg feminine hygiene commodities; also familiar tea and coffee in preference to 'pot luck', plus powdered milk.

Don't bring in 'pornographic' books or literature.

Don't photograph airports, railways, bridges or anything

Pamporovo, in the Rhodope mountains, a resort for skiers of all ages and abilities

military. It is forbidden. There are plenty of other good subjects for colour photography. Don't sunbathe or sea-bathe nude on the family beaches of the main resorts. Balkantourist can advise of naturist beaches around Sozopol, Primorsko, Kiten and Lozenets.

Don't change hard currency for leva in deals with street touts or waiters. It is illegal, and anyway the 200 per cent tourist currency bonus competes with many of the unofficial 'street' rates.

If you are an *independent* traveller, not on a package tour: Don't lose the *carte statistique* which is put in your passport on your arrival through Immigration — or the *bordereaux* (exchange receipts) for currency exchanged at official bureaux. You need to produce the *carte-statistique* to be date-stamped whenever you check in or out of accommodation, and the *bordereaux* when you pay for the accommodation in leva.

EVENTS

January

Wintersports competitions and carnivals in the ski resorts of Borovets, Pamporovo and Vitosha; Plovdiv Winter Music Festival

February

'Vinegrowers' Day', folklore in wine districts on 14th

March

Ruse International Music Festival

April

Bulgarian Music Days, Plovdiv

May

Plovdiv Spring Fair (consumer goods); Gabrovo Biennial

Festival of Humour and Satire, every odd-numbered year
May 24 — June 20: Sofia Music Weeks, leading international festival

June
Rose Festival, Valley of Roses, Kazanluk; Golden Orpheus Pop Festival, Sunny Beach, every odd-numbered year

June/July
Summer International Music Festival in Varna and Golden Sands

July
International Ballet Competition, Varna

August
Veliko Turnovo 'Scene of the Centuries' festival; sailing regatta, Duni, near Sozopol

September
Plovdiv Autumn Fair (machinery and technical equipment), and Plovdiv Old Town Arts Festival; Sozopol Arts Festival

October
International Television Drama Festival, Plovdiv

November
Katya Popova Laureate Days, Pleven; Jazz Parade, Sofia

December/January
Sofia International New Year's Music Festival

CHILDREN

Bulgaria's Black Sea resorts have gone to imaginative lengths to offer children attractions in addition to their clean, sandy beaches and safe bathing in clear, tideless sea. Trained staff will look after them and keep them amused for hours when parents want a break.
As to general practicalities:
A family with two children aged 2 — 12 enjoys big reductions on the holiday price. Hotels ensure an extra bed in the parents' room, and a separate room for two children. Restaurants offer special children's menus with popular preferences, at special prices. Kindergartens open round the clock. Qualified nurses look after the health and wellbeing of children. Excursion programmes provide entertainment for adults and children alike.
These are some facilities especially appealing to children at the three main resorts:

Sunny Beach
There are playgrounds with slides, climbing frames and swings in front of the Iskur Hotel, near Lazur discothèque, outside the Neptune and Ribarska Hizha restaurants. Swimming pools in front of the Neptune and Ribarska Hizha restaurants; mini-golf in front of the Strandja, Iskur, Yantra and Sever Hotels; water slide outside the Zheravi Hotel; kindergartens, karting, puppet theatre, etc.
Bicycles and rickshaws near the hotels Belassitsa, Strandja, Iskur, Continental, Sirena, Amphora and Kouban, as well as in the vicinity of the open-air theatre. Video games at the bowling centre.
Every week Balkantourist organises: Children's festivals at Bar Rusalka and Bar Astoria, camp fire sessions, child discos at the Rusalka café. There are donkey safaris in the forest, contests for the finest sandcastle, contests for the best asphalt drawing.
Excursions to Varna including visits to the Dolphinarium,

CHILDREN

Albena, a resort that has plenty on offer for the young

Aquarium and Zoo; scooter, transmobile and bobsleigh rides.

Golden Sands
The water slide outside the Metropol Hotel; two swimming pools in front of the Havana and Metropol Hotels; karting next to the Zlatna Kotva Hotel; electric train next to the Zlatna Kotva Hotel; tennis school behind the Lilia Hotel.

Bicycles — in the resort centre, next to the Rodina, Malina and Havana Hotels; at Druzhba resort — near Chernomorets restaurant and Grand Hotel Varna.

Rickshaws and pedalos at South, North and Central beach.

Kindergarten at the Strandja Hotel; Video games at the bowling centre, at the Moskva and Strandja Hotels.

Balkantourist organises: Matinées with video films at the Shipka and Ambassador cafeterias.

Special programmes at the Chaika children's club; drawing on asphalt, painting, contests and games, puppet shows, study of Bulgarian songs and dances.

Visit to the Zoo in the town of Aitos.

Competitions with roller skates, sack races, boat rides; courses in riding, swimming, tennis, waterskiing; trained instructor's programme adapted to children.

Albena
The water slide in front of the Dorostor Hotel, children's water-karting in front of the Tervel Hotel, paddling pools at the Tervel, Kaliakra and Kom Hotels; karting near Sever bazaar, next to the Cultural and Information Centre and near the Tervel and Kaliopa Hotels.

Mini-golf near the Kaliopa and Kardam Hotels, video games at Sever bazaar and near the Cultural and Information Centre;

donkey carts at the Slavyanka Hotel. Kiddie Kastle in front of the Rodina Hotel;
Kindergartens.
Balkantourist organises:
Family contests under the motto 'Mum, Daddy and I'
Fun competition 'Quick, Bold, Nimble' — weekly on the beach outside the Tervel Hotel
Swimming lessons under expert instructors
The Merry Rabbit pastryshop — venue for games, film shows, children's festivals, drawing and singing contests
The Sluntse (Sun) children's club organises the following events:
Banner of Peace — all about the International Children's Assembly
Chuchuliga (Lark) — children's singing contest
Vessel Horovod (Merry Dancing) — study of Bulgarian folk dances
Let the Sun Always Shine — meetings between children from different countries

In the World of Fairy-tales — making of dolls and fairy-tale heroes
There is also a children's play corner at the Cultural Information Centre.

TIGHT BUDGET

Bulgaria's 200 per cent currency bonus (as operating early in 1989) makes virtually the whole country a 'bargain basement' for the holidaymaker. This can make a three-course meal and good bottle of wine in an attractive restaurant seem incredibly cheap to the Westerner. And quite edible/drinkable fare can become progressively cheaper at a tavern called a *mehana*, or a *hanche*.
Package tourists on pre-booked holidays receive enough **meal vouchers** for their whole stay when they arrive in Bulgaria. And the flexible 'dine as you please' system does not tie them down to 'spending' them at any particular restaurant.
Also, for instance, they can buy a cheap mid-day snack at a beachfront café and save up the vouchers for a superior meal that night — or the next.
Independent tourists also can obtain meal vouchers when they book ongoing full-board accommodation through a Balkantourist office.
Many children's amusements come free of charge (or for just a few stotinki) in the seaside resorts.
Museum charges tend to be nominal and, in cities like Varna and Ruse, seats at the opera ridiculously cheap.

DIRECTORY

Traditional cuisine includes such dishes as stuffed peppers and vineleaves, meatballs and hotpots, cheese pastry and salads

DIRECTORY

Arriving

Passports and Visas

Bulgaria can be entered by any foreign citizen in possession of a valid passport or other document for travelling abroad (*passe-avant, laissez-passer,* etc), as well as a Bulgarian entry or transit visa, when required. No entry visa is required of the citizens of those states with which Bulgaria has signed inter-governmental agreements on visa-free travel or facilitated visa regime; of foreign citizens travelling in organised tourist groups of at least five persons; and of families travelling with their children, providing they have pre-paid tourist service vouchers for a minimum of two over-night stays in the country.

Instead of a visa, a unified Balkantourist voucher for a minimum of two over-night stays can be obtained at the country's border checkpoints.

Airlines

Sofia is directly linked with over 40 cities through regular flights of Balkan Airlines and foreign arilines.

There are also indirect flights via Athens, Amsterdam, Copenhagen, Frankfurt am Main, London, Madrid, Moscow, Paris, Rome and Zurich to all over the world.

During the summer season

direct flights operate to Varna and/or Burgas from 14 cities.

Balkan Airlines Offices
London
322 Regent Street, W1,
tel: 01-637 7637/8
New York
10017, 50 East 42nd Street,
tel: 661 5733

Overseas Airlines Offices
Aeroflot 2 Ruski Boulevard,
Sofia, tel: 87-90-80
Airport office, tel: 45-30-70
Lufthansa 9 A. Stamboliiski
Boulevard, Sofia, tel: 88-23-10,
88-42-23
Airport office, tel: 72-07-58
Lot — Poland 27 A. Stamboliiski
Boulevard, Sofia, tel: 87-45-62,
88-31-93
Airport office, tel: 72-06-44
SAS Scandinavian 24 A.
Stamboliiski Boulevard, Sofia,
tel: 88-37-05, 87-48-37
Malev Hungary 26 A.
Stamboliiski Boulevard, Sofia,
tel: 87-86-07
Airport office, tel: 72-07-90
Air France 2 A. Stamboliiski
Boulevard, Sofia, tel: 87-26-86,
88-19-39
CSA Czechoslovakia 9 A.
Stamboliiski Boulevard, Sofia,
tel: 88-55-88
Airport Office, tel: 72-05-22
Swissair 66 G. Dimitrov
Boulevard, tel: 32-81-81
Jat Yugoslavia 1 Vassil Levski
Street, Sofia, tel: 88-04-19,
87-25-67
Turkish Airlines 11A A.
Stamboliiski Boulevard, Sofia,
tel: 88-35-96, 87-42-20

Railways
These express trains pass through Bulgaria daily throughout the year:

DANUBE Sofia — Pleven — Ruse — Bucharest — Ungeny — Kiev — Moscow — Sofia (with direct coaches to Istanbul once a week)
SOFIA Sofia — Pleven — Ruse — Bucharest — Vadul — Siret — Kiev — Moscow — Sofia
BULGARIA Sofia — Pleven — Ruse — Bucharest — Vadul — Siret — Kiev (with daily direct coaches to Leningrad)
PANONIA Sofia — Bucharest — Budapest — Prague — Berlin/Leipzig — Sofia
PANONIA/CARPATI Sofia — Pleven — Ruse — Bucharest — Medica — Warsaw — Sofia
POLONIA Sofia — Belgrade — Budapest — Warsaw — Sofia
ISTANBUL Istanbul — Svilengrad — Sofia — Belgrade — Ljubljana (Venice — Dortmund — München — Vienna — Sofia — Istanbul)
SOFIA-ATHENS Sofia — Blagoevgrad — Kulata — Salonika — Athens — Sofia
The Rila international travel agency handles the sale of international railway tickets, sleeping cars included, tickets for Soviet domestic railways, food vouchers for Soviet railways, and arranges trips via Moscow to Japan and back.

Border Checkpoints
There are 24-hour border checkpoints as follows:
Bulgarian — Yugoslav border:
    Kalotina — on the Belgrade/Nis-Sofia motorway
    Gyueshevo — on the Skoplje/Kriva Palanka-Kyustendil motorway
Bulgarian — Greek border:
    Kulata — on the Salonika/Sidhirokastron-

DIRECTORY

Blagoevgrad motorway
Bulgarian — Turkish border:
 Kapitan Andreevo — on the
 Istanbul/Edirne-Svilengrad
 motorway
 Malko Turnovo — on the
 Istanbul/Kirklareli-Malko
 Turnovo motorway
Bulgarian — Romanian border:
 Vidin — connecting Calafat to
 Vidin by ferry boat
 Ruse — on the
 Bucharest/Giurgui-Ruse
 motorway
 Kardam — on the
 Constanta-Tolbukhin railroad
 crossing
 Durankulak — on the
 Constanta/Mangalia-Varna
 motorway
There are also border
checkpoints at Sofia, Varna and
Burgas international airports.
Hotel accommodation can be
booked at checkpoints.

Sea Routes
The Interbalkan travel agency,
an agent of IATA and the
general agent of
Morpasflot-Moscow (the Russian
shipping line) handles ticket
sales for the Soviet passenger
boats on the following
international routes:
Odessa-Marseilles;
Odessa-Alexandria and
Odessa-Algiers with visits to
Mediterranean sea ports;
Odessa-Batumi passing through
the Soviet Black Sea ports;
Baku-Enseli (Iran); Nak-
hodka-Yokohama-Nakhodka;
Leningrad-Stockholm.
Interbalkan also handles sales of
air tickets and hotel booking of
foreign visitors, organises
transfers from and to Sofia
Airport, Varna Airport and

Varna Passenger Docks,
transfers from inland to
international routes, issues hotel
and tourist services vouchers for
the Interhotels-Balkantourist
hotel chain.
Interbalkan travel agency, 127
Rakovski Street, Sofia, tel:
88-09-95, telex 23803.

Car Breakdown
The Shipka agency assures the
members of the agencies
associated with AIT and FIA
free road service for the span of
one working hour, legal
assistance, and repatriation of
the motor vehicle if the need
arises. The Shipka Agency also
organises tourist trips along
combined itineraries.
Road service is provided by the
Union of Bulgarian Motorists.
The telephone number to dial is
146.
Technical assistance is offered
by the service stations of
Mototehnika and Autoservisi
and at the repair shops of the
Union of Bulgarian Motorists in
all larger cities (see town
entries for addresses).

Car Hire
There are car rental offices as
follows:
Sofia — Sofia Airport, Hotel
Vitosha, The New Otani, Grand
Hotel
Plovdiv — Novotel Plovdiv
in the three largest Black Sea
resorts of Golden Sands, Sunny
Beach and Albena
Varna — Cherno More Hotel
Burgas — Bulgaria Hotel
Choice: Mercedes, Renault or
Lada.
Balkantourist is the Bulgarian
representative of the
international rent-a-car

companies of Avis, Hertz, Europcar and Interrent. For advance booking and additional information, contact Balkantourist or the nearest rent-a-car office.

Customs Regulations

Foreign citizens can import and export duty-free the following items:

(*a*) objects for personal use during their travel and stay in Bulgaria

(*b*) consumer goods, including foodstuffs in quantities satisfying the need of travellers up to the point of arrival, as well as 1 litre of spirits, 2 litres of wine, 250 cigarettes or 250g of other tobacco products

Hrelyo's defence tower at Rila Monastery, where fragments of murals can be seen

(*c*) presents and gifts not exceeding the total sum of 50 leva, according to retail prices in Bulgaria

(*d*) duty-free export of articles in unlimited quantities is permitted provided they have been bought against convertible currency at the specialised *Corecom* shops throughout the country, the purchase being certified by a receipt.

(*e*) persons travelling in their own vehicles can export the amount of fuel contained in their tanks. Duty-free export of fuel in excess of this amount is permitted only if it has been obtained within the country against special petrol vouchers bought against convertible currency at the border checkpoints or from the inland tourist offices.

Domestic Travel

Air

Regular internal flights operate from Sofia to Varna, Burgas, Gorna Oryahovitsa, Ruse, Silistra, Turgovishte and Vidin. Price reductions for children aged below 12.

Balkan Airlines Offices in Bulgaria
Sofia
    12 Narodno Subranie Square, tel: 87-57-24, 88-06-63
    19 Legue Street, tel: 88-49-89, tel: 88-41-92
    10 Sofiiska Comouna Street, tel: 88-44-36, 88-13-94
    National Palace of Culture, tel: 59-70-95/6
Burgas
    24 May First Street, tel: 4-50-36, 5-56-85, 4-56-05

DIRECTORY

Varna
15 Lenin Boulevard, tel:
22-54-08, 22-29-48
Plovdiv
4 Sasho Dimitrov Street, tel:
2-20-03, 3-30-81
Ruse
1 Tsurkovna Nezavisimost
Street, tel: 2-41-61, 2-89-59

Buses
Tickets for trams, trolleybuses
and buses may be bought in
advance from kiosks at stops, or

*Nesebur, a gem of a town, is
connected to the mainland by an
isthmus no wider than the road*

from the driver.
Balkantourist arranges coach
excursions.

Rail
Bulgaria has an electrified
railway network. Besides daily
trains which link Sofia with all
parts of the country, the
following express trains also
operate: Sofia-Varna-Sofia;
Sofia-Burgas-Sofia;
Sofia-Ruse-Sofia; Sofia-Gorna
Oryahovitsa-Sofia.
Additional express trains from
Sofia to Varna and Burgas run
during the summer.

City Railway Offices handle the advance sale of tickets and seat reservation, issue combined travel tickets, ensure taxis for passengers travelling with express and fast trains, and provide information:
Burgas 106 Purvi Mai Street, tel: 2-39-04, 2-40-47
Gabrovo Racho Kovacha block, tel: 2-53-39, 2-86-89
Gorna Oryahovitsa, 3 G Izmirliev Square, tel: 4-21-34
Pleven 2 Zamenhoff Street, tel: 2-32-56
Plovdiv 13 Gurko Street, tel: 2-27-32

Ruse 39 D. Blagoev Street, tel: 2-28-45
Sliven 5 G. Kirkov Street, tel: 8-36-56
Sofia 23 G. Dimitrov Boulevard, tel: 87-02-22
8 Slaveikov Square, tel: 86-57-42
In the underpass of the National Palace of Culture, Vitosha Boulevard: information — tel: 59-71-87: tickets — tel: 59-31-06: sleepers — tel: 59-71-24
Varna 10 Avram Gachev Street, tel: 22-30-53
13 July 27 Street, tel: 22-30-73
Vratsa 22 G. Dimitrov Street, tel: 22-35-06

Cars and Driving Information
These international motorways pass through Bulgaria:
E 80 Dubrovnik—Nis—Kalotina—
    Sofia—Kapitan
    Andreevo—Edirne—Istanbul
E 79 Oradea—Krajova—Vidin—
    Sofia—Kulata—Salonika
E 87 Tulcea—Duranlulak—
    Varna—Malko
    Turnovo—Babaeski
E 70
    Trieste—Zagreb—Belgrade—
    Turnu
    Severin—Bucharest—Ruse—
    Varna

Insurance A visitor may drive on a current domestic licence. Insurance providing third party liability cover, as well as the Green and Blue insurance cards, are obligatory. The latter may be bought at the border checkpoints.

Petrol vouchers Before entering Bulgaria you must buy vouchers for petrol and other fuel which cannot be bought for spot cash. These are sold for hard

DIRECTORY

currency by the offices of the Shipka Tourist Agency at the border checkpoints, and (if more are needed) in the Balkantourist hotels and motels along the main motorways, in all larger city hotels and at foreign tourist offices abroad which are partners of the Shipka agency.

Motorists' itineraries in Bulgaria can be handled by Balkantourist.

Traffic rules and the required documents conform to the International Road Traffic Convention signed in Vienna in 1968. Drive on the right.

Petrol stations are at an average distance of 18-25 miles (30-40km) from one another; 96, 93 and 86 octane petrol is available.

Road signs conform to the requirements of international conventions. Road directions are denoted in both Cyrillic and Latin letters.

Speed limits The permitted speed limit for cars is 74mph (120km/h) on express motorways, 50mph (80km/h) outside populated areas and 37mph (60km/h) in populated areas. The respective speed limits for coaches and caravans are 62mph (100km/h), 43mph (70km/h) and 31mph (50km/h). Driving after alcohol consumption, irrespective of quantity, is strictly prohibited, and there are heavy penalties.

Electricity
Voltage 220v. Two-pin plugs.

Emergency Telephone Numbers
Ambulance 150
Fire 160
Police 166

The climate and terrain mean there is an abundant supply of excellent fruits and vegetables

Road service 146
Telephone information 144

Embassies
Great Britain
65 Tolbukhin Boulevard, Sofia, tel: 88-53-61, 87-83-25
USA
1 A. Stamboliiski Boulevard, Sofia, tel: 88-48-01/05

Guidebooks
Bulgaria: Tourist Information is available from Bulgarian National Tourist Offices. The Sofia Press Agency publishes

books, albums and brochures in 21 languages, the *Sofia News* weekly, and the *Bulgaria* monthly magazine. The Bulgarian Association of Tourism and Recreation publishes the excellent *Discover Bulgaria* magazine in English, Russian, French and German. *Discover Bulgaria*, 127 Rakovski Street, Sofia.

Health

Bulgaria has a network of hospitals and polyclinics. No charge is made for the consultation and treatment of accident and emergency cases. Any longer treatment

administered to citizens from countries with which Bulgaria has no reciprocal agreements for medical treatment should be paid for. Check before leaving home whether there is a reciprocal charge-free arrangement with your country.

The prices of both medical treatment and medicines are reasonable.

In Sofia there is a Clinic for Foreign Citizens, Mladost 1, 1 Evgeni Pavlovski Street, tel: 75-361.

Spas There are over 600 springs in Bulgaria from which there are 190 mineral water sources. Water temperatures range from 50 to 212°F (10-100°C), but the majority of springs have temperatures between 85 and 140°F (30-60°C), ie, they are ranked in the warm and hot class.

Balkantourist offers treatment in the country's balneological and climatological resorts. Treatment is generally comprehensive, including climatotherapy, water cures, physiotherapy, remedial exercises, mud treatment, massages, slimming and fruit cures.

Before starting treatment, a case history and medical diagnosis should be presented to the centre.

Holidays — Public

January 1 New Year
March 3 Day of Liberation from Turkish rule
May 1 and 2 International Labour Holiday
May 24 Day of the Slav Script, Bulgarian Enlightment and Culture

DIRECTORY

September 9 – 10 National Days, marking the victory of the socialist revolution in Bulgaria
November 7 The Victory of the Great October Socialist Revolution

Money Matters

Credit Cards

Credit cards accepted in Bulgaria: American Express, Diners Club, Eurocard/Access/Mastercard, VISA and JCB.

Credit cards are accepted for payment of goods and services in more than 400 places throughout the country: by all Balkantourist hotels (over 250), by top restaurants and shops, by all *Corecom* shops; by all Balkantourist offices, hire car offices, Balkan Airways offices and Interhotels offices. Holders of Diners Club, Eurocard/Access/Mastercard and JCB are also entitled to a certain amount of cash advance in Bulgarian currency.

Currency

Import and export of Bulgarian banknotes and coins is prohibited. Convertible currency may be exchanged only at the tourist agency offices, hotels, bureaux de change, and the Bulgarian National Bank according to the official monthly exchange rate, plus a tourist bonus.

When currency is exchanged a *bordereau* is issued, which should be retained by clients until their departure from the country.

The exchange of currency outside the exchange offices is strictly prohibited and is a punishable offence.

The basic monetary unit is the *lev*, sub-divided into 100 *stotinki*. Coins of 1, 2, 5, 10, 20 and 50 *stotinki*, as well as of 1, 2 and 5 *leva*, and banknotes of 1, 2, 5, 10 and 20 *leva* are in circulation.

Nudism

Nudity on the beaches is forbidden, except on designated naturist beaches in the south, around Sozopol, Primorsko, Kiten and Lozenets.

Post Office

Offices offering postal, telegraph and telephone services can be found in all towns and villages in Bulgaria, and provide communications to all parts of the country and abroad.

Postal services have also been set up in the holiday resort complexes.

International and intercity calls can be placed from all hotels, and the larger ones offer telex connections.

The Central Post Office in Sofia is located on 6 Gurko Street; 24-hour telephone and telegram service.

Direct dialling to all European countries is possible from the post offices of all cities and resorts.

Telephones

See under **Post Office**

Time Difference

Local time equals GMT + 2 hours. Summer Time (GMT + 3 hours) lasts from the start of April until the end of September.

. . . except on certain designated beaches in some of the southern Black Sea coast resorts

Tourist Information Offices
In Sofia
(for other Balkantourist Offices see town entries)
Balkantourist, 1 Vitosha Boulevard, tel: 43-331
37 Dondukov Boulevard, tel: 88-44-30
Comprehensive Tourist Service Office, 35 Exarch Yossif Street, tel: 88-25-84
Underpass, National Palace of Culture, tel: 59-70-93
Bulgarian Association of Tourism and Recreation, 1 Lenin Square, tel: 84-131

At Border Checkpoints
There are tourist information offices at:
Durankulak, Kardam, Kulata, Malka Turnovo, Gyueshevo, Ruse, Silistra, Kalotina, Kapitan Andreevo

Overseas
Great Britain: Bulgarian Tourist Office, 18 Princes Street, London W1R 7RE, tel: 01-499 6988
Balkan Holidays, Sofia House, 19 Conduit Street, London WC1R 9LT, tel: 01-491 4499
USA: Bulgarian Tourist Office/ Balkan Holidays, 161 East 86 Street, New York, NY 10028, tel: 212/722-1110

Water
Tapwater is safe to drink almost everywhere, unless there are obvious contra-indications, and often uncommonly good.

LANGUAGE

Useful Words and Phrases

Meeting and Greeting

welcome dobré doshli
dear friends skápi priyáteli
dear guests skápi gósti
good morning dobró útro
good afternoon dóbar den
good evening dóbar vécher
good night léka nósht
hello zdravéite
please mólya
excuse me/I am sorry izvinéte
happy birthday chestit rozhdén dem
many happy returns of the day za mnógo godíni
happy New Year chestíta nóva godína
my congratulations móite pozdravléniya
how are you? kak ste?
very well, thank you blagodryá, mnógo dobré
do you speak Bulgarian/English/ French/German/Russian? govótite li bálgarski/anglíski/ fýrenski/némski/rúski?
I speak a little Bulgarian govórya málko bálgarski
do you understand? razbírate li?
I do not understand mólya, govoréte pó-bávno
yes da
no ne
where are you going? kadé otívate?
I am going to the seaside otívam na moré
I am going to the mountains otívam na planiná
I am interested in the history of Bulgaria interesuvam se ot istóriyata na Balgáriya
I am going to tour the country shte obikolyá stranáta
have a nice time priýyatno prekárvane

pleased to meet you priyátno mi e da se zapoznáya s vas
meet my husband/wife zapoznáite se s móya sapråg/móyata saprúga
how do you do priyátno mi e
what is your name? kak se kázvatez?
my name is... kázvam se...
what country do you come from? otkadé ste?
I come from Great Britain/ England /Scotland/Wales/ Ireland ot velikobritániya;/ Ángliya/Shotlándiya/Uéls/ Irlándiya
are you married? zhénen li ste?
no, I am single ne, ne sam
I hope I'll see you again nadyávam se da se vídim pak
so do I az sashto
when can I see you again? kogá shte vi vídya otnóvo?
here you are zapovyádaite
thank you blagodaryá
you are very kind mnógo ste lyubézna
goodbye dovizhdane
all the best vsíchko nái-húbavo
soon skóro
today dnes
tomorrow éutre
yesterday vchéra

Air Travel

how can I get to the airport? lal móga da otída do letíshteto?
where is the departure point for the airport buses? ot kadé trágvat avtobåsite za letíshteto?
what time does the next bus leave/arrive? kogá trágva/prístíga slédvashtiyat avtobús?
bus avtobús
ticket bilét
porter nossách
where are our seats, please? kadé sa ni mestáta, mólya?

here tuk
there tam
on the left-hand side v lyávo
on the right-hand side v dyásno
when will the plane take off? kogá islíta samolétat?
in ten minutes sled désset minúti
over Bulgaria nad Balgária
the plane is landing samolétat se prizemyáva
we had a very pleasant journey patåvaneto béshe mnógo priyátno

Days, Weeks
Sunday Nedélya
Monday Ponedélnik

Worn with pride by young and old;
national costumes are vibrant with
colour, rich in embroidery

Tuesday Vtórnik
Wednesday Sryáda
Thursday Chetvártak
Friday Pétak
Saturday Sábota
this week tázi sédmitsa
next week slédvashtata sédmitsa
last week mínalata sédmitsa
in several days' time sled nyákolko dni

In Hotels
where is the hotel? kadé e hotél...?
is my room ready? gotóva li e stáyata mi?
my name is... kázvam se...
your room is ready váshata stáya e gotóva
a suite apartamént
a single room stáya s edno legló

LANGUAGE

a double room stáya s dvóino legló
a twin-bedded room stáya s dva leglá
an extra bed dopalnítelno legló
your room number is... vie ste v stáya nómer...
on the first floor na párviya etázh
second vtóriya
third trétiya
fourth chetvártiya
fifth pétiya
sixth shéstiya
seventh sédmiya
eighth óssmiya
ninth devétiya
tenth dessétiya
eleventh edinádessetiya

the key, please klyúcha mólya
I have something to be laundered imam néshto za prané
could you please tell me where there is a toilet? kadé e toalétnata, mólya?
is there a hairdressing salon near here? ima li friziórski salón nablízo?
there is one in the hotel friziórski salón íma v hotéla
can I hire a car here? móga li da naéma kolá tuk?
yes, we have rent-a-car service da, imame slúzhba za kolí pod náem
is there a taxi rank near here? ima li taksíta nablízo?
will you please order a taxi for me for tomorrow at 7 o'clock? íhte li

Troyan Monastery, the country's third largest, founded in 1600 and a centre of Bulgarian nationalism during Ottoman domination. Visitors can stay here if they wish.

mi poráchali taksí za útre sutrintá v sédem chassá
will you wake me at 7 o'clock? sabudéte me v sédem chassa mólya?
where is the nearest restaurant? kadé e nái-blízkiyat restoránt
there is a restaurant in the hotel/ coffee bar/Evening bar/ cafeteria/discothéque v hotéla ima restoránt/dnéven bar/ nóshten bar/sladkárnitsa/ diskotéka
is there any post for me? ima li póshta za men?

would you post these cards for me? bíhte li púsnali tézi kártichki?
would you please send this letter registered/ordinary/air mail for me? bíhte li izpátili tová pismó preporáchana/obiknovéna/ vazdúshna póshta?
where can I buy stamps? kadé móga da kúpya póshtenski márki?
from any hotel vav vséki hotél
from the post office v póshtata
would you please book a telephone call for me at 17.00? bihte li mi poráchali telefónen rázgovor za pet chassá sled obyad?
number 64253 nómer 64253
engaged zaéto
no reply ne otgováryat
do you want to leave a message? da predám li néshto?
yes please da, mólya vi
no thank you ne, blagodaryá
sorry, wrong number izvinéte, gréshka
have you got a telephone directory? imate li telefónen ukazátel?
this line is bad lósho se chúva
please speak louder govoréte pó-silno mólya
please repeat once again mólya povtoréte
I do not feel well ne sam dobré
Have you anything for a headache? imate li néshto za glavobólie?
my wife is not well zhená mi ne e dobré
my husband is not well mazhát mi ne e dobré
my child is not well detéto mi ne e dobré
would you please send for the doctor mólya, povíkaite lékar
please may I have a map of the town/of the resort? daíte mi kárta na gradá/na kurórta, mólya?

LANGUAGE

museum muzéi
art gallery hudózhestvena galériya
exhibition izlózhba
open otvóreno
closed zatvóreno

At a Restaurant

restaurant restoránt
folkstyle restaurant mehaná
do you have a table for 2, 3, 4?
  ímate li mássa za dváma, tríma,
  chetiríma?
on the terrace na terássata
inside vátre
waiter servityór
may I please see the menu? dáyte
  mi menyúto, mólya?
knife nozh
fork vílitsa
spoon lazhítsa
napkin salféka
plate chiníya
glass/cup chásha
may I have something to drink?
  mólya vi, néshto za píene?
yes, of course da, rasbíra se
what would you like? kakvó
  zheláete?
tea chái
coffee kafé
wine víno
would you like? zheláete, li?
soft drinks bezalkohólni napítki
water vodá
soda water gazírana vodá
fruit juice plódov sok
drinks napítka
brandy konyák
white wine byálo víno
red wine chervéno víno
dry/medium/sweet wine
  súho/polúsúho/sládko víno
beer bíra
to your health! nazdráve!
tea with lemon chái s limón
tea with milk chái s mlyáko
black coffee shvárts kafé
white coffee kafé s mlyáko
turkish coffee túrsko kafé

bread hlyáb
toast prepéchen hlyáb
butter masló
eggs yaitsá
sandwich sándvich
salad saláta
soup súpa
fish ríba
sugar záhar
help yourself to the sugar
  zapvyádayte záhar
may I have another lump of sugar?
  bíhte li mi dáli óshe edná
  búchka záhar?
peppers chúshki
tomatoes domáti
cucumber krástavitsa
pickled cucumbers kísseli
  krástavichki
vegetarian dishes póstni yastiyá
meat dishes yasiyá s mesó
grills skára
omelette omlét
salt sol
pepper chéren pipér
vinegar otsét
Bulgarian yellow cheese
  kashkavál
dessert dessért
ice cream sladoléd
yoghurt kísselo mliyáko
apples yábalki
strawberries yágodi
pears krúshi
cherries cheréshi
raspberries malíni
water melon dínya
melon pápesh
apricots kaissíi
peaches práskovi
lemon limón
grapes grózde
Bulgarian food is very delicious
  Bálgarskata hraná e mnógo
  vkúsna
cigarettes tsigári
matches kíbrít
do you smoke? púshite li?
would you like a cigarette?

zheláete li tsigára?
may I have the bill please?
smétkata, mólya?

Travel by Car
petrol station benzinostántsiya
please fill it up mólya, zaredéte
I have had a breakdown íma
nyákakva povréda
**where is the nearest service
station?** kadé e nái-blízkiya
ávtoservíz?
I have a flat tyre spúkah gúma
I haven't got a spare tyre nyámam
rezérvna gúma
I have lost my way sbárkal sam
pátya
which is the road to Sofia? kói e
pátyat za Sófia?
Sofia is the capital of Bulgaria
Sófia e stólitsa na Balgáriya
driving is on the right-hand side
dvizhénieto e v dyásno
car park párking
free parking bezpláten párking
camping site kámping
motel motél
help! pomosht!

Numbers
one ednó
two dve
three tri
four chétiri
five pet
six shest
seven sédem
eight óssem
nine dévet
ten désset
eleven edinádesset
twelve dvanádesset
thirteen trinádesset
fourteen chetirinádesset
fifteen petnádesset
sixteen shestnádesset
seventeen sedemnádesset
eighteen ossemnádesset
nineteen devetnádesset

twenty dvádesset
twenty one dvádesset i ednó
twenty two dvádesset i dve
thirty trídesset
forty chetíridesset
fifty petdessét
sixty shestdessét
seventy sedemessét
eighty osedemdessét
ninety devetdessét
hundred sto

*An old woman on the streets of
Rila threads leaves of tobacco,
one of the country's main
products*

INDEX

ACKNOWLEDGEMENTS

The Automobile Association
would like to thank the following
photographers and libraries for
their assistance in the
compilation of this book

J ALLAN CASH
PHOTOLIBRARY 38 Rila
Monastery, 67 Stone Forest, 78
folk dancing, 113 Rila
Monastery, 125 old woman.
D ASH 63 Shiroka Luka, 122/3
Troyan Monastery.
P ATTERBURY Cover: Shipka
Pass, 7 nr Aitos, 9 Veliko
Turnovo, 54 Shipka, 72 Nesebur,
119 notice, Sunny Beach.
BULGARIAN TOURIST BOARD
4 nr Cape Kaliakra, 5 Location
Map, 11 Archaeology Museum,
Sofia, 23 Alexander Nevsky
Mem. Church, 24 souvenirs, 26/7
Bulgarian cuisine, 27 restaurant,
Sheraton Hotel, 29 Vitosha Hotel
Shtastlivetza, 31 Samokov
drinking fountain, 32 Ritlite
Rocks, 34/5 Belogradchik
Fortress, 36/7 Vidin, 40 Melnik,
43 Rila Mountains, 45 Khisar, 47
Plovdiv, 48 Plovdiv Roman
Theatre, 51 Valley of the Roses,
52 Etura, 56 Veliko Turnovo, 58
Preslav, 60 Kotel monument, 61
Pamporovo, 62 Map, 68 The
Black Sea, 69 Kamchiya, 70/1
Sozopol, 75 Hotel Varna,
Druzhba, 76 Golden Sands, 80/1
Sunny Beach, 83 Pleven, 86
tomb mural at Kazanluk, 99
market, 100/1 Bulgarian dishes,
103 Druzhba, 105 singers, 106
Pamporovo, 108/9 Albena, 110
traditional food, 114/5 Nesebur,
116/7 market, 121 Pirin singers.
MARY EVANS PICTURE
LIBRARY 12 Surrender of
Bulgarian Soldiers, 17 The
National Liberation Movement.
NATURE PHOTOGRAPHERS
LTD 87 wildcat (W S Paton), 89
eagle owl (E A Janes), 90 white
pelicans (R S Daniel), 93 ghost
orchid, 95 gentiana (C Grey-
Wilson), 96 wall lizard, 97 wood
ants, 98 white stork (P R Sterry).
ZEFA PICTURE LIBRARY (UK)
LTD 19 Ivan Vasov Nat. Theatre,
64/5 Bachkovo Monastery.

AUTHOR'S ACKNOWLEDGEMENTS

David Ash wishes to thank the
Bulgarian National Tourist
Office, Balkantourist, the
Bulgarian Association for
Tourism and Recreation,
Balkanair, and numerous guides
for their help during visits over
26 years which enabled him to
write this book. For incidental
information, he is particularly
grateful to Elisabeth Hussey of
the Ski Centre of Great Britain,
journalist Moira Rutherford,
guide George Poshtov, and
friends with 'Discover Bulgaria'.

W9-DET-752

C I T Y P A C K
R o m e

By Tim Jepson

2ND EDITION

Fodor's Travel Publications, Inc.
New York • Toronto • London • Sydney • Auckland

WWW.FODORS.COM/

Contents

About this book

KEY TO SYMBOLS

✚	map reference on the fold-out map accompanying this book (see below)	🚌	nearest bus route
✉	address	⛴	nearest riverboat or ferry stop
☎	telephone number	♿	facilities for visitors with disabilities
🕐	opening times	✋	admission charge
🍴	restaurant or café on premises or nearby	↔	other nearby places of interest
Ⓜ	nearest métro (underground) train station	❓	tours, lectures, or special events
🚆	nearest overground train station	►	indicates the page where you will find a fuller description
		ℹ	tourist information

Citypack Rome is divided into six sections to cover the six most important aspects of your visit to Rome. It includes:

- The author's view of the city and its people
- Itineraries, walks and excursions
- The top 25 sights to visit—as selected by the author
- Features on what makes the city special
- Detailed listings of restaurants, hotels, shops and nightlife
- Practical information

In addition, easy-to-read side panels provide extra facts and snippets, highlights of places to visit, and invaluable practical advice.

CROSS-REFERENCES

To help you make the most of your visit, cross-references, indicated by ► , show you where to find additional information about a place or subject.

MAPS

- **The fold-out map** in the wallet at the back of the book is a comprehensive street plan of Rome. All the map references given in the book refer to this map. For example, the Palazzo Corsini, on the Via della Lungara, has the following information: ✚ **dIV, C6**—indicating the grid squares of the large-scale map (**dIV**) and the main map (**C6**) in which the Palazzo Corsini will be found.
- **The city-center maps** found on the inside front and back covers of the book itself are for quick reference. They show the Top 25 Sights, described on pages 24–48, which are clearly plotted by number (**❶** – **㉕**, not page number) from west to east across the city.

PRICES

Where appropriate, an indication of the cost of an establishment is given by **$** signs: **$$$** denotes higher prices, **$$** denotes average prices, while **$** denotes lower charges.

ROME *life*

INTRODUCING ROME

Rome, more than most capitals, is a city of extremes. For the first day or so, particularly if you visit during a busy time, the noise, bustle, and traffic can seem almost Third World in their intensity. Arrival at Fiumicino airport or, worse still, the seedy confines of Stazione Termini, can be enough to make you think of turning tail for home. The streets appear places of confusion and wanton crowds, the city a labyrinth of belching cars and groaning inefficiency. Tackle the sights against this backdrop, and in the heat of a summer afternoon, and you will always emerge unenchanted, battered rather than enraptured by what—with the right approach—can be one of the most romantic cities in the world. For if you start slowly, and restrict yourself to a few sights, Rome reveals itself as the city of the Caesars, of languorous sunny days, the city of *la dolce vita*, of art and a galaxy of galleries, of religion, churches and museums, of fountain-splashed piazzas and majestic monuments to its golden age of Empire. To uncover this beguiling, but ever more beleaguered, face it is worth ignoring—at least initially—sights such as St. Peter's and the Colosseum (both likely to be besieged by visitors); start instead with a stroll around the Ghetto or Trastevere, or enjoy a quiet cappuccino in Campo de' Fiori or Piazza Navona. Or you might wander into some of the city's greener corners—the Villa Borghese and Pincio Gardens—oases of calm well away from the traffic and streams of people. Better still, start with one of the lesser-known churches, such as Santa Maria del Popolo or San Clemente. Only with this type of quiet beginning, and reassured of Rome's potential for enchantment, can you begin to uncover a city that keeps its magnificent past hidden beneath a brash and initially unsettling present.

Areas of the city

Rome's ancient heart is the Roman Forum, close to Piazza Venezia (its modern center). Via del Corso strikes north to Piazza del Popolo, with the busy

Piazza della Rotonda and (left) the side of the Pantheon

shopping streets around Piazza di Spagna to its east. Corso Vittorio Emanuele II runs west to St. Peter's, bisecting the core of the medieval city (or *centro storico*). Trastevere, a quaint area of restaurants and small streets, lies across the Tiber on the river's west bank. Testaccio, south of the old city, is an increasingly trendy area of bars and clubs. Prati (north of St. Peter's) and the area around Stazione Termini in the east are predominantly 19th-century creations.

Romans Rome itself, however, is not the only thing that can come as a shock: its citizens can be as startling as their city. In Italy's national mythology Romans are seen as lazy, stubborn, slovenly, and rude. As ever, there is some truth in the myth. Romans excel in the art of *menefreghismo*—not giving a damn—an infuriating knack when you want to be served in a bar or seek a little extra space in a bus. Of course there are exceptions, and in their defense Romans have had to develop thick skins to deal with the stresses of living in a city whose facilities barely match its needs, and whose overstretched resources are burdened further by tourists. This said, a smile and a little stuttered Italian may well be rewarded with courtesy, and after a while the Romans' fabled truculence can become almost endearing. You might also begin to enjoy the city's almost Fellini-esque cast of characters, from the pot-bellied restaurateurs and dog-walking old women to the fallen aristocrats, grumpy bartenders, and rough-fingered matriarchs of the market stalls.

Vatican City

Vatican City is the world's smallest independent sovereign state (just over 100 acres). Its 200 inhabitants (about 30 of whom are women) are presided over by the Pope, Europe's only absolute monarch. Around 800 "foreigners" commute in and out to work, but the general public is admitted only to areas like St. Peter's and the Vatican Museums. The city has its own civil service and judicial systems, shops, banks, currency, stamps, post office, garages—even its own helicopter pad, radio station, and newspaper (*L'Osservatore Romano*). Its official language is still Latin.

One of the matriarchs of the Roman market stalls

ROME IN FIGURES

HISTORY
- Official age of the city (in 2000): 2,753 years
- Number of emperors: 73
- Number of popes: 168
- Water delivered by aqueducts to Rome in the 2nd century AD: 312,000 gallons
- Number of obelisks: 20 (of which Egyptian: 7)
- Number of churches within the city walls: 280

GEOGRAPHY
- Number of historical hills: 7 (Palatine, Celian, Capitoline, Aventine, Quirnal, Esquiline, Viminal)
- Actual number of hills: 20
- Distance from the sea: 17 miles
- Area of the city: 577 square miles

PEOPLE
- Official population: 2,777,882
- Unofficial population: 4.5 million
- Estimated number of tourists annually: 15 million
- Size of average family: 2.7
- Number of people living in illegally built homes: 700,000
- Area covered by illegally built homes: 6,000 acres

RELIGION
- Percentage of Romans who have had their children baptized: 94
- Percentage of Romans who favor women priests: 40
- Percentage of Romans who do not condemn divorce: 80
- Percentage of Romans who believe in hell: 40
- Percentage of Romans who never go to confession: 60
- Percentage of Romans who sometimes go to mass: 23
- Percentage of Romans who go to both mass and confession weekly: 12
- Percentage of Romans who profess themselves Catholics, but who do not follow the Church's "moral teaching": 78
- Percentage of Romans who believe they have been affected by the "evil eye": 37

ROME PEOPLE

THE POPE

Rome's first bishop was St. Peter. Since then his successors have been considered Christ's representatives on earth and continue to hold sway over the world's Roman Catholics (who today number some 850 million). For centuries popes also ruled large areas of Italy (they only relinquished control of Rome in 1870). Papal election—conducted by a conclave of cardinals in the Sistine Chapel—is achieved by one of three methods: acclamation, in which divine intervention causes all present to call one name in unison (not common); by majority vote, with votes cast four times daily until a candidate has a two-thirds majority; and by compromise, on the recommendation of a commission.

VALENTINO

The doyen of Rome's fashion designers has no rivals in his home city. Having risen to prominence in the heady *dolce vita* days of the late 1950s, Valentino quickly established a name for exquisite (and exquisitely expensive) *haute couture*, dressing many stars of stage, screen, and high society. More recently, he has diversified into ready-to-wear and diffusion ranges. To visit his palatial showrooms around Piazza di Spagna, however, is to realize that the master's touch is still appreciated and bought.

Pope John Paul II

Devil's Advocate

The Vatican still has an office for the *Avvocato del Diavolo*—the Devil's Advocate—from which the expression derives. His job is to investigate the lives of prospective saints and those put forward for beatification to discover why they might *not* be acceptable.

The President

Rome is Italy's political capital, and as well as being home to the country's lower and upper chambers (housed in Palazzo Montecitorio—the Chamber of Deputies—and Palazzo Madama—the Senate) it is also home to her head of state, the President (whose offices are in the Palazzo del Quirinale). The post is largely symbolic.

9

A Chronology

1200–800 BC	First settlements on the banks of the Tiber
753 BC	Traditional date of the foundation of Rome by Romulus, first of the city's seven kings
616–578 BC	Tarquinius Priscus, Rome's first Etruscan king
509 BC	Etruscans expelled and the Republic founded
390 BC	Rome briefly occupied by the Gauls
264–241 BC	First Punic War: between Rome and Carthage
218–201 BC	Second Punic War: Rome threatened by Hannibal, leader of the Carthaginian army
149–146 BC	Third Punic War: Rome defeats Carthage
60 BC	Rome ruled by a triumvirate of Pompey, Crassus, and Julius Caesar
48 BC	Caesar declared ruler for life but assassinated by jealous rivals in 44 BC
27 BC–AD 14	Rule of Octavian, Caesar's great-nephew, who as Augustus becomes the first Roman emperor
AD 42	St. Peter the Apostle visits Rome
54–68	Reign of Emperor Nero. Great Fire in 64; "Nero fiddles while Rome burns." Christian persecutions
72	The Colosseum is begun
98–117	Reign of Emperor Trajan. Military campaigns greatly extend the Empire's boundaries
117–38	Reign of Emperor Hadrian
161–180	Reign of Emperor Marcus Aurelius, general and philosopher. Barbarians attack Empire's borders
284–286	Empire divided into East and West
306–337	The Emperor Constantine reunites the Empire and legalizes Christianity. St. Peter's and the first Christian churches are built

410	Rome is sacked by the Goths
476	Romulus Augustulus is the last Roman emperor
800	Charlemagne drives the Lombards from Italy and awards some of the conquered territories to the papacy, the germ of the Papal States. He is crowned Holy Roman Emperor by Pope Leo III
1378–1417	The Great Schism between rival papal claimants. Papacy to Avignon
1452–1626	The new St. Peter's is built
1508	Michelangelo begins the Sistine Chapel ceiling
1527	Rome is sacked and looted by German and Spanish troops under Charles V
1732–1735	Fontana di Trevi and Spanish Steps begun
1797	Napoleon occupies Rome until 1814, when power is restored to the Papal States
1848	Uprisings in Rome under Mazzini and Garibaldi force Pope Pius IX to flee. The new "Roman Republic" is ultimately defeated by the French
1861	A united Italy is proclaimed but Rome remains under papal control
1870	Rome joins a united Italy
1922	Fascists march on Rome; Mussolini becomes Prime Minister. Fascists rule Italy 1924–1943
1929	The Lateran Treaty recognizes the Vatican as a separate state
1940	Italy enters World War II with the Axis powers. The Allies liberate Rome from the Nazis in 1944
1960	Rome hosts the Olympic games
1978	Karol Wojtyla is elected Pope John Paul II
1990	Soccer's World Cup Final held in Rome

PEOPLE & EVENTS FROM HISTORY

Capitoline Wolf, suckling Romulus and Remus, Palazzo dei Conservatori (► 37)

ROMULUS AND REMUS

The myth of Rome's birth was recorded by Livy (Titus Livius, 59 BC–AD 17), and begins in the old Latin capital Alba Longa with the king Numitor, whose throne was stolen by his brother Amulius. To prevent rival claims Amulius forced Numitor's daughter, Rhea, to become a vestal virgin. The god Mars then appeared to Rhea and left her pregnant with Romulus and Remus. The twins, when born, were cast adrift by Amulius, but were guided by the gods to the Velabrum, the old marshes under the Palatine Hill. Here they were suckled by a she-wolf and eventually adopted by a shepherd. In adulthood, fulfilling a prophecy made by Mars, they founded Rome in 753 BC. Both wished to rule, but neither could agree on a name for the new city. Remus favored Rema, while Romulus preferred Roma. Romulus eventually murdered his brother and built the city's first walls.

The Sack of Rome

One of the single most traumatic events in Rome's long history took place in 1527, when the city was sacked by German and Spanish troops from the imperial army of Charles V. Countless buildings and works of art were destroyed while Pope Clement VII took refuge in the Castel Sant'Angelo. Over 4,000 people died in the siege. The plunder of the city then went on for several weeks.

JULIUS CAESAR

Caesar originally intended to become a priest, joining the army in 81 BC to pay his debts. He eventually became Pontifex Maximus, Rome's high priest, and then joined Pompey and Crassus in 60 BC in ruling Rome as the "First Triumvirate." Over the next ten years he fought military campaigns in Gaul and Germany, and launched two short invasions of Britain. His successes aroused the envy of Pompey, who eventually fled Rome at the news that Caesar had crossed the Rubicon with his returning army. For six months Caesar pursued Pompey across Spain, Greece, and Africa, and also spent time with Cleopatra. In 48 BC he was appointed Rome's absolute ruler. He was assassinated in 44 BC on March 15 (the "Ides of March"), murdered by a group of envious conspirators that included Brutus, his adopted son.

ROME
how to organize your time

ITINERARIES

Rome is best enjoyed during a short visit by concentrating on a few sights in a single area (having considered opening times) because it is possible only to skim the surface of this great city's cultural and artistic heritage.

ITINERARY ONE	**ANCIENT ROME**
Breakfast	Latteria del Gallo (➤ 68) or an outdoor café in Campo de' Fiori (➤ 29)
Morning	Stroll through the Ghetto district (➤ 18) to Piazza del Campidoglio Santa Maria in Aracoeli (➤ 38) and Capitoline Museums (➤ 37) Roman Forum and the Palatine (➤ 41) Colosseum (➤ 43) Arch of Constantine (➤ 50)
Lunch	Picnic lunch in the Colle Oppio park (➤ 56); snack in Enoteca, Via Cavour 313; or lunch in Da Valentino (➤ 64) or Nerone (➤ 63)
Afternoon	San Pietro in Vincoli (➤ 44) San Clemente (➤ 46) San Giovanni in Laterano (➤ 48) Metro to Termini then Santa Maria Maggiore (➤ 47)
ITINERARY TWO	**PANTHEON TO ST. PETER'S**
Breakfast	In Piazza della Rotonda or a bar nearby (La Tazza d'Oro, Sant'Eustachio or Camilloni: ➤ 69)
Morning	Santa Maria sopra Minerva (➤ 34) Pantheon (➤ 33) San Luigi dei Francesi (➤ 30) Piazza Navona (➤ 30) Coffee at Bar della Pace (➤ 68) Via dei Coronari or Via del Governo Vecchio Castel Sant'Angelo (➤ 27)
Lunch	Picnic in the Parco Adriano
Afternoon	St. Peter's (➤ 24), then Vatican Museums (➤ 25) and Sistine Chapel (➤ 26)
Evening	Dine and stroll in Trastevere (➤ 18)

ITINERARY THREE	**THE CORSO TO THE VATICAN**
	To Via del Corso and Column of Marcus Aurelius (► 51); walk to Fontana di Trevi (► 39)
Breakfast	Bar by the Fontana di Trevi (► 39)
Morning	Walk up Via delle Scuderie and Via Rasella to the Palazzo Barberini (► 42) Piazza di Spagna and Spanish Steps (► 40), Museo Keats–Shelley (► 40, 52) Coffee at Caffè Greco or Babington's Tea Rooms (► 69), or Casina Valadier (► 68) Pincio Gardens (► 56) Santa Maria del Popolo (► 32)
Lunch	Picnic in the Pincio Gardens (► 56) or Villa Borghese (► 57); or snack at the Casina Valadier, Rosati or Canova bars (► 68)
Afternoon	Altar of Peace (► 31) Walk to Piazza del Risorgimento or take bus 49 from Piazza Cavour Vatican Museums (► 25), Sistine Chapel (► 26)
Evening	Stroll and dine near Piazza di Spagna (► 40)
ITINERARY FOUR	**TOWARDS TRASTEVERE**
Breakfast	Antico Caffè Brasile (► 69)
Morning	Trajan's Markets (► 51) Palazzo-Galleria Colonna (► 53) Palazzo-Galleria Doria Pamphili (► 36) Piazza Venezia: Santa Maria in Aracoeli (► 38) and Capitoline Museums (► 37)
Lunch	Light lunch in Birreria Fratelli Tempera (► 64)
Afternoon	Walk to Santa Maria in Cosmedin (► 60) via Piazza del Campidoglio and Piazza della Consolazione Circus Maximus (► 51) Explore the Isola Tiberina. Cross to Trastevere: visit Santa Cecilia in Trastevere (► 16) and Santa Maria in Trastevere (► 28)

15

WALKS

Temple of Vesta

THE SIGHTS

INFORMATION

FROM PIAZZA VENEZIA TO ST. PETER'S THROUGH THE HISTORIC CITY CENTER AND TRASTEVERE

Start at Piazza Venezia. Walk to Piazza del Campidoglio and exit at the rear left-hand corner for a view over the Forum. Return to the piazza: from its rear right-hand corner, follow the alley to Via della Consolazione and Piazza Bocca della Verità. Follow Lungotevere dei Pierleoni north and explore the Isola Tiberina.

Cross Ponte Cestio and follow Via Anicia south to Santa Cecilia in Trastevere. Cut west to Viale Trastevere and Piazza S. Sonnino, and follow Via della Lungaretta to Piazza Santa Maria in Trastevere. Leave the piazza to the north, and follow the alleys to Vicolo dei Cinque and Piazza Trilussa. If you have time, walk west to Via della Lungara to see the Villa Farnesina.

Cross the Ponte Sisto, follow Via dei Pettinari north, and then turn left on to Via Capo di Ferro to Piazza Farnese and Campo de' Fiori. (Detour south from Piazza Farnese on to Via dei Farnesi to look at elegant Via Giulia and Santa Maria della Orazione e Morte; ➤ 29.) Take Via dei Cappellari west from Campo de' Fiori, turn left on to Via del Pellegrino and then right on to Via dei Cartari to reach Corso Vittorio Emanuele II.

Pick up Via dei Filippini to the left of the Chiesa Nuova. Turn left on to Via dei Banchi Nuovi and then right on to Via del Banco Santo Spirito. Cross the Ponte Sant'Angelo. Follow Via della Conciliazione to St. Peter's.

A CIRCULAR WALK FROM PIAZZA NAVONA THROUGH THE HEART OF THE MEDIEVAL CITY

Begin in Piazza Navona. Leave via the alley in the southeast corner, cross Corso del Rinascimento and follow Via Staderari past Sant'Ivo (in Palazzo di Sapienza) and Sant'Eustachio. Take Via Santa Chiara to Piazza della Minerva and then Via Minerva to Piazza della Rotonda.

Take Via del Seminario east from the Piazza and then turn right on to Via Sant'Ignazio and into Piazza Collegio Romano. Cross Via del Corso and wind northeast through Via Santi Apostoli, Via San Marcello, and Via dell'Umiltà to emerge by the Fontana di Trevi.

Follow Via del Lavatore, Via delle Scuderie, and Via Rasella east to Palazzo Barberini. Walk north to Piazza Barberini; detour briefly up Via Vittorio Veneto to see Santa Maria della Concezione in the Convento dei Cappuccini, then head west on Via Sistina to explore the Spanish Steps (Piazza di Spagna) and the chic shopping streets nearby. Climb back up to the top of the steps and take Viale Trinità dei Monti and Viale A. Mickievicz to the Pincio Gardens (and Villa Borghese).

Piazza del Popolo

Drop down west to Piazza del Popolo and walk south along Via di Ripetta to the Altar of Peace and the Mausoleum of Augustus. From Piazza di Porta di Ripetta follow Via Borghese and Via Divino Amore to Piazza Firenze. Then continue south to Piazza della Rotonda by way of Piazza in Campo Marzio and Via Maddalena. Take Via Giustiniani west to San Luigi, and then follow Via della Scrofa north to Sant'Agostino before returning to Piazza Navona.

THE SIGHTS

INFORMATION

Time 4–6 hours
Distance 3½ miles (circular tour)
Start/end point Piazza Navona

🚌 e1, C5

🚌 46, 62, 64 to Corso Vittorio Emanuele II, or 71, 81, 87, 90,186 to Corso del Rinascimento

🕐 Start early with Palazzo-Galleria Doria Pamphili and Palazzo Barberini. Churches at the end of the walk are open late afternoon

🍴 Bar della Pace, Doney, Rosati and Canova (➤ 68). For ice-cream: Tre Scalini and the Gelateria della Palma (➤ 67)

EVENING STROLLS

INFORMATION

Ghetto
Start point Via Arenula
✠ e/fIII/IV, C/D6
🚌 44, 46, 56, 60, 61, 64, 65, 70, 75, 81, 87, 90 to Largo di Torre Argentina, or 44, 46, 56, 60, 61, 64, 65, 70, 75, 170, 181 to Via Arenula, or all services to Piazza Venezia
🕐 The empty, echoing streets of the Ghetto are best seen late at night

Trastevere
Start point Piazza S. Sonnino
✠ eIV, C6
🚌 44, 56, 60, 75, 170, 181 to Piazza S. Sonnino

THE GHETTO

The old Jewish Ghetto occupies the quaint quadrangle of streets and alleys formed by Via delle Botteghe Oscure, Via Arenula, Lungotevere dei Cenci, and Via del Teatro di Marcello. Many descendants of the Jews who were first forced to move here in 1556 still live and work in the district (there is a synagogue overlooking the Tiber at Lungotevere dei Cenci). Any combination of routes through the area offers intriguing little corners, though the one sight you should be sure not to miss is the charming Fontana delle Tartarughe in Piazza Mattei. This can be seen by walking down Via dei Falegnami from Via Arenula. Thereafter you might wander south on Via Sant'Ambrogio to Via Portico d'Ottavia, where you can see the remains of a 2nd-century BC gateway and colonnade. Striking north from here to Piazza Campitelli and Piazza Margana will also reveal some enchanting nooks and crannies. At night the area is almost deserted, but it is well lit and should be perfectly safe, though women on their own—as ever—should take special care.

TRASTEVERE

Almost every city has an area like Trastevere, a district whose tight-knit streets and intrinsic charm single it out as a focus for eating and nightlife. Trastevere (literally "across the Tiber") was once the heart of Rome's 19th-century working-class suburbs, and parts of its fringes are still slightly rough and ready (and so worth avoiding in the dead of night). A good way to get to know the area is to take the Via della Lungaretta to Piazza di Santa Maria in Trastevere from Piazza S. Sonnino and then explore some of the smaller streets to the north, such as Vicolo dell' Cinque and Via del Moro. At night be sure to take in the floodlit façade of Santa Maria in Trastevere (► 28). During the day, visit the Villa Farnesina (► 53), the Botanical Gardens (► 56), and the market in Piazza San Cosimato (► 73). Time your stroll for the early morning or late afternoon if you want to see the churches in Trastevere, especially Santa Cecilia (► 16).

ORGANIZED SIGHTSEEING

AMERICAN EXPRESS

American Express runs bus tours around Rome, Tivoli, and farther afield to Pompeii, Naples, and Capri. The "Tivoli" tour (Tue, Thu, Sun, Apr–Sep 2:30PM, Oct 2PM; ► 21) includes Hadrian's Villa and the Villa d'Este. The company also organizes three- to four-hour walks of the city with English-speaking guides: the "Vatican City" tour (Apr–Oct daily, Nov–Mar Mon–Sat; 9:30AM), which takes in the Vatican Museums (► 25), Sistine Chapel (► 26), and St. Peter's (► 24); "Rome of the Caesars" (all year, daily 2:30PM); and "Religious Rome" (May–Sep Wed, Fri 2:30PM), which visists the Catacombs, Pantheon (► 33), Piazza Navona (► 30), and St. Peter's.

✚ D5 ✉ Piazza di Spagna 38 ☎ 67 641 🕲 Mon–Fri 9–5:30, Sat 9–12:30 🚇 Spagna 🚌 119 to Piazza di Spagna

The Tiber and two of its bridges

APPIAN LINE

Many travel agents organize guided tours (try those in Piazza della Repubblica). Appian Line, close to Santa Maria Maggiore, is one of the best known. The prices of its tours of the city and destinations farther out are a little cheaper than those of American Express. Booking is unnecessary for local itineraries: simply turn up at the office 15 minutes before your tour departs.

✚ E5 ✉ Piazza Esquilino 6 ☎ 487 861 🕲 Mon–Fri 9–1, 2–6 🚇 Termini 🚌 4,9,14,16,27 to Piazza Esquilino

GREEN LINE TOURS

Green Line operates trips similar to those organized by American Express and Appian Line at prices about midway between the two.

✚ E5 ✉ Via Farini 5a ☎ 482 7480 🕲 Daily 7AM–9PM 🚇 Termini 🚌 4,9,14,16,27 to Piazza Esquilino

Other reputable firms that run bus tours and guided walks include **CIT** (✉ Piazza della Repubblica 64 ☎ 47 941), and **Carrani Tours** (✉ Via V. E. Orlando 95 ☎ 474 2501). CIT, Appian, and Carrani all organize trips to the Pope's Sunday blessing at Castel Gandolfo in the Appian Hills. Carrani will also organize papal audiences and (like Appian) a tour of Rome at night with accordianists.

Cheap tours

One of the cheapest and most relaxed tours of Rome can be enjoyed, albeit without commentary, by boarding tram No.19 or 30, both of which meander through some of the most interesting parts of the city. Or take ATAC's official public transportation tour: at 3:30PM daily between April and October (2:30 in winter) the 110 bus makes a three-hour circuit from Piazza dei Cinquecento (with five stops *en route*). A brief multilingual commentary and a free multilingual brochure are included with tickets, which are available from the ATAC kiosk in Piazza dei Cinquecento from 3PM.

EXCURSIONS

INFORMATION

Frascati

🚆 Regular trains from Termini: travel time 30min

🍴 Enoteca Carlo Taglienti, Via Sepolcro di Lucullo 8 (for wine)
Ristorante Cacciani, Via Armando Diaz 13 (☎ 942 0378 ⊙ Closed Mon)

Ostia Antica

✉ Viale dei Romagnoli 717 (15 miles southwest of Rome)

☎ 565 0022; 565 1405

⊙ Excavations: daily 9AM–1hr before dusk.
Museum: daily 9AM–2PM.
Closed public holidays

🚇 Metro Line B to Magliana, then train to Ostia Antica

♿ Large outdoor site

💰 Expensive

Ostia Antica

FRASCATI

Frascati, cradled in the Alban Hills, makes the easiest and most accessible day (or half-day) trip from Rome. Lauded for its white wine, it is also known for its broad views and cooling summer breezes. Small trains ply the branch line to the town, rattling though vineyards and olive groves beyond the city's sprawling suburbs. There is little to do—most pleasure is to be had wandering the streets—but you should see the gardens of the Villa Aldobrandini (above the main Piazza Marconi) and sample a refreshing glass of Frascati in one of the town's many wine cellars.

OSTIA ANTICA

Untrumpeted Ostia Antica is Italy's best-preserved Roman town after Pompeii and Herculaneum, its extensive ruins and lovely rural site as appealing as any in Rome itself. Built at the mouth (*ostium*) of the Tiber as ancient Rome's seaport, it became a vast and bustling colony before silt and the Empire's decline together hastened its demise. Among the many excavated buildings are countless *horrea*, or warehouses, and several multi-story apartment blocks known as *insulae*. Other highlights at the site include the Piazzale delle Corporazioni, the heart of the old business district; the 4,000-seat amphitheater; and the small Ostiense Museum.

TIVOLI

Tivoli is by far the most popular excursion from Rome (19 miles), thanks to the town's lovely wooded position, the superlative gardens of the Villa d'Este, and the ruins and grounds of Hadrian's vast Roman villa (4 miles southwest). The Este gardens were laid out in 1550 as part of a country retreat for Cardinal Ippolito d'Este, son of Lucrezia Borgia and the Duke of Ferrara. The highlights among the beautifully integrated terraces and many fountains are Bernini's elegant Fontana di Bicchierone and the vast Viale delle Cento Fontane ("Avenue of the Hundred Fountains"). Hadrian's Villa, the largest ever conceived in the Roman world, was built between AD 118 and 135 and covered an area as great as the center of imperial Rome.

Villa d'Este gardens, Tivoli

TARQUINIA

Of great appeal if you have an interest in the Etruscans, Tarquinia (ancient Tarquinii; 70min by train) was one of three major Etruscan cities—the others are present-day Vulci and Cerveteri—and was the cultural, artistic, and probably political capital of the civilization. Founded in the 10th century BC, its population once touched 100,000, declining from the 4th century BC with the rise of Rome. The town's Museo Nazionale houses a fascinating assortment of Etruscan art and artifacts, including the famous winged horses, though it is the number of nearby Etruscan tombs, the Necropoli (many beautifully painted), that draw most visitors (1–3 miles from town).

INFORMATION

Tivoli

✉ Villa d'Este: Piazza Trento.
Villa Adriana: Via Tiburtina

☎ Villa d'Este: 0774/22 070.
Villa Adriana: 0774/530 203

◷ Villa d'Este: Tue–Sun
9AM–1hr before sunset.
Villa Adriana: daily
9AM–90min before sunset

🍴 Refreshments at both Villa
d'Este and Villa Adriana;
Sibilla, Via della Sibilla 50,
Tivoli

🚌 COTRAL bus from Via Gaeta
or Metro Line B to Rebibbia,
and COTRAL bus to Tivoli

🚆 Train to Tivoli (40min) from
Termini, then 30min walk or
Villa d'Este (Villa Adriana)
local bus No. 4

💶 Villa d'Este: expensive.
Villa Adriana: expensive

Tarquinia

✉ Museo Nazionale, Palazzo
Vitelleschi

☎ Tourist office: 0766/856 384

◷ Museum: all year Tue–Sun
9–7.
Necropoli: Apr–Sep Tue–Sun
9–7. Oct–Mar Tue–Sun 9–5

🚌 Metro Line A to Lepanto,
then COTRAL bus from
corner of Viale Giulio Cesare
and Via Lepanto

🚆 Train to Tarquinia from
Termini, then shuttle bus

💶 Expensive (ticket includes
museum and tombs).
Contact Museo Nazionale
ticket office for tombs

WHAT'S ON

JANUARY *La Befana* (Jan 6): Epiphany celebrations; fair and market in Piazza Navona

FEBRUARY *Carnevale* (week before Lent): costume festivities on the streets; parties on Shrove Tuesday

MARCH *Festa di San Giuseppe* (Mar 19): street stalls in the Trionfale area north of the Vatican

Festa della Primavera (late Mar–Apr): thousands of azaleas arranged on the Spanish Steps

APRIL *Good Friday* (Mar/Apr): Procession of the Cross at 9PM to the Colosseum, led by the Pope

Easter Sunday (Mar/Apr): Pope addresses the crowds at midday in Piazza di San Pietro

Rome's Birthday (Apr 21): flags and pageantry on Piazza del Campidoglio

MAY *International Horse Show* (early May): Concorso Ippico in Villa Borghese

JUNE *Feste della Repubblica* (Jun 2): military parade along Via dei Fori Imperiali

Festa di San Giovanni (Jun 23–24): fair, food, and fireworks around San Giovanni in Laterano

JULY *Tevere Expo* (last week Jun/Jul): food and handicrafts fair on the banks of the Tiber between the Cavour and Sant'Angelo bridges

Festa dei Noiantri (week beginning third Sunday in July): street fairs and processions, Trastevere

Jazz Festival di Roma (end of Jun/Jul)

AUGUST *Ferragosto* (Aug 15): Feast of the Assumption; everything closes

SEPTEMBER *Art Fair* (Sep): Via Margutta

Sagra dell'Uva (early Sep): wine and harvest festival in the Basilica di Massenzio

OCTOBER *Antiques Fair* (mid-Oct): Via dei Coronari

NOVEMBER *Festa di Santa Cecilia* (Nov 22): in the catacombs and church of Santa Cecilia in Trastevere

Ognissanti (Nov 1–2): All Saints' Day

DECEMBER *Festa della Madonna Immacolata* (Dec 8): Pope and other dignitaries leave flowers at the statue of the Madonna in Piazza di Spagna

Nativity Scenes (mid-Dec–mid-Jan): crèches (*presepi*) in many Rome churches

Christmas Eve: Midnight Mass in many churches, especially Santa Maria Maggiore and Santa Maria in Aracoeli

Christmas Day: papal address and blessing in Piazza San Pietro

New Year's Eve: firework displays

ROME's
top 25 sights

These sights are shown on the maps on the inside front cover and inside back cover, numbered **1–25** *from west to east across the city*

BASILICA DI SAN PIETRO

HIGHLIGHTS

- Façade
- Dome
- *Pietà*, Michelangelo
- *Baldacchino*, Bernini
- *St. Peter*, Arnolfo di Cambio
- Tomb of Paul III, Guglielmo della Porta
- Tomb of Urban VIII, Bernini
- Monument to Alexander VII, Bernini
- Monument to the Last Stuarts, Canova
- View from the dome

INFORMATION

- ✚ bIII, B5
- ✉ Piazza San Pietro, Vatican City
- ☎ 698 4466; 698 4866
- ⌚ Basilica: mid-Mar–Oct daily 7–7. Nov–mid-Mar daily 7–6.
  Dome: mid-Mar–Oct daily 8–6. Nov–mid-Mar daily 8–4.
  Grottoes: Apr–Sep daily 7–6. Oct–Mar daily 7–5.
  Treasury: Apr–Sep daily 9–6. Oct–Mar daily 9–5
- 🍴 Shop
- Ⓜ Ottaviano
- 🚌 64 to Piazza San Pietro, or 19, 23, 49, 81, 492, 991 to Piazza del Risorgimento
- ♿ Wheelchair access
- 🎫 Basilica: free. Dome & Treasury: moderate. Grottoes: expensive
- ↔ Vatican Museums (➤ 25), Sistine Chapel (➤ 26), Castel Sant'Angelo (➤ 27)

Although the works of art in St. Peter's are rather disappointing—a Michelangelo sculpture aside—the interior still manages to impress as the spiritual capital of Roman Catholicism with an overwhelming sense of scale and decorative splendor.

History The first St. Peter's was built by Constantine around AD 326, reputedly on the site where St. Peter was buried following his crucifixion in AD 64. Much later, between 1506 and 1626, it was virtually rebuilt to plans by Bramante, and then to designs by Antonio da Sangallo, Giacomo della Porta,

Baldacchino *and dome*

Michelangelo, and Carlo Maderno. Michelangelo was also responsible for much of the dome, while Bernini finished the façade and the interior.

What to see Michelangelo's unforgettable *Pietà* (1499), behind glass following an attack in 1972, is in the first chapel of the right nave. At the end of the same nave stands a statue of St. Peter: his right foot has been caressed by millions since 1857 when Pius IX granted a 50-day indulgence to anyone kissing it after confession. Bernini's high altar canopy, or *baldacchino* (1624–1633), was built during the papacy of Urban VIII, a scion of the Barberini family; it is decorated with bees, the Barberinis' dynastic symbol. To its rear are Guglielmo della Porta's Tomb of Paul III (left) and Bernini's influential Tomb of Urban VIII (right). Rome seen from the dome (entrance at the end of the right nave) is *the* highlight of a visit.

MUSEI VATICANI

The Vatican Museums make up the world's largest museum complex. The 1,400 rooms abound in riches: Greek, Roman, and Etruscan sculptures, Renaissance paintings, books, maps and tapestries, and frescoes in the Raphael Rooms and the Sistine Chapel.

Treasures of 12 museums Instead of the two days (and 4 miles of walking) needed to do justice to the Vatican Museums, you can follow one of the color-coded walks, designed to ease your way through the crowds and match the time you have available. Or you might decide on your own priorities, choosing between the collections according to your interest: Egyptian and Assyrian art (the Museo Gregoriano Egizio); Etruscan artifacts (Museo Gregoriano-Etrusco); the more esoteric anthropological collections (Museo Missionario Etnologico); or modern religious art (Collezione d'Arte Religiosa Moderna).

Celebrated works of art Whatever your priorities, several sights should not be missed. Most obvious are the Sistine Chapel (► 26), with Michelangelo's recently restored *Last Judgment*, and the four rooms of the Stanze di Raffaello, each of which is decorated with frescoes by Raphael. Further fresco cycles by Pinturicchio and Fra Angelico adorn the Borgia Apartment and Chapel of Nicholas V, and are complemented by an almost unmatched collection of paintings in the Vatican Art Gallery (or Pinacoteca). The best of the Greek and Roman sculpture is the breathtaking Laocoön group in the Cortile Ottagono of the Museo Pio-Clementino. The list of artists whose work is shown in the Gallery of Modern Religious Art is a rollcall of the most famous in the last 100 years, from Gauguin and Picasso to Dali and Henry Moore.

HIGHLIGHTS

- Sistine Chapel (► 26)
- Laocoön
- Apollo del Belvedere (Museo Pio-Clementino)
- Marte di Todi (Museo Gregoriano-Etrusco)
- Maps Gallery (Galleria delle Carte Geografiche)
- Frescoes by Pinturicchio
- Frescoes by Fra Angelico
- Stanze di Raffaello
- Pinacoteca
- Room of the Animals (Museo Pio-Clementino)

INFORMATION

- ✛ bl, B5
- ✉ Vatican Museums, Viale Vaticano, Città del Vaticano
- ☎ Recorded message: 6988 3333
- 🕐 Apr–mid-Jun and Sep–Oct Mon–Fri 8:45–4; Sat, last Sun of month 8:45–1. Rest of year Mon–Sat, last Sun of month 8:45–1. Closed public and religious holidays
- 🍴 Café, restaurant and shop
- Ⓜ Ottaviano
- 🚌 19, 23, 81, 492 to Piazza del Risorgimento, or 64 to Piazza San Pietro
- ♿ Wheelchair-accessible routes
- 💰 Very expensive (includes entry to all other Vatican museums); free last Sun of month
- ⟷ St. Peter's (► 24), Sistine Chapel (► 26), Castel Sant'Angelo (► 27)

25

3

CAPPELLA SISTINA

INFORMATION

- bI, B5
- Vatican Museums, Viale Vaticano, Città del Vaticano
- Recorded message: 6988 3333
- Opening times as Vatican Museums (➤ 25)
- Café, restaurant, and shop
- Ottaviano
- 19, 23, 81, 492 to Piazza del Risorgimento, or 64 to Piazza San Pietro (there is a connecting bus from Piazza San Pietro to museums)
- Wheelchair-accessible routes
- Very expensive (includes entry to all other Vatican Museums)
- St. Peter's (➤ 24), Vatican Museums (➤ 25), Castel Sant'Angelo (➤ 27)

In Michelangelo's frescoes the Sistine Chapel has one of the world's supreme masterpieces. Recently and controversially restored, the paintings of this modest-sized, hall-like chapel at the heart of the Vatican Museums draw a ceaseless stream of pilgrims.

The chapel The Cappella Sistina (Sistine Chapel) was built by Pope Sixtus IV between 1475 and 1480. The Vatican Palace's principal chapel, it is used by the conclave of cardinals when they assemble to elect a new pope. Decoration of its lower side walls took place between 1481 and 1483, the work, among others, of Perugino, Botticelli, Ghirlandaio, Pinturicchio, and Luca Signorelli. From the chapel entrance their 12 paintings compose *Scenes from the Life of Christ* (on the left wall as you face away from the high altar) and *Scenes from the Life of Moses* (on the right wall).

Michelangelo's frescoes Michelangelo was commissioned by Pope Julius II to paint the ceiling in 1508. The frescoes, comprising over 300 individual figures, were completed in four years, most of which Michelangelo spent in appalling conditions, lying on his back and in extremes of heat and cold. Their narrative describes in nine scenes the story of Genesis and the history of humanity before the coming of Christ. In the center is the *Creation of Adam*. The fresco behind the high altar, the *Last Judgment*, was begun for Pope Paul III in 1534 and completed in 1541. An extraordinary work of art, it is densely crowded with figures, conveying a powerful sense of movement. It also shows Michelangelo in a more somber mood, with the righteous rising to paradise accompanied by angels on Christ's right, and the damned drawn irrevocably toward hell on his left.

CASTEL SANT'ANGELO

Castel Sant'Angelo, rising above the river, has served as an army barracks, papal citadel, imperial tomb, and medieval prison. Today its 58-room museum traces the castle's near 2,000-year history and makes for a less demanding visit after the Vatican's riches.

Many incarnations The Castel Sant'Angelo was built by the Emperor Hadrian in AD 130 as a mausoleum for himself, his family, and his dynastic successors. It was crowned by a gilded chariot driven by a statue of Hadrian disguised as the sun god Apollo. Emperors were buried in its vaults until about AD 271, when under threat of invasion from Germanic raiders it became a citadel and was incorporated into the city's walls. Its present name arose in 590, after a vision by Gregory the Great, who while leading a procession through Rome to pray for the end of plague saw an angel sheathing a sword, an act thought to symbolize the end of the pestilence.

Castle and museum In 847 Leo IV converted the building into a papal fortress, and in 1277 Nicholas III linked it to the Vatican by a (still visible) passageway, the *passetto*. A prison in the Renaissance, and then an army barracks, the castle became a museum in 1933. Exhibits are spread over four floors, scattered around a confusing but fascinating array of rooms and corridors. Best of these is the beautiful Sala Paolina, decorated with stucco, fresco, and *trompe-l'oeil*, though the most memorable sight is the all-round view from the castle's terrace, the setting for the last act of Puccini's *Tosca*.

HIGHLIGHTS

- Spiral funerary ramp
- Staircase of Alexander VI
- Armory
- Hall of Justice
- Fresco: *Justice*, attributed to Domenico Zaga
- Chapel of Leo X: façade by Michelangelo
- Sale di Clemente VII with wall paintings
- Cortile del Pozzo: wellhead
- Prisons (Prigione Storiche)
- Sala Paolina
- View from Loggia of Paul III

INFORMATION

- ✚ dI, C5
- ✉ Lungotevere Castello 50
- ☎ 687 5036
- ◔ Daily 9–2
- 🍴 Café
- Ⓜ Lepanto
- 🚌 23, 64, 87, 280 to Lungotevere Castello, or 34, 49, 70, 81, 186, 926, 990 to Piazza Cavour
- ♿ Poor
- 💲 Expensive
- ↔ St. Peter's (► 24), Vatican Museums (► 25), Sistine Chapel (► 26), Piazza Navona (► 30), Altar of Peace (► 31)

A Bernini angel on the Ponte Sant'Angelo

27

5

SANTA MARIA IN TRASTEVERE

HIGHLIGHTS

- Romanesque campanile
- Façade mosaics
- Portico
- Ceiling, designed by Domenichino
- Cosmati marble pavement
- Wall tabernacle by Mino del Reame (central nave)
- Byzantine mosaics, upper apse
- Mosaics: *Life of the Virgin* (lower apse)
- *Madonna della Clemenza* in Cappella Altemps
- Cappella Avila: baroque chapel

INFORMATION

- ✚ dIV, C6
- ✉ Piazza Santa Maria in Trastevere
- ☎ 581 4802
- ◷ Daily 7:30–12:30, 4–7
- 🚌 44, 56, 60, 75, 97, 170, 280, 710, 718, 719, 774, 780 to Viale di Trastevere, or 23, 65 to Lungotevere Raffaello Sanzio
- ♿ Wheelchair accessible
- 🎫 Free

One of the most memorable sights of nighttime Rome is the 12th-century gold mosaics that adorn the façade of Santa Maria in Trastevere, their floodlit glow casting a gentle light over the milling nocturnal crowds in the piazza below.

Early church Santa Maria in Trastevere is among the oldest officially sanctioned places of worship in Rome. It was reputedly founded in AD 222, allegedly on the spot where a fountain of olive oil had sprung from the earth on the day of Christ's birth (symbolizing the coming of the grace of God). Much of the present church was built in the 12th century during the reign of Innocent II, a member of the Papareschi, a prominent Trastevere family. Inside, the main colonnade of the nave is composed of reused and ancient Roman columns. The portico, containing fragments of Roman reliefs and inscriptions and medieval remains, was added in 1702 by Carlo Fontana, who was also responsible for the fountain that graces the adjoining piazza.

Mosaics The façade mosaics probably date from the mid-12th century, and depict the Virgin and Child with ten lamp-carrying companions. Long believed to portray the parable of the Wise and Foolish Virgins, their subject-matter is now contested, as several "virgins" appear to be men and only two are carrying unlighted lamps (not the five of the parable). The mosaics of the upper apse inside the church, devoted to the glorification of the Virgin, date from the same period and represent Byzantine-influenced works by Greek or Greek-trained craftsmen. Those below, depicting scenes from the life of the Virgin (1291), are by the mosaicist and fresco-painter Pietro Cavallini.

CAMPO DE' FIORI

There is nowhere more relaxing in Rome to sit down with a cappuccino and watch the world go by than Campo de' Fiori, a lovely old piazza whose fruit, vegetable, and fish market makes it one of the liveliest and most colorful corners of the old city.

Ancient square Campo de' Fiori—the "Field of Flowers"—was turned in the Middle Ages from a meadow facing the old Roman Theater of Pompey (55 BC; now Palazzo Pio Righetti) into one of the city's most exclusive residential and business districts. By the 15th century it was surrounded by busy inns and bordellos, some run by the infamous courtesan Vanozza Cattenei, mistress of the Borgia pope, Alexander VI. By 1600 it had also become a place of execution: Giordano Bruno was burned for heresy on the spot marked by his cowled statue.

Present day Crowds of students, foreigners, and tramps mingle with stallholders shouting their wares. Cafés, bars, and the wonderfully dingy wine bar at No. 15 allow for fascinated observation. One block south lies Piazza Farnese, dominated by the Palazzo Farnese, a Renaissance master-piece partly designed by Michelangelo and begun in 1516; it is now home to the French Embassy. One block west is the Pal-azzo della Cancelleria (1485), once the papal chancellery. The near-by streets (Via Giulia,

Knife-grinder

Via dei Baullari and the busy Via dei Cappellari and Via del Pellegrino) reward exploration.

HIGHLIGHTS

- Street market
- Wine bar Vineria Reggio
- Statue of Giordano Bruno
- Palazzo Farnese, Piazza Farnese
- Palazzo della Cancelleria, Piazza della Cancelleria
- Palazzo Pio Righetti
- Via Giulia
- Santa Maria dell'Orazione e Morte: church door decorated in stone skulls
- Via dei Baullari

INFORMATION

PIAZZA NAVONA

HIGHLIGHTS

- Fontana dei Quattro Fiumi
- Fontana del Moro (south)
- Fontana del Nettuno (north)
- Sant'Agnese in Agone
- Palazzo Pamphili
- San Luigi dei Francesi (Via Santa Giovanna d'Arco)
- Santa Maria della Pace (Vicolo dell'Arco della Pace 5)
- Santa Maria dell'Anima (Via della Pace)

INFORMATION

- ✚ el, C5
- ✉ Piazza Navona
- ☎ Sant'Agnese: 679 4435. San Luigi: 6880 3629. Santa Maria della Pace: 686 1156. Santa Maria dell'Anima: 683 3729
- 🕐 Sant'Agnese: Mon–Sat 5–6:30PM; Sun 10–1. San Luigi: Fri–Wed, Sun 8–12:30, 3:30–7. Santa Maria della Pace (cloister): Tue–Sat 10–12, 4–6; Sun 9–11. Santa Maria dell'Anima: Mon–Sat 7:30–7; Sun 8–1, 3–7. Palazzo Pamphili: closed
- Ⓜ Spagna
- 🚌 70, 81, 87, 90, 186, 492 to Corso del Rinascimento, or 46, 62, 64 to Corso Vittorio Emanuele II
- ♿ Good (Santa Maria della Pace: two steps)
- 🎟 Free to piazza and churches
- ↔ Castel Sant'Angelo (▶ 27), Campo de' Fiori (▶ 29), Pantheon (▶ 33)

Piazza di Spagna may be more elegant and Campo de' Fiori more vivid, but the Piazza Navona, with its atmospheric echoes of a 2,000-year history, is a place to amble, watch the world, and stop for a drink at a sun-drenched wayside table.

History Piazza Navona owes its unmistakable elliptical shape to a stadium and racetrack built here in AD 86 by the Emperor Domitian. From the Circus Agonalis—the stadium for athletic games—comes the piazza's present name, rendered in medieval Latin as *in agone*, and then in Rome's strangulated dialect as *'n 'agona*. The stadium was used until well into the Middle Ages for festivals and competitions. The square owes its present appearance to its rebuilding by Pope Innocent X in 1644.

Around the piazza Bernini's Fontana dei Quattro Fiumi (1651), the "Fountain of the Four Rivers" (▶ 54), dominates the center. On the west side is the baroque Sant' Agnese (1652–1657), whose façade was designed by Borromini. Beside it stands the Palazzo Pamphili, commissioned by Innocent X and now the Brazilian Embassy. Further afield, San Luigi dei Francesi is famous for three superlative Caravaggio paintings, and Santa Maria della Pace for a cloister by Bramante and Raphael's frescoes of the four Sybils.

Fontana dei Quattro Fiumi

ARA PACIS AUGUSTAE

Few ancient bas-reliefs are as beautiful or as striking as those on the marble screens protecting the Altar of Peace, painstakingly but triumphantly reconstructed and restored in its present position from disparate fragments over many years.

Monument to peace Now sheltered from Rome's marble-rotting pollution by a glass pavilion, the Ara Pacis Augustae (Altar of Peace) was built between 13 and 9 BC on the orders of the Senate as a memorial to the military victories in Gaul and Spain of the Emperor Augustus, and in celebration of the peace ("*pacis*") he brought to the Empire after years of conquest and civil war. Its panels were buried or dispersed over the centuries; the first fragments were recovered in the 16th century, the last over 300 years later (some were found as far away as Paris).

Reliefs While the altar at the heart of the monument is comparatively plain, the walls around it are covered with finely carved bas-reliefs. The best occupy the exterior north and south walls: they depict processional scenes of the altar's consecration and show the family of Augustus (including his wife, Livia) with 12 *lictors* (with their rods, or *fasces*, symbols of authority) and four *flamine* (who lit the sacred fires tended in the Forum by the Vestal Virgins). Other scenes include the Lupercalium—the grotto where the she-wolf suckled Romulus and Remus—and Aeneas Sacrificing the Sow (both west panel), and the Earth Goddess Tellus (east panel). The delicate ornamentation below includes floral motifs. Nearby is the Piazza del Popolo, with monuments ranging from a 3,000-year-old Egyptian obelisk to twin baroque churches and a 16th-century gateway.

HIGHLIGHTS

- *Emperor Augustus and Family* (south wall)
- *Emperor Augustus and Family* (north wall)
- *Aeneas Sacrificing the Sow*
- *Lupercalium*
- *Earth Goddess Tellus*
- Mausoleum of Augustus (Piazza Augusto Imperatore), to the east
- Piazza del Popolo
- Santa Maria di Montesanto and Santa Maria dei Miracoli (Piazza del Popolo)
- Egyptian obelisk (Piazza del Popolo)
- Porta del Popolo (Piazza del Popolo)

INFORMATION

- ✚ el, D5
- ✉ Via di Ripetta
- ☎ 6710 3569, 6710 2475
- 🕐 Tue–Sat 9–5; Sun 9–1
- 🚌 81, 90, 926 to Lungotevere in Augusta and Via di Ripetta, or 119 to Via di Ripetta
- ♿ Poor
- 🎨 Moderate
- ↔ Santa Maria del Popolo (➤ 32), Pantheon (➤ 33), Piazza di Spagna & Spanish Steps (➤ 40)

9

SANTA MARIA DEL POPOLO

HIGHLIGHTS

- Cappella Chigi
- *Conversion of St. Paul* and *Crucifixion of St. Peter*, Caravaggio
- *Coronation of the Virgin*, Pinturicchio
- Tombs of Ascanio Sforza and Girolamo Basso della Rovere
- *Nativity*, Pinturicchio
- Fresco: *Life of San Girolamo*, Tiberio d'Assisi
- *Delphic Sybil*, Pinturicchio
- Altar, Andrea Bregno
- Stained glass
- *Assumption of the Virgin*, Annibale Carracci

INFORMATION

- ✚ D4
- ✉ Piazza del Popolo 12
- ☎ 361 0836
- ◉ Daily 7–12:15, 4–7
- 🍴 Rosati and Canova (➤ 68)
- Ⓜ Flaminio
- 🚌 90, 90b, 95, 119, 490, 495, 926 to Piazza del Popolo
- ♿ Few
- 🎫 Free
- ↔ Altar of Peace (➤ 31), Villa Giulia (➤ 35), Piazza di Spagna & Spanish Steps (➤ 40), Pincio Gardens (➤ 56), Villa Borghese (➤ 57)

Santa Maria del Popolo's appeal stems from its intimate size and location, and from a wonderfully varied and rich collection of works of art that ranges from masterpieces by Caravaggio to some of Rome's earliest stained-glass windows.

Renaissance achievement Founded in 1099 on the site of Nero's grave, Santa Maria del Popolo was rebuilt by Pope Sixtus IV in 1472 and extended later by Bramante and Bernini. The right nave's first chapel, the Cappella della Rovere, is decorated with frescoes—*Life of San Girolamo* (1485–1490)—by Tiberio d'Assisi, a pupil of Pinturicchio whose *Nativity* (c. 1490) graces the chapel's main altar. A doorway in the right transept leads to the sacristy, noted for its elaborate marble altar (1473) by Andrea Bregno.

Apse The apse contains two fine stained-glass windows (1509) by the French artist Guillaume de Marcillat. On either side are the greatest of the church's monuments: the tombs of the cardinals Ascanio Sforza (1505, left) and Girolamo Basso della Rovere (1507, right). Both are the work of Andrea Sansovino. High on the walls are superb and elegant frescoes (1508–1510) of the Virgin, Evangelists, the Fathers of the Church, and Sybils by Pinturicchio.

Left nave The frescoed first chapel, the Cappella Cerasi, also contains three major paintings: the altarpiece, *Assumption of the Virgin*, by Annibale Carracci (above); and Caravaggio's dramatic *Conversion of St. Paul* and the *Crucifixion of St. Peter* (all 1601). The famous Cappella Chigi (1513) was commissioned by the wealthy Sienese banker Agostino Chigi, while its architecture, sculpture, and paintings were designed as a unified whole by Raphael.

PANTHEON

No other monument suggests the grandeur of ancient Rome as magnificently as the Pantheon, a temple whose early conversion to a place of Christian worship has rendered it the most perfect of the city's ancient monuments.

Temple and church Built in its present form by the Emperor Hadrian in AD 119–128, the Pantheon replaced a temple of 27 BC by Marcus Agrippa, son-in-law of Augustus (though Hadrian modestly retained Agrippa's original inscription proclaiming it as his work, which is still picked out in bronze on the façade). Becoming a church in AD 609, it was named Santa Maria ad Martyres (the bones of martyrs were brought here from the Catacombs). It is now a shrine to Italy's "immortals," including the artist Raphael and two Italian kings, Vittore Emanuele II and Umberto I.

An engineering marvel Massive and simple externally, the Pantheon (AD 118–125) is even more breathtaking inside, where the scale, harmony, and symmetry of the dome in particular are more apparent. The world's largest dome until 1960, it has a diameter of 142 feet (equal to its height from the floor). Weight and stresses were reduced by rows of coffering in the ceiling, and the use of progressively lighter materials from the base to the crown. The central oculus, 29 feet in diameter, lets in light to flood the marble panels of the walls, and the floor paving far below.

HIGHLIGHTS

- Façade inscription
- Interior of the dome
- The pedimented portico
- Original Roman doors
- The interior pavement
- The open oculus
- Ceiling coffering
- Tomb of Raphael
- Royal tombs

INFORMATION

- ✚ ell, D5
- ✉ Piazza della Rotonda
- ☎ 6830 0230
- 🕐 Mon–Sat: Apr–Jun 9–5:30; Jul–Sep 9–6; Oct–Mar 9–4:30. Sun: all year 9–1
- 🚇 Spagna
- 🚌 119 to Piazza della Rotonda, or 64, 70, 75 to Largo di Torre Argentina
- ♿ Good
- 💷 Free
- ↔ Piazza Navona (➤ 30), Santa Maria sopra Minerva (➤ 34)

The Pantheon

11

SANTA MARIA SOPRA MINERVA

HIGHLIGHTS

- Egyptian obelisk atop an elephant, Bernini (outside)
- Porch to the Cappella Carafa
- Frescoes: *St. Thomas Aquinas* and *The Assumption*, Filippino Lippi, in the Cappella Carafa
- *Risen Christ*, Michelangelo
- Relics of St. Catherine of Siena, and preserved room in sacristy where she died
- Tombs of Clement VII and Leo X, Antonio da Sangallo
- Tomb-slab of Fra Angelico
- Tomb of Giovanni Alberini, Mino da Fiesole or Agostino di Duccio
- Monument to Maria Raggi
- Tomb of Francesco Tornabuoni, Mino da Fiesole

INFORMATION

- ✚ fII, D5
- ✉ Piazza della Minerva 42
- ☎ 679 3926
- ⊙ Daily 7–12, 4–7
- Ⓢ Spagna
- 🚌 44, 46, 56, 60, 61, 64, 65, 70, 75, 81, 87, 90, 170 to Lago di Torre Argentina, or 119 to Piazza della Rotonda
- ♿ Stepped access to church
- 💵 Free
- ↔ Pantheon (➤ 33), Palazzo-Galleria Doria Pamphili (➤ 36), Fontana di Trevi (➤ 39)

Almost unique in having retained (perhaps too well) many Gothic features despite Rome's love for the baroque, behind its plain façade Santa Maria sopra Minerva is a cornucopia of tombs, paintings, and Renaissance sculpture.

Florentine influences
Founded in the 8th century over (*sopra*) the ruins of a temple to Minerva, this church was built in 1280 to a design by a pair of Florentine Dominican monks. The connections with Florence continued, not least in the rash of Florentine artists whose works are richly represented within: works such as Michelangelo's calm statue *The Risen Christ* beside the high altar; and the Cappella

Elephant supporting an obelisk

Carafa, whose finely carved porch is attributed to Giuliano da Maiano. Filippino Lippi painted the celebrated frescoes (1488–1493) *St. Thomas Aquinas* and the *Assumption*. Among other sculptures are the tombs of Francesco Tornabuoni (1480) and that of Giovanni Alberini, the latter decorated with reliefs of Hercules (15th century). Both are attributed to Mino da Fiesole. Other works include: Fra Angelico's tomb-slab (1455); the tombs of the Medici popes Clement VII and Leo X (1536) by Antonio da Sangallo the Younger; and Bernini's monument to Maria Raggi (1643). St. Catherine of Siena, one of Italy's patron saints, is also buried here.

VILLA GIULIA

The Museo Nazionale di Villa Giulia houses the world's greatest collection of Etruscan art and artifacts. Although the exhibits are not always perfectly presented, it remains a revelation for anyone keen to know about the mysterious civilization that preceded ancient Rome.

The villa Built for the hedonistic Pope Julius III in 1550–1555 as a country house and garden, the Villa Giulia was designed by some of the leading architects of the day, including Michelangelo and the biographer Vasari. Recent restoration has renovated its frescoed loggia and the Nympheum, a sunken court in the villa gardens by the Mannerist architect Vignola.

The collection The exhibits range over two floors and 34 rooms, generally divided between finds from Etruscan sites in northern Etruria (Vulci, Veio, Cerveteri, and Tarquinia) and from excavations in the south (Nemi and Praeneste), including artifacts made by the Greeks. Most notable are the Castellani exhibits, which include vases, cups, and ewers, and jewelry from the Minoan period; the latter is one of the villa's special treasures. Otherwise be selective, picking through the numerous vases, such as the *Tomba del Guerriero* and the *Cratere a Volute*, to see the most striking works of art. These include the *Sarcofago degli Sposi*, a 6th-century BC sarcophagus with figures of a married couple reclining together on a banqueting couch; the engraved marriage coffer known as the *Cista Ficoroni* (4th century BC); the giant terracotta figures, *Hercules and Apollo*; the temple sculptures from Falerii Veteres; and the valuable 7th-century BC relics in gold, silver, bronze, and ivory from the Barberini and Bernardini tombs in Praeneste.

HIGHLIGHTS

- *Lamine d'Oro*, Sala di Pyrgi: a gold tablet (left of entrance)
- Vase: *Tomba del Guerriero* (room 4)
- Terracottas: *Hercules and Apollo* (room 7)
- *Sarcofago degli Sposi* (room 9)
- Castellani Collection (rooms 19–22)
- Vase: *Cratere a Volute* (room 26)
- Finds from Falerii Veteres (room 29)
- Tomb relics: Barberini and Bernardini (room 33)
- Marriage coffer: *Cista Ficoroni* (room 33)
- Gardens with Nympheum and reconstructed "Temple of Alatri"

INFORMATION

- ✚ D3
- ✉ Piazzale di Villa Giulia 9
- ☎ 322 6571; 320 1951
- 🕐 Tue–Sat 9–7; Sun 9–1
- 🍴 Café and shop
- Ⓜ Flaminio
- 🚌 52, 926 to Viale Bruno Buozzi, or 95, 490, 495 to Viale Washington, or 19, 19b, 30b to Piazza Thorwaldsen
- ♿ Good: wheelchair access with assistance
- 💰 Expensive
- ↔ Santa Maria del Popolo (➤ 32), Galleria Borghese (➤ 45)

35

PALAZZO-GALLERIA DORIA PAMPHILI

HIGHLIGHTS

- *Religion Succored by Spain* (labeled 10) and *Salome* (29), Titian
- *Portrait of Two Venetians* (23), Raphael
- *Maddalena* (40) and *Rest on the Flight into Egypt* (42), Caravaggio
- *Birth* and *Marriage of the Virgin* (174/176), Giovanni di Paolo
- *Nativity* (200), Parmigianino
- *Innocent X*, Velázquez
- *Innocent X*, Bernini
- *Battle of the Bay of Naples* (317), Pieter Brueghel the Elder
- Salone Verde
- Saletta Gialla

INFORMATION

- fIII, D6
- Piazza del Collegio Romano 1a
- 679 7323
- Tue, Fri, Sat, Sun 10–1. Closed public holidays
- Barberini
- 56, 60, 62, 85, 90, 95, 160, 492 to Piazza Venezia
- Good
- Gallery: expensive. Private apartments: moderate
- Pantheon (➤ 33), Santa Maria sopra Minerva (➤ 34), Capitoline Museums (➤ 37), Santa Maria in Aracoeli (➤ 38), Fontana di Trevi (➤ 39)

The Palazzo Doria Pamphili is among the largest of Rome's palaces, and is still privately owned. It contains one of the city's finest patrician art collections and offers the chance to admire some of the sumptuously decorated rooms of its private apartments.

Palace Little in the bland exterior of the Palazzo Doria Pamphili prepares you for the splendor of the beautifully decorated rooms that lie within. Built over the foundations of a storehouse dating back to classical times, the core of the building was erected in 1435, though it has withstood countless alterations and owners. The Doria Pamphili a dynasty was formed by yoking together the Doria, a famous Genoa seafaring clan, and the Pamphili, an ancient Roman-based patrician family. Most people come here for the paintings, but for an additional fee you can enjoy a guided tour around some of the private apartments in the 1,000-room palace. The most impressive is the Saletta Gialla ("Yellow Room"), decorated with ten Gobelin tapestries made for Louis XV. In the Salone Verde ("Green Room") are three major paintings: *Annunciation* by Filippo Lippi, *Portrait of a Gentleman* by Lorenzo Lotto, and *Andrea Doria* (a famous admiral) by Sebastiano del Piombo.

Paintings The Pamphili's splendid art collection is displayed in ranks of paintings in four broad galleries; these are numbered, not labeled, so a catalogue from the ticket office is a worthwhile investment. The finest painting by far is the famous Velázquez portrait, *Innocent X*, a likeness that captured the pope's weak and suspicious nature so adroitly that Innocent is said to have lamented that it was "too true, too true." The nearby bust by Bernini of the same pope is more flattering.

MUSEI CAPITOLINI

With their outstanding but limited number of Greek and Roman sculptures, the Capitoline Museums (Palazzo Nuovo and Palazzo dei Conservatori) make a far more accessible introduction to the subject than the rambling Vatican Museums.

Palazzo Nuovo The Capitoline Museums occupy two separate palaces on opposite sides of the piazza. Designed by Michelangelo, the Palazzo Nuovo (on the north side) contains most of the finest pieces, none greater than the magnificent 2nd-century AD bronze equestrian statue of Marcus Aurelius (just off the main courtyard). Moved from outside San Giovanni in Laterano to the piazza here in the Middle Ages, it has recently been restored and placed under cover. Among the sculptures inside are celebrated Roman copies in marble of Greek originals, including the *Dying Gaul*, *Wounded Amazon*, *Capitoline Venus*, and the discus thrower *Discobolus* (► 52). In the Sala degli Imperatori is a portrait gallery of busts of Roman emperors.

Palazzo dei Conservatori Former seat of Rome's medieval magistrates, this palazzo (a detail from the courtyard is illustrated above) contains an art gallery (Pinacoteca Capitolina) on the third floor and a further rich hoard of classical sculpture (second floor). Bronzes include the 1st-century BC *Spinario*, a boy removing a thorn from his foot, and the 5th-century BC Etruscan *Capitoline Wolf*, the famous she-wolf suckling Romulus and Remus (added later). Paintings in the Pinacoteca include *St. John the Baptist* by Caravaggio and works by Velázquez, Titian, Veronese, and Van Dyck.

HIGHLIGHTS

Palazzo Nuovo
- Statue of Marcus Aurelius
- Sculpture: *Capitoline Venus*
- Sculpture: *Dying Gaul*
- Sculpture: *Wounded Amazon*
- Sculpture: *Discobolus*
- Sala degli Imperatori

Palazzo dei Conservatori
- *St. John the Baptist*, Caravaggio
- Bronze: *Capitoline Wolf*
- Bronze: *Spinario*
- Marble figure: *Esquiline Venus*

INFORMATION

- ✚ fIV/gIV, D6
- ✉ Musei Capitolini (Capitoline Museums), Piazza del Campidoglio 1
- ☎ 6710 2071
- ⏲ Tue–Sat 9–7; Sun 9–1
- 🚌 44, 46, 64, 70, 81, 110 and all services to Piazza Venezia
- ♿ Poor: stepped ramp to Piazza del Campidoglio
- 💰 Expensive (entry to both museums)
- 🔗 Santa Maria in Aracoeli (► 38), Roman Forum (► 41)

Statue of Constantine, Palazzo dei Conservatori

37

SANTA MARIA IN ARACOELI

INFORMATION

fIII, D6

Piazza d'Aracoeli

679 8155

Jun–Sep daily 7–12, 4–6:30. Oct–May daily 7–12

44, 46, 56, 60, 64, 65, 70, 75, 90, 90b,170, 492 and all other services to Piazza Venezia

Poor: steep steps to main entrance or steps to Piazza del Campidoglio

Free

Palazzo-Galleria Doria Pamphili (➤ 36), Capitoline Museums (➤ 37), Roman Forum (➤ 41)

Perched atop the Capitol Hill—long one of Rome's most sacred spots—Santa Maria in Aracoeli, with its glorious ceiling, fine frescoes and soft chandelier-lit interior, makes a calm retreat from the ferocious traffic and hurrying crowds of Piazza Venezia.

Approach There are 124 steep steps in Santa Maria's staircase, built in 1348 to celebrate either the end of the plague epidemic of 1348 or the Holy Year proclaimed for 1350. Today it is traditionally climbed by newly married couples.

Ancient foundation The church was first recorded in AD 574, but even then it was old. Emperor Augustus raised an altar here, the Ara Coeli (the Altar of Heaven), with the inscription now on the church's triumphal arch (*Ecce ara primogeniti Dei*—"Behold the altar of the firstborn of God"). Most of the present structure dates from 1260.

Interior Although only one work of art stands out (Pinturicchio's frescoes, the *Life of St. Bernard of Siena*, 1486), the church's overall sense of grandeur is achieved by the magnificent gilded wooden ceiling, built in 1572–1575 to celebrate the naval battle of Lepanto (1571), and by the nave's enormous columns, removed from lost ancient Roman buildings. Tombs to see include those of Cardinal d'Albret, Giovanni Crivelli, Luca Savelli, and Filippo Della Valle.

Detail from the Life of St. Bernard of Siena

FONTANA DI TREVI

There is no lovelier surprise in Rome than that which suddenly confronts you as you emerge from the tight warren of streets around the Fontana di Trevi, the city's most famous fountain—a sight "silvery to the eye and ear" in the words of Charles Dickens.

Virgin discovery In its earliest guise the Fontana di Trevi marked the end of the Aqua Virgo, or Acqua Vergine, an aqueduct built by Agrippa in 19 BC (supposedly filled with Rome's sweetest waters). The spring that fed it was reputedly discovered by a virgin, hence its name. (She is said to have shown her discovery to some Roman soldiers, a scene—along with Agrippa's approval of the aqueduct's plans—described in bas-reliefs on the fountain's second tier.) The fountain's liveliness and charm is embodied in the pose of *Oceanus*, the central figure, and the two giant tritons and their horses (symbolizing a calm and a stormy sea) drawing his chariot. Other statues represent Abundance and Health and, above, the Four Seasons, which each carry gifts.

Fountains A new fountain was built in 1453 on the orders of Pope Niccolò V, who paid for it by levying a tax on wine—Romans sneered that he "took our wine to give us water." Its name came from the three roads (*tre vie*) that converged on the piazza. The present fountain was commissioned by Pope Clement XII in 1732 and finished 30 years later: its design was inspired by the Arch of Constantine and is attributed to Nicola Salvi, with possible contributions from Bernini (though the most audacious touch—combining a fountain with a palace-like façade—was probably the work of Pietro da Cortona). Visitors wishing to return to Rome throw a coin (preferably over the shoulder) into the fountain. The money goes to the Italian Red Cross.

HIGHLIGHTS

- *Oceanus* (Neptune)
- *Allegory of Health* (right of *Oceanus*)
- *Virgin Indicating a Spring to Soldiers*
- *Allegory of Abundance* (left of *Oceanus*)
- *Agrippa Approving the Design of the Aqueduct*
- *Triton with Horse* (on the right, symbolizing the ocean in repose)
- *Triton with Horse* (on the left, symbolizing a tempestuous sea)
- Façade of Santi Vincenzo e Anastasio
- Baroque interior of Santa Maria in Trivio

INFORMATION

- fII/gII, D5
- Piazza Fontana di Trevi
- Always open
- Spagna or Barberini
- 52, 53, 56, 58, 60, 61, 62, and other routes to Via del Corso and Via del Tritone
- Access via cobbled street
- Free
- Pantheon (➤ 33), Santa Maria sopra Minerva (➤ 34), Palazzo-Galleria Doria Pamphili (➤ 36), Piazza di Spagna & Spanish Steps (➤ 40)

17

PIAZZA DI SPAGNA & SPANISH STEPS

HIGHLIGHTS

- Spanish Steps
- Museo Keats–Shelley
  (➤ 52)
- Trinità dei Monti
- Fontana della Barcaccia
  (➤ 54)
- Babington's Tea Rooms
  (➤ 69)
- Caffè Greco (➤ 69)
- Villa Medici gardens
- Pincio Gardens (➤ 56)
- Roffi Isabelli: wine bar and
  shop, Via della Croce 76a

INFORMATION

- ✚ fl/gl, D5
- ✉ Piazza di Spagna
- ☎ Museo Keats–Shelley: 678
  4235. Babington's Tea
  Rooms: 678 6027. Caffè
  Greco: 678 2554. Villa
  Medici: 679 8381
- 🕐 Spanish Steps: always open.
  Museo Keats–Shelley:
  Mon–Fri 9–1, 3–6.
  Trinità dei Monti: daily
  10–12:30, 4–6.
  Villa Medici: occasionally
  open for exhibitions.
  Gardens: apply to the French
  Academy
- 🍴 Caffè Greco, Babington's
  Tea Rooms
- 🚇 Spagna
- 🚌 119 to Piazza di Spagna
- ♿ None for the Spanish Steps
- 💰 Free except to Museo
  Keats–Shelley (moderate)
- ↔ Santa Maria del Popolo
  (➤ 32), Palazzo Barberini
  (➤ 42)

Neither old nor particularly striking, the Spanish Steps are nonetheless one of Rome's most famous sights, thanks largely to their popularity as a meeting point, to their views, and to their position at the heart of the city's most exclusive shopping district.

Spanish Steps Despite their name, the Spanish Steps were commissioned by a Frenchman, Gueffier (the French ambassador), who in 1723 sought to link Piazza di Spagna with the French-owned church of Trinità dei Monti on the hill above. A century earlier the piazza had housed the headquarters of the Spanish ambassador to the Holy See, hence the name of both the steps and the square.

Around the steps At the base of the steps sits the Fontana della Barcaccia, commissioned in 1627 by Urban VIII and designed either by Gian Lorenzo Bernini or by his less famous father, Pietro. The eccentric design represents a half-sunken boat (➤ 54). To the right of the steps stands the Museo Keats–Shelley (➤ 52), a fascinating collection of literary memorabilia and a working library housed in the lodgings where the poet John Keats died in 1821. To the left are the famed Babington's Tea Rooms (➤ 69) and to the south the Via Condotti, Rome's most exclusive shopping street. At the top of the steps turn to enjoy the views past the Palazzo Barberini and towards the Quirinal Hill, walk into the simple Trinità dei Monti, with its outside double staircase by Domenico Fontana, and visit the beautiful gardens of the 16th-century Villa Medici (open one or two days each week), the seat of the French Academy, where students can study painting, sculpture, architecture, engraving, and music.

FORO ROMANO

The civic and political heart of the Roman Empire was the Roman Forum. Its ruins can be difficult to decipher, but the site is one of the most evocative in the city, the standing stones and fragments conjuring up echoes of a once all-powerful state.

History The Forum (Foro Romano) started life as a marsh between the Palatine and Capitoline hills, taking its name from a word meaning "outside the walls." Later it became a rubbish dump, and (after drainage) a marketplace, and religious shrine. In time it acquired all the structures of Rome's burgeoning civic, social and political life. Over the centuries consuls, emperors, and senators embellished it with magnificent temples, courts, and basilicas.

Forum and Palatine A 1,000-year history, and two millennia of plunder and decay, have left a mishmash of odd pillars and jumbled stones, which nonetheless can begin to make vivid sense given a plan and some imagination. This strange, empty space is romantic, especially on the once palace-covered Palatine Hill to the south. Today orange trees, oleanders, and cypresses line the paths; grasses and wildflowers flourish among the ancient remains. Worth a visit are the Temple of Antoninus and Faustina, the Colonna di Foca, the Curia, the restored Arch of Septimius Severus, the Portico of the Dei Consentes, the Temple of Saturn, Santa Maria Antiqua (the oldest church in the Forum), the House of the Vestal Virgins (who tended the sacred fire), the aisle of the Basilica of the Emperor Maxentius, and the Arch of Titus.

HIGHLIGHTS

- Temple of Antoninus and Faustina (Tempio di Antonino e Faustina, AD 141, a church in medieval times)
- Colonna di Foca (AD 608)
- Curia (Senate House, 80 BC)
- Arch of Septimius Severus (Arco di Settimio Severo, AD 203)
- 12 columns from the Portico of the Dei Consentes (AD 367)
- 8 columns from the Temple of Saturn (Tempio di Saturno, 42 BC, AD 284)
- House of the Vestal Virgins

INFORMATION

- ✚ gIV, D6/E6
- ✉ Entrances from Via di San Gregorio and at Largo Romolo e Remo on Via dei Fori Imperiali
- ☎ 699 0110
- 🕐 Apr–Sep Mon–Sat 9–6; Sun 9–1. Oct–Mar Mon–Sat 9–3; Sun 9–1
- 🚇 Colosseo
- 🚌 11, 27, 81, 85, 87, 186 to Via dei Fori Imperiali
- ♿ Access only from Largo Romolo e Remo
- 💶 Expensive; includes entry to the Palatine and Farnese Gardens (➤ 56)
- ↔ Capitoline Museums (➤ 37), Colosseum (➤ 43), San Clemente (➤ 46), Arch of Constantine (➤ 50)

Pillar and capital from the Forum

41

19

PALAZZO BARBERINI

INFORMATION

The magnificent Palazzo Barberini—designed by Bernini, Borromini, and Carlo Maderno—also houses a stupendous ceiling fresco and one of Rome's finest art collections, the Galleria Nazionale d'Arte Antica (the earlier works of the Galleria Nazionale).

The palace The Palazzo Barberini (Galleria Nazionale d'Arte Antica) was commissioned by Maffei Barberini for his family when he became Pope Urban VIII in 1623. The epitome of Rome's high baroque style, it is a maze of suites, apartments, and staircases, many still swathed in their sumptuous original decoration. Overshadowing all is the Gran Salone, dominated by Pietro da Cortona's rich ceiling frescoes, glorifying Urban as an agent of Divine Providence. The central windows and oval spiral staircase (Scala Elicoidale) are Borromini's creation.

The collection *Antica* here means old rather than ancient, and embraces the earlier works of the nation's art collection. Probably its most popular painting is Raphael's *La Fornarina* (also attributed

to Giulio Romano). It is reputedly a portrait of one of the artist's mistresses, identified later as the daughter of a baker (*fornaio* means baker). It was executed in the year of the painter's death, a demise brought on, it is said, by his mistress's unrelenting passion. Else-

Raphael's La Fornarina

where, eminent Italian works from Filippo Lippi, Andrea del Sarto, Caravaggio, and Guido Reni are contrasted with foreign artists.

COLOSSEO

The Pantheon may be better preserved, the Forum more historically important, but for me no other monument in Rome rivals the majesty of the Colosseum, the world's largest surviving structure from Roman antiquity.

History The Colosseum was begun by the Emperor Vespasian in AD 72 and inaugurated by his son, Titus, in AD 80 with a gala that saw 5,000 animals slaughtered in a day (and 100 days of continuous games thereafter). Finishing touches to the 55,000-seat stadium were added by Domitian (AD 81–96). Its walls are made of brick and volcanic tufa faced with travertine marble blocks, which were bound together by metal clamps (removed AD 664), while three types of columns support the arcades. Its long decline began in the Middle Ages, with the pillaging of stone for churches and palaces. The desecration ended in 1744, when the structure was consecrated in memory of the Christians supposedly martyred in the arena. Clearing of the site and excavations began late in the 19th century and restoration was carried out in the 20th.

Games Unlike the Christian martyrdoms, which were rare events, the gladitorial games continued for some 500 years. Criminals, slaves, gladiators, and wild animals kept underground, often fought to the death. Women and dwarfs also wrestled, and mock sea battles were waged (the arena could be flooded via underground drains). Spectators could exercise the power of life and death over defeated combatants, by waving handkerchiefs to signify mercy, or by displaying a down-turned thumb to demand the finishing stroke. Survivors often had their throats cut anyway, and even the dead were poked with red-hot irons to make sure they had actually expired.

HIGHLIGHTS

- Circumference walls
- Arches: 80 lower arches for the easy admission of crowds
- Doric columns: lowest arcade
- Ionic columns: central arcade
- Corinthian columns: upper arcade
- Underground rooms for animals
- The "holes" used by the binding metal clamps
- *Vomitoria*: interior exits and entrances
- Views from the upper levels
- Arch of Constantine nearby (➤ 50)

INFORMATION

- ✚ hIV, E6
- ✉ Piazza del Colosseo, Via dei Fori Imperiali
- ☎ 700 4261
- 🕐 Mon, Tue, Thu–Sat 9–2hrs before sunset; Wed, Sun 9–1
- 🚇 Colosseo
- 🚌 11, 13, 15, 27, 30b, 81, 85, 87, 118, 186, 673 to Piazza del Colosseo
- ♿ Poor to the interior: limited access from Via Celio Vibenna entrance
- 🎟 Ground floor: free. Upper levels: moderate
- ↔ Capitoline Museums (➤ 37), Roman Forum (➤ 41), San Pietro in Vincoli (➤ 44), San Clemente (➤ 46), Arch of Constantine (➤ 50)

43

21

SAN PIETRO IN VINCOLI

HIGHLIGHTS

- *Moses*, Michelangelo
- Profile self-portrait in the upper part of Moses' beard
- Chains of St. Peter
- Carved paleochristian sarcophgus (crypt)
- Mosaic: *St. Sebastian*
- Tomb of Niccolò da Cusa
- *Santa Margherita*, Guercino
- Tomb of Antonio and Piero Pollaiuolo
- Torre dei Margani (Piazza San Pietro in Vincoli), once believed to have been owned by the Borgias

INFORMATION

- hIII, E6
- Piazza di San Pietro in Vincoli 4a
- 488 2865
- Mon–Sat 7–12:30, 3:30–7 (Oct–Mar 6PM); Sun 8:45–11:30AM
- Colosseo or Cavour
- 11, 27, 81 to Via Cavour, or 11, 27, 81, 85, 87, 186 to Piazza del Colosseo
- Good
- Free
- Roman Forum (▶ 41), Colosseum (▶ 43), Santa Maria Maggiore (▶ 47)

San Pietro in Vincoli, hidden in a narrow back street, is a thoroughly appealing church. Drop by for the chance to admire Michelangelo's statue of Moses, one of the most powerful of all the artist's monumental sculptures.

Chains San Pietro in Vincoli takes its name from the chains (*vincoli*) proudly clasped in the coffer with bronze doors under the high altar. According to tradition they are the chains used to bind St. Peter while he was held captive in the Mamertine prison (remnants of which are preserved under the church of San Giuseppe near the Forum). Part of the chains found their way to Constantinople, while the rest were housed in San Pietro by Pope Leo I (who had the church specially reconstructed from a 4th-century building for the purpose). When the two parts were eventually reunited, they are said to have miraculously fused together. The church has often been transformed and restored. The 20 columns of its interior arcade came originally from a Roman temple.

Works of art Michelangelo's majestic sculpture (of a patriarchal Moses receiving the Tablets of Stone) was originally designed as part of a 42-figure ensemble for the tomb of Julius II. Michelangelo spent years scouring the Carrara mountains for suitable pieces of stone, but the project never came close to completion, and he was to describe the work as "this tragedy of a tomb"; much of his time was instead spent (reluctantly) on the Sistine Chapel. Also make sure you see the Byzantine mosaic *St. Sebastian* (*c.* 680), the monument to the Pollaiuolo brothers (*c.* 1498) by Luigi Capponi, and the tomb of Cardinal da Cusa (1464), attributed to Andrea Bregno.

GALLERIA BORGHESE

Normally only the collection of the Vatican Museums would surpass the sculptures and paintings of the Galleria Borghese. Since subsidence in 1985, however, only the sculptures now reside here, the paintings being housed at San Michele a Ripa.

Seductress The Villa Borghese was designed in 1613 as a summer retreat for Cardinal Scipione Borghese, nephew of Pope Paul V, who accumulated most of the collection (acquired by the state in 1902). Scipione was an enthusiastic patron of Bernini, whose works dominate the gallery. The museum's first masterpiece, however, is Antonio Canova's *Paolina Borghese* (above), Napoleon's sister, and wife of Camillo Borghese. Depicted bare-breasted, with a come-hither hauteur, Paolina was just as slyly seductive in life. She excited much gossip, being renowned for her jewels, clothes, and lovers, and the servants she used as footstools.

Temple of Aesculapius, Villa Borghese

Bernini His *David* (1623–1624) is said to be a self-portrait, while *Apollo and Daphne* (1622–1625), in the next room, is considered his masterpiece. Other Bernini works include the *Rape of Proserpine* (1622) and *Truth Unveiled by Time* (1652).

The paintings Foremost among this treasure trove are works by Raphael (*The Deposition of Christ*), Titian (*Sacred and Profane Love*), Caravaggio (*Boy with a Fruit Basket* and *Madonna dei Palafrenieri*), and Correggio (*Danae*).

HIGHLIGHTS

Galleria Borghese
- *Paolina Borghese*, Canova
- *David*, Bernini
- *Apollo and Daphne*, Bernini

Quadreria della Galleria Borghese al San Michele a Ripa
- *Madonna dei Palafrenieri*, Caravaggio
- *Sacred and Profane Love*, Titian
- *Deposition of Christ*, Raphael

INFORMATION

Galleria Borghese
- 🗓 E4
- ✉ Piazzale Scipione Borghese 5
- ☎ 854 8577
- 🕐 Tue–Sat 9–7; Sun 9–1. Closed public holidays
- Ⓜ Spagna or Flaminio
- 🚌 52, 53, 910 to Via Pinciana, or 3, 4, 56, 57, 319 to Via Po, or 19, 30b to Via delle Belle Arti
- ♿ Steps to front entrance
- 💷 Moderate
- ↔ Villa Giulia (➤ 35), Piazza di Spagna & Spanish Steps (➤ 40), Palazzo Barberini (➤ 42)

San Michele a Ripa in Trastevere
- 🗓 C7
- ✉ Via di San Michele in Trastevere 22
- ☎ 581 6732
- 🕐 Tue–Sat 9–7; Sun 9–1
- 🚌 13, 23 to Viale di Trastevere
- 💷 Moderate

45

23

SAN CLEMENTE

No site in Rome suggests as vividly the layers of history that underpin the city as San Clemente, a beautiful medieval ensemble built over a superbly preserved 4th-century church and the remains of a 3rd-century Mithraic temple.

Upper church The present San Clemente—named after Rome's fourth pope—was built between 1108 and 1184 to replace an earlier one that was sacked by the Normans in 1084. Almost untouched since, its medieval interior is dominated by the earlier 12th-century marble panels of the choir screen and pulpits and the glittering 12th-century apse mosaic, *The Triumph of the Cross*. Equally captivating are the *Life of St. Catherine* frescoes (1428–1431), by Masolino da Panicale.

Mithraic temple

To the underground sanctuaries Steps descend to the lower church, which retains traces of its 8th- to 11th-century frescoes of San Clemente, and the legends of saints Alessio and Sisinnio. More steps lead deeper into the twilight world of the best-preserved of the 12 Mithraic temples uncovered in Rome (Mithraism was a popular, male-only cult eclipsed by Christianity.) Here are an altar with a bas-relief of Mithras, and the Triclinium, used for banquets and rites. Excavations are revealing parts of the temple, and the 1,900-year-old remains of other buildings, streets, and an (audible) underground stream that perhaps formed part of ancient Rome's drainage system.

INFORMATION

- hIV, E6
- Via di San Giovanni in Laterano
- 7045 1018
- Apr–Sep daily 9–12:30, 3:30–6:30. Oct–Mar daily 9–12:30, 3:30–6
- 15, 81,85, 87, 93,118, 186 to Via Labicana, or 13, 30b to Colosseum
- Church: free. Excavations: cheap

SANTA MARIA MAGGIORE

Santa Maria Maggiore is Rome's finest early Christian basilica, with a magnificent interior that celebrates its long history; it is the only church in the city where mass has been celebrated every single day since the 5th century.

History According to myth, the Virgin appeared to Pope Liberius on August 5, AD 352, telling him to build a church exactly where snow would fall the next day. Although it was summer, the snow fell, marking the outlines of a basilica on the Esquiline Hill. Legend aside, the church probably dates from AD 430, though the campanile (at 246 feet the tallest in Rome) was added in 1377, and the interior and exterior were altered in the 13th and 18th centuries. The coffered ceiling, attributed to Giuliano da Sangallo, was reputedly gilded with the first gold to arrive from the New World, a gift from Spain to Alexander VI (note his Borgia bull emblems).

Interior Beyond the splendor of its general decoration, the main treasures are mosaics: in the architraves of the nave are 36 5th-century mosaic panels on the lives of Moses, Abraham, Isaac, and Jacob (framed below by some 40 ancient columns); on the Triumphal Arch the mosaics are the *Annunciation* and *Infancy of Christ*; in the 13th-century apse are Jacopo Torriti's mosaics, including the *Coronation of the Virgin* (1295), the pinnacle of Rome's medieval mosaic tradition; and those in the entrance loggia are by Filippo Rusuti. Other highlights include the Cappella Sistina (tomb of Sixtus V, by Domenico Fontana, 1588) and Cappella Paolina, built by rival popes, and Giovanni di Cosima's tomb of Cardinal Rodriguez (1299). The high altar reputedly contains relics of Christ's crib, the object of devotion of countless pilgrims.

HIGHLIGHTS

- Mosaics: upper tier of entrance loggia
- Coffered ceiling
- Mosaic cycle: 36 Old Testament scenes
- Mosaics: Triumphal Arch
- Apse mosaic: *Coronation of the Virgin*, Jacopo Torriti
- Four reliefs from a papal altar, Mino del Reame
- Fresco fragments: *Prophets*, attributed to Cimabue, Pietro Cavallini, or Giotto (apse)
- Cappella Sistina
- Cappella Paolina
- Tomb of Cardinal Rodriguez, Giovanni di Cosima

INFORMATION

- ✚ E6
- ✉ Piazza di Santa Maria Maggiore and Piazza dell'Esquilino
- ☎ 483 195
- ◔ Apr–Sep daily 7AM–8PM. Oct–Mar daily 7AM–7PM
- Ⓠ Termini or Cavour
- ▤ 16, 27, 70, 71, 93, 93b to Piazza di Santa Maria Maggiore
- ♿ Poor: access is easiest from Piazza di Santa Maria Maggiore
- ▓ Free
- ↔ Palazzo Barberini (▶ 42), San Pietro in Vincoli (▶ 44)

SAN GIOVANNI IN LATERANO

INFORMATION

🚩 F7
✉ Piazza di San Giovanni in
  Laterano
☎ 6988 6433; fax 6988 6452
🕐 Church & Cloister: Apr–Sep
  daily 7AM–7PM. Oct–Mar
  closes 6PM.
  Scala Santa: daily
  6–midday, 2:30–6:30.
  Baptistery: daily 9–1, 4–6.
  Museum: Apr–Sep Mon–Fri
  9–6. Oct–Mar closes 5PM
🚇 San Giovanni
🚌 4, 15, 16, 85, 87, 93, 93b,
  tram 13, 30b to Piazza di
  San Giovanni in Laterano
♿ Poor: steps to church
🎫 Church, Scala Santa,
  Baptistery: free.
  Museum & Cloister:
  inexpensive
↔ Colosseum (➤ 43), San
  Pietro in Vincoli (➤ 44),
  San Clemente (➤ 46)

San Giovanni's façade can be seen from afar, its statues rising over the rooftops—a deliberate echo of St. Peter's—reminding us that this is the cathedral church of Rome and the Pope's titular see in his role as Bishop of Rome.

History A 4th-century palace here provided a meeting place for Pope Miltiades and Constantine (the first Christian emperor), later becoming a focus for Christianity. Barbarians, earthquakes, and fires destroyed the earliest churches on the site; the façade (modeled on St. Peter's) dates from 1735, Borromini's interior from 1646. It was the papal residence in Rome until the 14th century (when the popes moved to the Vatican), though pontiffs were crowned here until the 19th century.

Nave with statues of the Apostles

Interior Bronze doors from the Forum's Curia usher you into the cavernous interior, its chill whites and grays redeemed by a fabulously ornate ceiling. The cloister provides the main attraction, the alfresco *Boniface VIII*, attributed to Giotto, and an apse mosaic is by Jacopo Torriti. A high altar reliquary is supposed to contain the heads of saints Peter and Paul, and a frescoed tabernacle is attributed to Arnolfo di Cambio and Fiorenzo de Lorenzo. Outside are the Scala Santa, reputedly the steps ascended by Christ at his trial in Jerusalem (the faithful climb up on their knees). The octagonal baptistery dates back to the time of Constantine and was the model for many subsequent baptisteries.

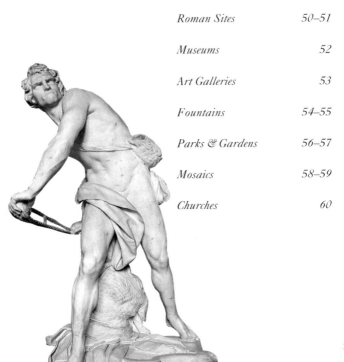

ROME's *best*

49

ROMAN SITES

See Top 25 Sights for
ALTAR OF PEACE ➤ 31
CASTEL SANT'ANGELO ➤ 27
COLOSSEUM ➤ 43
PANTHEON ➤ 33
ROMAN FORUM ➤ 41

Triumphal arches

Two of Rome's greatest contributions to architecture were the basilica and the triumphal arch, the latter raised by the Roman Senate on behalf of a grateful populace to celebrate the achievements of victorious generals and emperors. Returning armies and their leaders would pass through the arches, bearing the spoils of war past a cheering crowd. Only three major arches still survive in Rome—the arches of Constantine, Titus, and Septimius Severus (the last two are in the Forum)—but their continuing influence can be seen in London's Marble Arch and Paris's Arc de Triomphe.

ARCH OF CONSTANTINE

Triumphal arches, like celebratory columns, were usually raised as monuments to military achievement, in this case the victory of Constantine over his rival Maxentius at Milvian Bridge in AD 312 (making it one of the last great monuments to be built in ancient Rome). At 69 feet high and 85 feet wide it is the largest and best-preserved of the city's arches, and has recently been magnificently restored. Most of its reliefs were taken from earlier buildings, partly out of pragmatism and partly out of a desire to link Constantine's glories with those of the past. The battle scenes of the central arch show Trajan at war with the Dacians, while another describes a boar hunt and sacrifice to Apollo, carved in the time of Hadrian (2nd century AD).

🔲 hIV, E6 🖂 Piazza del Colosseo-Via di San Gregorio, Via dei Fori Imperiali 🕐 Always open 🚇 Colosseo 🚌 11, 13, 15, 27, 30b, 81, 85, 87, 118, 186, 673 to Piazza del Colosseo 💷 Free

BATHS OF CARACALLA

Although the Terme di Caracalla were not the largest baths *(terme)* in ancient Rome (those of Diocletian near the present-day Piazza della Repubblica were bigger), the Baths of Caracalla were the city's most luxurious (and could accommodate as many as 1,600 bathers at one time). Started by Septimius Severus in AD 206, and completed by his son, Caracalla, 11 years later, they were designed as much for social meeting as for hygiene, since they were complete with gardens, libraries, sports facilities, stadiums, lecture rooms, shops— even hairdressers. They were open to both sexes, but bathing for men and women took place at different times. Something of the Terme's scale can still be gauged from today's ruins, although the site is perhaps now best known as the stage for outdoor opera in the summer (➤ 81).

🔲 E8 🖂 Via delle Terme di Caracalla 52 ☎ 575 8626 🕐 Tue–Sat 9AM–2hrs before sunset; Sun, Mon 9–1. Closed public holidays 🚇 Circo Massimo 🚌 90, 90b, 118, 613, 617, 714, 715 to Piazzale Numa Pompilio 💷 Moderate

Carving from the Baths of Caracalla

CIRCUS MAXIMUS

This enormous grassy arena follows the outlines of a stadium capable of seating 300,000 people. Created to satisfy the passionate Roman appetite for chariot racing, and the prototype for almost all subsequent race courses, it was begun around 326 BC and modified frequently before the occasion of its last recorded use under Totila the Ostrogoth in AD 549. Much of the original structure has long been quarried for building stone, but there remains the *spina* (the arena's old dividing wall), marked by a row of cypresses, the ruins of the imperial box, and the open arena, now a public park (avoid after dark).
🚩 D7 ✉ Via del Circo Massimo 🕐 Always open 🚇 Circo Massimo 🚌 11, 13, 15, 27, 30b, 90, 94, 118, 673 to Piazza di Porta Capena 🎟 Free

COLUMN OF MARCUS AURELIUS

The Column of Marcus Aurelius (AD 180–196) was built to celebrate Aurelius's military triumphs over hostile northern European tribes. It is composed of 27 separate drums of Carraran marble welded into a seamless whole, and is decorated with a continuous spiral of bas-reliefs commemorating episodes from the victorious campaigns. Aurelius is depicted no fewer than 59 times, though curiously never actually in battle. The summit statue is of St. Paul, and was crafted by Domenico Fontana in 1589 to replace the 60th depiction of Aurelius.
🚩 fII, D5 ✉ Piazza Colonna, Via del Corso 🕐 Always open 🚇 Barberini 🚌 56, 60, 85, 90, 90b, 119, 492 to Via del Corso 🎟 Free

TRAJAN'S MARKETS (MERCATI TRAIANEI)

Lack of space in the Roman Forum prompted the building of the new Imperial Fora (Fori Imperiali). They were begun in the 1st century BC by Julius Caesar and augmented by emperors Augustus, Vespasian, Nerva, and Trajan (the ruins of the buildings constructed during their rule lie either side of the Via dei Fori Imperiali). Part of the largest, Trajan's Forum, was the Mercati Traianei, constructed at the beginning of the 2nd century AD as a semicircular range of halls on three levels. Two survive in excellent condition, together with many of the 150 booths that once traded rare and expensive commodities; look in particular at the Via Biberata, named after *pipera* (pepper).
🚩 gIII, D6 ✉ Via IV Novembre 94 ☎ 679 0048 🕐 Oct–Mar Tue–Sat 9–1:30; Sun 9–1. Apr–Sep Tue–Sat 9–7; Sun 9–1 🚇 Cavour 🚌 57, 64, 65, 70, 75, 170 and other routes to Via IV Novembre 🎟 Moderate; free last Sun of month

Trajan's Forum

At the races

Going to the races was as much a social event in ancient times as it is today. All types of people attended meetings, but different classes were kept rigidly separated. The emperor and his entourage sat on the imperial balcony, or *pulvinar*, while senators sat in the uppermost of the marble stalls. Lesser dignitaries occupied tiers of wooden seats, while the common rabble scrambled for standing room in open stands. The sexes, however, were unsegregated (unlike at the Colosseum), and the races became notorious for their sexual license. Ovid recorded that at the Circo there was "no call for the secret language of fingers: nor need you depend on a furtive nod when you set upon a new affair."

51

Museums

John Keats

It was in what is now the Museo Keats–Shelley that the young English poet John Keats died on February 23, 1821, aged just 25. He had arrived in Rome the previous September, sent south to seek a cure for consumption. He described his time in Rome, however, as a "posthumous life," lamenting that he "already seemed to feel the flowers growing over him." (He was buried in the Protestant Cemetery ➤ 56.)

See Top 25 Sights for
CAPITOLINE MUSEUMS ➤ 37
CASTEL SANT'ANGELO ➤ 27
GALLERIA BORGHESE ➤ 45
VATICAN MUSEUMS ➤ 25
VILLA GIULIA ➤ 35

MUSEO BARRACCO (PICCOLA FARNESINA)
This modest collection of Assyrian, Egyptian, Greek, Etruscan, and Roman artifacts is housed in the charming Piccola Farnesina, a miniature Renaissance palace.
✚ elII, C6 ✉ Corso Vittorio Emanuele II 166–8 ☎ 6880 6848 ⏰ Tue–Sat 9–7; Sun 9–1 🚌 46, 62, 64, 79, 81, 87, 90, 186, 492, 926 to Corso Vittorio Emanuele II 🎫 Moderate

MUSEO DEL FOLKLORE
Paintings, prints, and artifacts that illuminate the lives and times of past Romans.
✚ C7 ✉ Piazza Sant'Egidio 1b, Trastevere ☎ 581 6563 ⏰ Tue–Sat 9–7; Sun 9–1 🚌 44, 56, 60, 75, 170, 181, 280, 717 to Piazza S. Sonnino 🎫 Moderate

MUSEO KEATS–SHELLEY
Since 1909 this has been a museum and a library for students of fellow Romantics Keats and Shelley, both of whom died in Italy (see panel). Books, pamphlets, pictures, and essays lie scattered around the 18th-century house.
✚ gI, D5 ✉ Piazza di Spagna ☎ 678 4235 ⏰ Mon–Fri 9–1, 3–6 🚇 Spagna 🚌 119 to Piazza di Spagna 🎫 Moderate

MUSEO NAZIONALE ROMANO
Once one of the city's greatest museums, this state collection of ancient sculpture has an uncertain future. Its magnificent, but previously badly displayed collection of antiquities, is to be rehoused in the Palazzo Massimo in Piazza dei Cinquecento.
✚ E5 ✉ Viale Enrico de Nicola 79 ☎ 4890 3507 or 488 0530 ⏰ Tue–Sat 9–2; Sun 9–1 🚇 Repubblica 🚌 All services to Termini and Piazza dei Cinquecento 🎫 Expensive

MUSEO DEL PALAZZO VENEZIA
Built in 1455 for Pietro Barbi (later Pope Paul II), the Palazzo Venezia was among the first Renaissance palaces in Rome. For years it was the Venetian Embassy (hence its name), becoming the property of the state in 1916. (Mussolini harangued the crowds from the balconies.) Today the museum hosts traveling exhibitions and a fine permanent collection that includes Renaissance paintings, sculpture, armor, ceramics, silverware, and countless *objets d'art*.
✚ fIII, D6 ✉ Palazzo Venezia, Via del Plebiscito 118 ☎ 679 8865 ⏰ Tue–Sat 9–1:30; Sun 9–1. Closed public holidays 🚌 All services to Piazza Venezia 🎫 Expensive

Discobolus *(the discus thrower)*

ART GALLERIES

GALLERIA DELL'ACCADEMIA NAZIONALE DI SAN LUCA

An interesting collection of 18th- and 19th-century paintings, with earlier masterpieces by Raphael, Titian, Van Dyck, and Guido Reni.

➕ D5 ⊠ Piazza dell'Accademia 77 ☎ 678 9243 ⏰ Mon, Wed, Fri, and the last Sun of every month 10–1 🚌 52, 53, 56, 58, 60, 61, 62, 71, 81, 95, 119 to Via del Tritone-Piazza Colonna 👷 Moderate

A ceiling in the Villa Farnesina

PALAZZO CORSINI

Though in a separate building, this gallery is part of the Palazzo Barberini's Galleria Nazionale. It houses later paintings from the national collection, with pictures by Rubens, Van Dyck, Murillo, and Caravaggio.

➕ dIV, C6 ⊠ Via della Lungara 10 ☎ 6880 2323 ⏰ Tue–Sat 9–2; Sun and public holidays 9–1 🚌 23, 65, 280 to Lungotevere Farnesina 👷 Expensive

PALAZZO SPADA

The pretty Palazzo Spada, with its creamy stucco façade (1556–1560), contains four rooms of paintings by Guido Reni, Guercino, Cerquozzi, Dürer, Andrea del Sarto, and others.

➕ eIII, C6 ⊠ Piazza Capo di Ferro 3 ☎ 686 1158 ⏰ Tue–Sat 9–7; Sun 9–1 🍴 Café 🚌 44, 56, 60, 65, 75, 170, 181 to Via Arenula 👷 Moderate

PALAZZO-GALLERIA COLONNA

The best painting of this mostly 16th- to 18th-century (and rarely open) collection is Carracci's *Bean Eater*.

➕ gIII, D5 ⊠ Via della Pilotta 17 ☎ 679 4362 ⏰ Sep–Jul Sat only 9–1. Closed Sun–Fri and Aug 🚌 57, 64, 65, 70, 75, 81, 170, and other buses to Piazza Venezia 👷 Moderate

VILLA FARNESINA

This lovely Renaissance villa was completed in 1511 for Agostino Chigi (see panel) by Baldassare Peruzzi (and later sold to the Farnese). It is best known for the Loggia of Cupid and Psyche, decorated with frescoes (1517) by Raphael; for Sodoma's masterpiece, *Scenes from the Life of Alexander the Great*; and for the Salone delle Prospettive, Peruzzi's *trompe-l'oeil* views of Rome.

➕ dIII, C6 ⊠ Via della Lungara 230 ☎ 6880 1767 ⏰ Tue–Sat 9–1 🚌 23, 65, 280 to Lungotevere Farnesina 👷 Free

Agostino Chigi

Agostino Chigi (d. 1512), from Siena, made his banking fortune by securing Rome's prize business —the papal account. He became renowned for flinging the family silver into the Tiber after gargantuan feasts at the Villa Farnesina. This extravagant gesture was not all it seemed, however, for Chigi omitted to tell his admiring diners that a net strung below the water caught the loot for the next banquet.

FOUNTAINS

Fontana delle Naiadi

Fontana delle Naiadi

The "Fountain of the Naiads" in Piazza della Repubblica is of little historical interest or even of great artistic value. Nonetheless it is probably one of the most erotic works of art on public display anywhere in Italy. Designed by Mario Rutelli, the sculptures were added in 1901. Water plays seductively over four frolicking and suggestively clad bronze nymphs, each entwined in the phallic-like tentacles of a marine creature so as to leave little to the imagination. Each creature represents water in one of its forms: a swan for lakes, a sea-horse for the oceans, a water snake for rivers, and a lizard for underground streams.

See Top 25 Sights for
FONTANA DI TREVI ➤ 39

FONTANA DELLE API
Bernini's small but captivating fountain was commissioned in honor of Pope Urban VIII, leading light of the Barberini clan. It depicts a scallop shell, a symbol of life and fertility—a favorite Bernini conceit—at which three bees (*api*), taken from the Barberini coat of arms, have settled to drink.
🔲 gll, E5 ✉ Piazza Barberini 🚇 Barberini 🚌 52, 53, 56, 58, 60, 95, 119, 492 to Piazza Barberini

FONTANA DELLA BARCACCIA
Commissioned in 1627–1629 by Pope Urban VIII, this eccentric little fountain at the base of the Spanish Steps (➤ 40) is the work of either Gian Lorenzo Bernini or his father Pietro. It represents a half-sunken ship and, translated literally, its name means the "Fountain of the Wretched Boat." Bernini was unable to create a greater aquatic display because of the low water pressure in the aqueduct feeding the fountain.
🔲 fl, D4/5 ✉ Piazza di Spagna 🚇 Spagna 🚌 119 to Piazza di Spagna

FONTANA DEL MORO
Designed in 1575 by Giacomo della Porta, the fountain at Piazza Navona's southern end shows a "Moor" (actually a marine divinity) grappling with a dolphin, a figure added by Antonio Mori from a design by Bernini.
🔲 ell, C5 ✉ Piazza Navona 🚌 70, 81, 87, 90, 186, 492 to Corso del Rinascimento, or 46, 62, 64 to Corso Vittorio Emanuele II

FONTANA PAOLA
The five arches and six granite columns of the monumental façade fronting this majestic fountain were built between 1610 and 1612 to carry the waters of Pope Paul's recently repaired Trajan Aqueduct. The columns were removed from the old St. Peter's, while many of the precious marbles were filched from the Temple of Minerva in the Imperial Fora.
🔲 clV, C6/7 ✉ Via Garibaldi 🚌 41, 44, 75, 710 to the Gianicolo

FONTANA DEI QUATTRO FIUMI
Bernini's spirited "Fountain of the Four Rivers" at the heart of Piazza Navona was designed for Pope Innocent X in 1648 as part of a scheme to improve the approach to the Palazzo Doria Pamphili. It was unveiled in 1651. Its four figures represent the four rivers of Paradise (the Nile, Ganges, Danube, and Plate), and the four "corners" of the world (Africa, Asia, Europe, and America). The dove atop the

central obelisk is a symbol of the Pamphili family, of which Innocent was a member.

✚ ell, C5 ☒ Piazza Navona 🚌 70, 81, 87, 90, 186, 492 to Corso del Rinascimento, or 46, 62, 64 to Corso Vittorio Emanuele II

FONTANA DELLE TARTARUGHE

This tiny creation (1585) is one of the most delightful sights in Rome, thanks largely to the tortoises added by Bernini in the 17th century.

✚ fIII, D6 ☒ Piazza Mattei 🚌 44, 56, 60, 65, 75, 170, 181, 710, 718, 719 to Via Arenula

FONTANA DEL TRITONE

Like its companion piece the Fontana delle Api (▶ 54), the "Fountain of Triton" (1643) was also designed by Bernini for Urban VIII. One of the sculptor's earliest fountains, the Fontana del Tritone is made of travertine rather than the more usual marble. It depicts four dolphins supporting twin scallop shells (bearing the Barberini coat of arms) on which the triumphant Triton is enthroned.

✚ gI, E5 ☒ Piazza Barberini 🚇 Barberini 🚌 52, 53, 56, 58, 60, 95, 119, 492 to Piazza Barberini

LE QUATTRO FONTANE

These four linked fountains (1585–1590) sit at a busy crossroads close to Via Nazionale. Each contains a reclining deity: the two female figures are probably Juno and Diana; the male figure is the Nile or Aniene; and the last figure, shown with the she-wolf, is a river god representing the Tiber.

✚ hII, E5 ☒ Via delle Quattro Fontane-Via del Quirinale 🚇 Repubblica 🚌 57, 64, 65, 70, 75, 81, 170 to Via Nazionale

Artistic rivalry

Well-worn Roman myths surround Bernini's Fontana dei Quattro Fiumi. One suggests the veiled figure of the Nile symbolizes the sculptor's dislike for the church of Sant'Agnese, designed by his fierce rival, Borromini (the veil actually symbolizes the river's unknown source). Another claims the figure representing the Plate is holding up his arm as if in horror of the church (either appalled by its design or afraid it is about to fall down). However, neither theory is correct, for Bernini finished the fountain before Borromini had even begun work on his church.

Fontana dei Quattro Fiumi

PARKS & GARDENS

The Protestant Cemetery

"...the cypress trees cast their long shadows upon the most extraordinary collection of exiles ever assembled in one place."
H. V. Morton, *A Traveller in Rome.*

"The Cemetery is an open space among the ruins, covered in winter with violets and daisies. It might make one in love with death to know that one should be buried in so sweet a place." Percy Bysshe Shelley, Preface to *Adonis.*

Via Appia Antica

BOTANICAL GARDENS (ORTO BOTANICO)

Trastevere has few open spaces, so these university gardens and their 7,000 or so botanical species—originally part of the Palazzo Corsini—provide a welcome slice of green shade.

✚ clV, C6 ✉ Largo Cristina di Svezia, off Via Corsini ☎ 686 4193 ⏰ Mon–Sat 9–6. Closed Sun and public holidays 🚌 23, 65, 280 to Lungotevere Farnesina 💷 Free

COLLE OPPIO

This homey area of park, once part of a palace complex built by Nero and redeveloped by Trajan, rests the eyes and feet after visits to the Colosseum, San Clemente or San Giovanni in Laterano. A community meeting place, it's a welcoming mixture of grass and walkways (and feral cats), complete with promenading mothers, a small café, and a children's playground.

✚ hlV, E6 ✉ Via Labicana-Viale del Monte Oppio ⏰ Always open 🚌 11, 15, 16, 27, 81, 85 to Via Labicana 💷 Free

PALATINE AND FARNESE GARDENS (PALATINO E ORTI FARNESIANI)

After a stroll around the Forum it's worth finding time to climb the Palatine Hill to enjoy a lovely garden haven, designed in the 16th century by the great Renaissance architect Vignola. Orange groves, cypresses, and endless drowsy corners, all speckled with flowers and ancient stones, make up the Orti Farnesiani, which were laid out over the ruins of the palace that once stood here.

✚ glV, D6 ✉ Entrances from Via di San Gregorio and for the Roman Forum at Largo Romolo e Remo on Via dei Fori Imperiali ☎ 699 0110 ⏰ Mon, Wed–Sat 9AM–2hrs before sunset; Tue, Sun 9–2 🚇 Colosseo 🚌 11, 27, 81, 85, 87, 186 to Via dei Fori Imperiali 💷 Expensive (includes entry to Roman Forum)

PARCO SAVELLO

Close to Santa Sabina (a pretty church in its own right), the Parco Savello is another little-known Roman park that lies closer to the center than you might expect. Its hilly position provides a lovely panorama over the Tiber and the city beyond.

✚ D7 ✉ Via Santa Sabina, Aventino ⏰ Daily dawn–dusk 🚌 94 💷 Free

PINCIO GARDENS

Even if you cannot face the longer trip to the nearby Villa Borghese, be sure to walk to these gardens from Piazza del Popolo or Piazza di Spagna to enjoy the wonderful views (best at sunset) across the rooftops to St. Peter's.

✚ D4 ✉ Piazza del Pincio ⏰ Daily dawn–dusk 🚌 90, 90b, 95, 119, 926 to Piazzale Flaminio or Piazza del Popolo 💷 Free

PROTESTANT CEMETERY (CIMITERO PROTESTANTE)

Described more than once as the "most beautiful cemetery in the world," this bucolic oasis is also something of a literary shrine (see panel opposite), thanks to the graves of poets like John Keats, whose tombstone bears the epitaph "Here lies One whose Name was Writ in Water." As late as the 19th century, burials here had to take place at night to avoid provoking attacks from outraged Catholics.

Villa Doria Pamphili

🔲 D8 ✉ Via Caio Cestio 6, Testaccio ☎ 574 1141 🕐 Mar–Sep Thu–Tue 8–11:30, 3:20–5:30. Oct–Feb Thu–Tue 8–11:30, 2:20–4:30 🚌 13, 23, 27, 30b, 57, 94, 95, 716 to Piazza di Porta San Paolo 💰 Free but donation expected

VIA APPIA ANTICA

Once an imperial highway, this old roadway so close to the city center is now an evocative cobbled lane fringed with ancient monuments, tombs, catacombs, and lovely open country (see panel).

🔲 F9 ✉ Via Appia Antica 🕐 Always open 🚌 118 from the Colosseum, San Giovanni in Laterano, or the Baths of Caracalla 💰 Free

VILLA BORGHESE

Rome's largest central park was laid out between 1613 and 1616 as the grounds of the Borghese family's summer villa. Smaller now, and redesigned in the 18th century to suit the then-fashionable penchant for "English parkland," it still offers a shady retreat from the rigors of sightseeing. Walkways, woods, and lakes are complemented by fountains, a racetrack, children's playgrounds and a (rather tawdry) zoo.

🔲 D4/E4 ✉ Porta Pinciana–Via Flaminia 🕐 Daily dawn–dusk 🚇 Flaminio 🚌 3, 4, 52, 53, 57, 95, 490, 495, 910 💰 Free

VILLA CELIMONTANA

This is one of Rome's lesser-known parks, but is easily accessible from the Colosseum and San Giovanni in Laterano.

🔲 E7 ✉ Piazza della Navicella 🕐 Daily 7AM–dusk 🚌 15, 673 to Via Claudia, or 90, 90b to Via Druso 💰 Free

VILLA DORIA PAMPHILI

This huge area of parkland—laid out for Prince Camillo Pamphili in the mid-17th century—is probably too far from the center if you are just making a short visit to Rome. If you have time to spare, however, and fancy a good long walk away from the hordes, there is nowhere better.

🔲 A7 ✉ Via di San Pancrazio 🕐 Daily dawn–dusk 🚌 31, 41, 75, 144 to the Gianicolo 💰 Free

The Appia Antica

The Appia Antica was built in 312 BC by Appius Claudius Caecus to link Rome with Capua; in 194 BC it was extended to Brindisi (320 miles and 13 days' march away). In 71 BC it was the spot where 6,000 of Spartacus's troops were crucified during a slaves' revolt; it bore witness to the funeral processions of Sulla (78 BC) and Augustus (AD 14); it was the road along which St. Paul was marched as prisoner in AD 56; and close to the city walls was the point at which St. Peter (fleeing Rome) encountered Christ and, famously, asked him *"Domine, quo vadis?"* ("Lord, where are you going?").

MOSAICS

See Top 25 Sights for
SAN CLEMENTE ➤ 46
SAN GIOVANNI IN LATERANO ➤ 48
SANTA MARIA MAGGIORE ➤ 47
SANTA MARIA IN TRASTEVERE ➤ 28

Sant'Agnese (St. Agnes)

St. Agnes, who was martyred in Piazza Navona and buried near Sant'Agnese, was one of the most popular early Christian martyrs—despite the recorded fact that she failed to take a bath in the 13 years she was alive (such was her modesty). According to legend, this beautiful girl was martyred

Santa Prassede ceiling mosaics

for refusing to marry the son of a pagan governor of the city. As an earlier punishment she was thrown into a brothel, but as she was about to be paraded naked her hair grew miraculously to spare her blushes. St. Agnes' steadfastness made her a symbol of Christian chastity, and her tomb became a place of pilgrimage particularly venerated by Roman women.

SANT'AGNESE FUORI LE MURA

Compare the outstanding Byzantine 7th-century mosaics in the apse of Sant'Agnese with the earlier mosaics in Santa Costanza (see below). The church was built in AD 342 by Constantia to be close to the tomb of the martyred Sant'Agnese (see panel). Although they were rather clumsily restored in 1855, the mosaics have survived intact. They show Agnes, with the sword of her martyrdom at her feet, flanked by the church's 7th-century rebuilder Pope Honorius I.

➕ G3 ✉ Via Nomentana 349 ☎ 861 0840 🕐 Daily 8–12, 4–7:30 🚌 36, 36b, 37, 60, 136, 137 to Via Nomentana-Via di Santa Costanza 🎟 Free

SANTA COSTANZA

In this church, originally built as a mausoleum for Constantia and Helena (daughters of the Emperor Constantine), are exquisite 4th-century mosaics. Note their white background, in contrast to the gold in Byzantine work of later centuries. Note, too, the pagan icons adapted to Christian use—especially the lamb and peacock, symbols of innocence and immortality respectively.

➕ G3 ✉ Via Nomentana 349 ☎ 861 0840 🕐 Mon 9–12; Tue–Sat 9–12, 4–6; Sun 12–6 🚌 36, 36b, 37, 60, 136, 137 to Via Nomentana-Via di Santa Costanza 🎟 Cheap

SANTA MARIA IN DOMNICA AND SANTO STEFANO ROTONDO

Like those in Santa Prassede (➤ 59), the glorious mosaics in the apse of the 9th-century Santa Maria in Domnica were commissioned by Pope Paschal I, depicted at the foot of the Virgin and Child (his square halo indicates he was alive when the mosaic was created). Almost opposite this church is Santo Stefano Rotondo, with a 7th-century mosaic commemorating two martyrs buried nearby, and some eye-opening frescoes (see panel opposite).

➕ E7 ✉ Piazza della Navicella 1 and Via di Santo Stefano 7 ☎ Santa Maria: 700 1519. Santo Stefano: 7049 3717 🕐 Santa Maria: daily 8:30–12, 3:30–6. Santo Stefano: Oct–Mar Mon 2–4:30; Tue–Sat 9–1, 2–4:30. May–Jun, Sep Mon–Sat 9–1, 3:30–6. Jul–Aug Tue–Sat 9–12:30 🚌 15, 673 to Via della Navicella 🎟 Free

SANTA PRASSEDE

The treasure of this church is the stunning mosaic work commissioned by Pope Paschal I in 822 to decorate his mother's mausoleum in the Cappella di San Zeno. So beautiful were the mosaics that in the Middle Ages the gold-encrusted chapel became known as the Garden of Paradise. Similar Byzantine mosaics adorn the church's apse and triumphal arch.

🕂 E6 ✉ Via Santa Prassede 9a ☎ 488 2456 🕐 Daily 7:30–12, 4–6:30 🚌 11, 27 to Via Cavour-Piazza Esquilino 💵 Free

SANTA PUDENZIANA

Built in the 4th century (but much altered over the years), this church was reputedly raised over the house of the Roman senator Pudens, site of St. Peter's conversion of the senator's daughters, Pudenziana and Prassede (see above). Its prized apse mosaic dates from this period, an early Christian depiction of a golden-robed Christ, the Apostles, and two women presumed to be Prassede and Pudenziana.

🕂 hII, E5 ✉ Via Urbana 160 ☎ 481 4622 🕐 Apr–Sep daily 8–12, 3–6. Oct–Mar daily 3–6 🚇 Termini 🚌 70, 71 to Via A de Pretis, or 11, 27 to Via Cavour-Piazza Esquilino 💵 Free

SANTI COSMA E DAMIANO

This church is housed in part of the former Forum of Vespasian, one of the Imperial Fora, though its rebuilding in 1632 wiped out all but a few vestiges of its original classical and medieval splendor. Chief among the surviving treasures is the magnificent 6th-century Byzantine mosaic in the apse, *The Second Coming*, a work that influenced Roman and other mosaicists for centuries to come.

🕂 gIV, D6 ✉ Via dei Fori Imperiali ☎ 699 1540 🕐 Daily 8–1, 4–7 🚌 All routes to Piazza Venezia and 11, 27, 81, 85, 87, 186 to Via Fori dei Imperiali 💵 Free

Mosaics in Cappella di San Zeno, Santa Prassede

Santo Stefano's frescoes

"...hideous paintings...such a panorama of horror and butchery no man could imagine in his sleep, though he were to eat a whole pig, raw, for his supper. Grey-bearded men being boiled, fried, crimped, singed, eaten by wild beasts, worried by dogs, buried alive, torn asunder by horses, chopped up small with hatchets; women having their breasts torn off with iron pincers, their tongues cut out, their ears screwed off, their jaws broken, their bodies stretched on the rack, or skinned on the stake, or crackled up and melted in the fire —these are among the mildest subjects." Charles Dickens, *Pictures from Italy.*

Mosaics in Santa Prassede

CHURCHES

SANTA MARIA DELLA CONCEZIONE

Rome's most ghoulish sight lurks behind an unassuming façade in the unlikely surroundings of

Santa Maria in Cosmedin

the Via Vittorio Veneto. Lying in the crypt of Santa Maria della Concezione are the remains of 4,000 Capuchin monks, some still dressed in jaunty clothes, the bones of others crafted into macabre chandeliers and bizarre wall decorations. The bodies were originally buried in soil especially imported from Jerusalem. When this ran out they were left uncovered, a practice that continued until 1870. The church was built in 1624 by Cardinal Antonio Barberini, brother of Urban VIII, a Capuchin friar who lies buried before the main altar under a cheerful legend: *"hic jacet pulvis cinis et nihil"* ("here lie dust, ashes, and nothing"). The church is known for Guido Reni's painting *St. Michael Tempting the Devil*, in which the Devil is reputedly a portrait of the Pamphili Pope Innocent X.

✚ gI, E5 ✉ Via Vittorio Veneto 27 ☎ 487 1185 🕐 Church: daily 7–12, 4–7. Crypt (Cimitero dei Cappuccini): daily 9–12, 3–6 🚌 52, 53, 56, 58, 58b, 490, 495, and others to Via Vittorio Veneto 🚇 Church: free. Crypt: donation

La Bocca della Verità

The "Mouth of Truth" is a gaping marble mouth set in a stone face. Anyone suspected of lying—particularly a woman accused of adultery—would have his or her right hand forced into the maw. Legend claims that in the case of dissemblers the mouth would clamp shut and sever their fingers. To give credence to the story a priest supposedly hid behind the stone to hit the fingers of those known to be guilty.

SANTA MARIA IN COSMEDIN

This lovely old medieval church—one of the most atmospheric in the city—is best known for the Bocca della Verità (see panel), a weatherbeaten stone face (of the seagod Oceanus) once used by the ancient Romans as a drain cover. Inside, the church has a beautiful pavement, twin *ambos* (pulpits), a bishop's throne, and a stone choir screen, all decorated in fine Cosmati stone inlay. Most date from the 12th century, a little earlier than the impressive *baldacchino* (altar canopy), which was built by Deodato di Cosma in 1294. Tucked away in a small room off the right aisle is the mosaic *Adoration of the Magi*, almost all that remains of an 8th-century Greek church on the site.

✚ D7 ✉ Piazza Bocca della Verità ☎ 678 1419 🕐 Daily 9–12, 3–5 🚌 15, 23, 57, 90, 92, 94, 95, 160, 716 to Piazza Bocca della Verità 🚇 Free

ROME
where to...

EXPENSIVE RESTAURANTS

ALBERTO CIARLA
Among Rome's best fish restaurants, with a fine wine list. The food is elegantly presented, to go with the candlelight ambience and the impeccable service.
✚ C7 ✉ Piazza San Cosimato 40 ☎ 581 8668 🕐 Mon–Sat 12:30–3, 8:30–11:30; Sun 8:30–11:30. Closed 15 days in Aug, Christmas, and 15 days in Jan 🚌 44, 75, 170, 181, 280, 717 to Viale di Trastevere

CHECCHINO DAL 1887
Robust appetites are required for this menu. Quintessential Roman dishes relying largely on offal are its specialty. Booking recommended.
✚ C/D8 ✉ Via Monte Testaccio 30 ☎ 574 3816 🕐 Jun–Jul, Sep Tue–Sat 12:30–3, 8:30–11. Oct–May Tue–Sat 12:30–3, 8:30–11; Sun 12:30–3. Closed Aug and Christmas 🚌 13, 23, 27, 57, 95, 716 to Piramide and Via Marmorata

EL TOULÀ
Considered by many to be Rome's best restaurant, the food is inspired by a mixture of Venetian and international cuisine. Service is formal, in keeping with the traditional atmosphere.
✚ el, D5 ✉ Via della Lupa 29b ☎ 687 3498 🕐 Mon–Fri 1–3, 8–11; Sat 8–11PM. Closed Aug and Christmas 🚌 81, 90 to Via del Corso-Largo Carlo Goldini

IL CONVIVIO
The Troiani brothers from Italy's Marche region have created a tranquil little restaurant with a reputation for innovative and subtly flavored modern dishes.
✚ ell, C5 ✉ Via dell'Orso 44 ☎ 686 9432 🕐 Mon–Sat 1–2:30, 8–10:30. Closed May 🚌 70, 81, 90, 90b, 186 to Ponte Umberto-Lungotevere Marzio

LA ROSETTA
An exclusive fish and seafood restaurant whose popularity means booking is a must.
✚ ell, D5 ✉ Via della Rosetta 8–9 ☎ 6830 8841 🕐 Mon–Fri 1–3, 8–11:30; Sat 8–11:30. Closed 3 weeks in Aug and Christmas 🚌 119 to Piazza della Rotonda, or 70, 81, 87, 90 to Corso del Rinascimento

SABATINI
Once Rome's most famous restaurant, Sabatini is still favored for its reliable food and lovely setting, though prices are higher than the cooking deserves. Reservations essential.
✚ dIV, C6 ✉ Piazza Santa Maria in Trastevere 13 ☎ 581 2026.
✚ dIV, C6 ✉ Vicolo Santa Maria in Trastevere 18 ☎ 581 8307 🕐 Mon, Tue, Thu–Sun 12–2:30; 7:30–11. Closed Wed and Aug 🚌 44, 56, 60, 75, 170, 181, 280 to Piazza S. Sonnino

VECCHIA ROMA
In a pretty piazza and perfect for an alfresco meal on a summer evening. Though the 18th-century interior is also captivating, prices are high for what is only straightforward and reliable Roman cooking.
✚ fIV, D6 ✉ Piazza Campitelli 18 ☎ 686 4604 🕐 Mon, Tue, Thu–Sun 1–3, 8–11 🚌 44, 46, 56, 60, 75, 85, 87, 94 and all other services to Piazza Venezia

---

Change of career

According to a legend—whose origins are now some 25 years old—La Rosetta's famous owner, the Sicilian Carmelo Riccioli, abandoned a career as a boxer and a sports writer when he won this restaurant as payment for a bet.

MID-PRICE RESTAURANTS

AL 34

A popular restaurant, known for its Roman and southern Italian-based cooking, and its romantic and candelit intimacy. Close to Via Condotti and the Spanish Steps. Reservation recommended.

fl, D5 ⊠ Via Mario de' Fiori 34 ☎ 679 5091 ⏰ Tue–Sun 12:30–3, 7:30–11. Closed 3 weeks in Aug Ⓜ Spagna 🚌 119

AL MORO

Fellini's favorite restaurant in the 1960s. A rambunctious, busy trattoria near the Fontana di Trevi (in an alley off Via delle Muratte) with close tables and good traditional cooking. Reservation essential.

fII, D5 ⊠ Vicolo delle Bollette 13 ☎ 678 3495 ⏰ Mon–Sat 1–3:30, 8–11:30. Closed Aug 🚌 56, 60, 62, 85, 90, 160 to Via del Corso

NERONE

A small, friendly, old-fashioned trattoria just a few steps north of the Colosseum that is best known for its buffet of antipasti and simple Abruzzese cooking. Has a handful of outside tables.

hIV, E6 ⊠ Via delle Terme di Tito 96 ☎ 474 5207 ⏰ Mon– Sat 12:30–2:30, 7:30–10:30. Closed Aug 🚌 11, 13, 27, 30, 81, 85, 87, 186 to Piazza del Colosseo

PAPÀ GIOVANNI

Currently among the city's best restaurants, with light and often innovative cooking— and prices higher than they are at some other mid-price choices. Located off Corso del Rinascimento.

eIII, C5 ⊠ Via dei Sediari 4 ☎ 686 5308 ⏰ Mon–Sat 1–3, 8–11. Closed Sun and Aug 🚌 70, 81, 87, 90 to Corso del Rinascimento

PARIS

An extremely popular and elegant little restaurant located just south of Piazza Santa Maria in Trastevere, and known for its fish, pastas, and the quality of its Roman-based cooking. Outside tables for alfresco dining. Reservations are essential.

dIV, C7 ⊠ Piazza San Callisto 7a ☎ 581 5378 ⏰ Tue–Sat 12:30–3, 8–11; Sun 12:30–3. Closed 3 weeks in Aug 🚌 44, 56, 60, 75, 170, 181, 280, 717 to Piazza S. Sonnino

ROMOLO

A long-established fixture in Trastevere, housed in what was reputedly the home of Raphael's model and mistress, the "Fornarina" (baker's daughter). An outside courtyard is candlelit for dinner.

dIV, C7 ⊠ Via Porta Settimiana 8 ☎ 581 8284 ⏰ Tue–Sun 12:30–2:30, 7:30–11:30. Closed 3 weeks in Aug 🚌 23, 65, 280 to Lungotevere Farnesina

Expect to pay L40,000–75,000 per person, with wine, for a meal in a mid-price restaurant.

Roman specialties

Roman favorites— though they are by no means confined to the city— include pastas like *bucatini all'Amatriciana* (tomato sauce, salt pork, and chilli peppers); *spaghetti alla carbonara* (egg, bacon, pepper, and cheese); and *gnocchi alla Romana* (small potato or semolina dumplings with tomato or butter). The best-known main course is *saltimbocca alla Romana* (veal escalopes with ham and sage, cooked in wine and butter). Less familiar perhaps to tourists but nevertheless traditional are *trippa* (tripe), *cervelli* (brains) and *coda alla vaccinara* (oxtail).

BUDGET RESTAURANTS

Meals in a budget restaurant may cost anything up to L40,000 per person, with wine.

The menu

Starters are called *antipasti*; first course (soup, pasta, or risotto) is *il primo*; and main meat and fish dishes are *il secondo*. Salads (*insalata*) and vegetables (*contorni*) are ordered (and often eaten) separately. Desserts are *dolci*, with cheese (*formaggio*) or fruit (*frutta*) to follow. If no menu card is offered, ask for *la lista* or *il menù*. A set-price menu (*un menù turistico*) may seem good value, but portions are small and the food is invariably poor—usually just spaghetti with a tomato sauce, followed by a piece of chicken and fruit.

AUGUSTO

One of the last remaining cheap and authentic family-run trattorias in Trastevere.
☩ dIV, C6 ⊠ Piazza de' Renzi 15 ☎ 580 3798 ⏰ Mon–Sat 1–3:30, 8–11. Closed Aug 🚌 23, 65, 280 to Lungotevere Sanzio, or 44, 56, 60, 75, 170 to Piazza S. Sonnino

BIRRERIA FRATELLI TEMPERA

Ideal for a simple lunch or early evening meal. Original art nouveau interior and a large and easy-going beer-hall atmosphere. Especially busy at lunchtimes.
☩ fII, D5 ⊠ Via di San Marcello 19 ☎ 678 6203 ⏰ Mon–Sat 12:30–2:45, 7:30–11 🚌 44, 46, 64, 75, 85, 87, 94 and all other buses to Piazza Venezia

DA LUCIA

Tiny and basic Trastevere hideaway. The Roman atmosphere and local cooking are first rate. Outdoor tables.
☩ dIV, C6 ⊠ Via del Mattonato 2b ☎ 580 3601 ⏰ Tue–Sun 12:30–2:30, 7:30–11. Closed 3 weeks in Aug 🚌 23, 65, 280 to Lungotevere Farnesina, or 44, 56, 60, 75, 170 to Piazza S. Sonnino

DA VALENTINO

A tiny, old-fashioned Roman trattoria close to the Forum.
☩ hIII, E6 ⊠ Via Cavour 293 ☎ 488 1303 ⏰ Mon–Thu, Sat, Sun 12–3, 7–10 🚇 Cavour 🚌 11, 27, 81 to Via Cavour, or 85, 87, 186 to Via dei Fori Imperiali

FIASCHETTERIE BELTRAMME DA CESARETTO

Housed in a historical monument, and with a fine outside courtyard. Inside, shared tables have a bustling atmosphere. Convenient to the Spanish Steps.
☩ fI, D5 ⊠ Via della Croce 39 ⏰ Mon–Sat 12:15–3, 7:30–11. Closed 2 weeks in Aug 🚇 Spagna 🚌 119 to Piazza di Spagna, or 81, 90 to Via del Corso

FILETTI DI BACCALÀ

At this tiny place with Formica tables, filets of cod (and little else) are washed down with plenty of beer or crisp local wine. Close to Campo de' Fiori.
☩ eIII, C6 ⊠ Largo dei Librari ⏰ Mon–Sat 12:30–2:30, 7–10:30 🚌 44, 56, 60, 65, 75, 170, 181, 710, 718, 719 to Via Arenula

GRAPPOLO D'ORO

This unspoilt Roman trattoria has been a favorite for decades with locals and foreign residents. The menu features *pasta all'amatriciana* and *scaloppine* any way you want them.
☩ eIII, C6 ⊠ Piazza della Cancelleria 80 ☎ 689 7080 ⏰ Mon–Sat. Closed Aug 🚌 46, 62, 64 to Corso Vittorio Emanuele II

MARIO ALLA VITE

Simple Tuscan cooking. Crowded and slightly chaotic, but conveniently located near the Via Condotti and the Spanish Steps.
☩ fI, D5 ⊠ Via della Vite 55 ☎ 678 3818 ⏰ Mon–Sat 12:30–3, 7:30–11. Closed Aug 🚇 Spagna 🚌 119 to Piazza di Spagna

PIZZERIAS

BAFFETTO ($)

Rome's most famous pizzeria. A tiny, hole-in-the-wall classic that has retained its atmosphere and low prices despite its fame. Expect lines.

🖬 dll, C5 ⊠ Via del Governo Vecchio 11 ☎ 686 1617 🕔 Mon–Sat 6:30PM–12:45AM 🚍 46, 62, 64 to Corso Vittorio Emanuele II

CORALLO ($)

Rather up-scale, this popular and occasionally chaotic pizzeria is convenient to Piazza Navona. Full meals are also available.

🖬 dll, C5 ⊠ Via del Corallo 10, off Via del Governo Vecchio ☎ 6830 7703 🕔 Tue–Sun 7:30PM–1:30AM. Closed 1 week in Aug 🚍 46, 62, 64 to Corso Vittorio Emanuele II

DA VITTORIO ($)

Tiny Neapolitan-run Trastevere pizzeria that makes a good standby if Ivo is busy.

🖬 C7 ⊠ Via di San Cosimato 14a, off Piazza San Callisto ☎ 580 0353 🚍 44, 56, 60, 75, 170, 181, 280, 717 to Viale di Trastevere

EST! EST! EST! ($)

Among the oldest pizzerias in Rome; worth the slight walk if you are around Stazione Termini.

🖬 hlll, E5 ⊠ Via Genova 32 ☎ 488 1107 🕔 Tue–Sun 6:30–11:30PM. Closed Aug 🚇 Repubblica 🚍 57, 64, 65, 70, 71, 75, 170 to Via Nazionale

IVO ($)

The best-known and most authentic of Trastevere's pizzerias.

Lines are common but turnover is quick.

🖬 C7 ⊠ Via di San Francesco a Ripa 158 ☎ 581 7082 🕔 Mon, Wed–Sun 7PM–1AM. Closed 3 weeks in Aug 🚍 44, 56, 60, 75, 170, 181, 280, 717 to Viale di Trastevere

LA CAPRICCIOSA ($)

Reputedly the birthplace of the *capricciosa* pizza. A full restaurant service complements the pizzeria (though pizzas are available only at dinner). Boasts a roomy, rather stylish dining room, plus a terrace for alfresco eating.

🖬 fI, D5 ⊠ Largo dei Lombardi 8, Via del Corso ☎ 687 8480 🕔 Mon, Wed–Sun 12:15AM–3PM, 7PM–12:30AM. Closed 3 weeks in Aug 🚇 Spagna 🚍 81, 90, 119 to Via del Corso-Via della Croce

LEONCINO ($)

Nothing has changed in the wonderful old-fashioned interior for over 30 years. Authentic food and atmosphere. Expect a line. Open at lunch.

🖬 fI, D5 ⊠ Via del Leoncino 28, Piazza San Lorenzo in Lucina ☎ 687 6306 🕔 Mon–Fri 1–2:30PM, 7PM–12; Sat 7PM–12 🚇 Spagna 🚍 81, 90, 119 to Via del Corso-Via Tomacelli

PANATTONI ($)

Big, bright, and often busy place known locally as L'Obitorio ("The Morgue") on account of its cold marble tables. Seating also outside on Viale di Trastevere.

🖬 eIV, C7 ⊠ Viale di Trastevere 53 ☎ 580 0919 🕔 Mon, Tue, Thu–Sun 6:30PM–2AM. Closed 3 weeks in Aug 🚍 44, 56, 60, 75, 170, 181, 280, 717 to Viale di Trastevere

The check

The check is *il conto* and usually includes extras such as service (*servizio*). Iniquitous cover charges (*pane e coperto*) have recently been outlawed, but some restaurants still try to get round the new regulations. Only pay for bread (*pane*) if you have asked for it. Proper checks—not a scrawled piece of paper—must be given by law. If you receive a scrap of paper—and you are more likely to in a pizzeria—and have doubts about the total be sure to ask for a proper receipt (*una fattura* or *una ricevuta*).

ETHNIC & INTERNATIONAL RESTAURANTS

Unusual waitresses

You are served at the L'Eau Vive by nuns from a Third World order known as the Vergini Laiche Cristiane di Azione Cattolica Missionaria per Mezzo del Lavoro (Christian Virgins of Catholic Missionary Action though Work). With restaurants in several parts of the world, their aim is to spread the message of Christianity through the medium of French food. To this end dining is interrupted by prayers each evening at 9PM.

AFRICA ($)

A long-established restaurant close to Termini catering mainly to Rome's Ethiopian and Eritrean population.
🎯 F5 ✉ Via Gaeta 26 ☎ 494 1077 ⏰ Tue–Sun 9AM–1PM. Closed 2 weeks in Aug 🚌 38, 57, 319 to Via Volturno and all buses to Termini

BIRRERIA VIENNESE ($)

An authentic Austrian beer house with a wide range of beers and Austro-German specialties.
🎯 fl, D5 ✉ Via della Croce 21 ☎ 679 5569 ⏰ Mon, Tue, Thu–Sun 11:30–4, 6–12 🚇 Spagna 🚌 81, 90 to Via del Corso, or 119 to Piazza di Spagna

CHARLY'S SAUCIÈRE ($$)

Well-established restaurant offering reliable French and Swiss staples in a cozy setting.
🎯 hIV, F7 ✉ Via di San Giovanni in Laterano 270 ☎ 7049 5666 ⏰ Mon–Sat 8PM–midnight. Closed 2 weeks in Aug 🚌 85 to Via San Giovanni in Laterano

GEORGE'S ($$$)

One of the city's leading restaurants, established 50 years ago, though its splendor of its *dolce vita* heyday is now slightly faded. Good but rarely exceptional French, Italian and international cuisine. Polished service and a refined and elegant ambience. Jacket, tie, and reservations essential.
🎯 E4 ✉ Via Marche 7 ☎ 474 5204 ⏰ Mon–Sat 12:30–3, 7:30PM–1AM. Closed Aug 🚇 Spagna 🚌 52, 53, 56, 58, 95 to Via Vittorio Veneto

GIGGETTO ($)

A famous Romano-Jewish restaurant in the Ghetto district, which comes a close (and slightly cheaper) second to the Piperno.
🎯 flV, D6 ✉ Via Portico d'Ottavia 21a ☎ 686 1105 ⏰ Tue–Sun 12:30–2:30, 7:30–10:30 🚌 44, 56, 60, 65, 75, 170, 181, 710, 718, 719 to Via Arenula

L'EAU VIVE ($$–$$$)

A pleasantly bizarre dining experience. The (predominantly) French food is served by nuns (see panel). Politicians, celebrities, and locals alike all come to enjoy the food, the ambience, and the beautiful 16th-century frescoed dining rooms.
🎯 elII, D6 ✉ Via Monterone 85 ☎ 654 1095 or 6880 1095 ⏰ Mon–Sat 12:30–3:30, 7:30–10. Closed first week of Aug 🚌 44, 46, 56, 60, 61, 64, 65, 70, 75, 81, 87, 90, 170 to Largo di Torre Argentina

PIPERNO ($$)

Much Roman cuisine is based on the city's extensive Jewish culinary traditions. The famous and resolutely traditional Piperno has been a temple to Romano-Jewish cuisine for over a century. Be sure to book well ahead.
🎯 elV, D6 ✉ Via Monte de' Cenci 9 ☎ 6880 6629 or 6880 2772 ⏰ Tue–Sat 12:15–2:30, 8–10:30; Sun 12:15–3. Closed Aug, Christmas and Easter 🚌 44, 56, 60, 65, 75, 170, 181, 710, 718, 719 to Via Arenula

GELATERIE

ALBERTO PICA

Only 20 flavors, but of excellent quality; try the house specialties like green apple (*mele verde*) and Sicilian citrus (*agrumi di Sicilia*).

🔲 elV, C6 ✉ Via della Seggiola 12 (off Via Arenula opposite Piazza Cenci) ☎ 687 5990 🕔 Mon–Sat 8AM–1:30AM 🚌 44, 56, 60, 65, 75, 170, 181, 710, 718, 719 to Via Arenula

DA MIRELLA

Sells *granita*: crushed ice drenched in juice or syrup. In this kiosk, the flavorings are based on years of experience; the ice is still hand ground.

🔲 elV, D6 ✉ Lungotevere Anguillara, Ponte Cestio 🕔 Daily 8AM–late 🚌 23, 717, 774, 780

GELATERIA DELLA PALMA

A big, brash place behind the Pantheon. Cakes and chocolates, plus over 100 flavors of ice cream—many of them wild and wonderful.

🔲 ell, D5 ✉ Via della Maddalena 20 ☎ 654 0752 🕔 Thu–Tue noon–midnight 🚌 119 to Piazza della Rotonda

GIOLITTI

For years Giolitti was the king of Roman ice cream. Standards have slipped slightly, but the ice cream, coffee, and cakes are still of excellent value.

🔲 fII, D5 ✉ Via Uffici del Vicario 40 ☎ 699 1243 🕔 Tue–Fri, Sun 7AM–12:30AM; Sat 7AM–2AM 🚌 119 to Piazza della Rotonda, or 52, 53, 56, 60, 62, 81, 85, 90, 160 to Via del Corso

LA FONTE DELLA SALUTE

At the so-called "Fount of Health", ice creams are made with fresh cream, sugar, eggs, and other far from healthy ingredients.

🔲 C7 ✉ Via Cardinale Marmaggi 2–6 🕔 Tue–Sun 8AM–10PM 🚌 44, 56, 60, 75, 170, 181, 280 to Viale di Trastevere

PREMIATE GELATERIE FANTASIA

A good port of call near the church of San Giovanni in Laterano.

🔲 G7 ✉ Via La Spezia 100–2 🕔 Mon–Sat 8AM–11PM 🚌 San Giovanni 🚌 4, 13, 16, 30, 81, 85, 87 to Piazzale Appio

SACCHETTI

Family-run bar also good for cakes and pastries.

🔲 C7 ✉ Piazza San Cosimato 61–2 ☎ 581 5374 🕔 Tue–Sun 5AM–11PM 🚌 44, 75, 170, 181, 280, 717 to Viale di Trastevere

SAN FILIPPO

This quiet-looking bar in Parioli is for many the best *gelateria* in the city. Zabaglione is emperor of the 60-odd flavors.

🔲 E2 ✉ Via di Villa San Filippo 8–10 ☎ 807 9314 🕔 Tue–Sun 7:30AM–midnight 🚌 3, 19, 30, 53, 168 to Piazza Ungheria, or 4 to Via di Villa San Filippo

TRE SCALINI

Tre Scalini is celebrated for its chocolate-studded *tartufo*, the ultimate in chocolate chip ice cream.

🔲 ell, C5 ✉ Piazza Navona 28–32 ☎ 6880 1996 🕔 Thu–Tue 8AM–1AM 🚌 70, 81, 87, 90, 186, 492 to Corso del Rinascimento

Buying ice cream

Ice cream (*gelato*) in a proper *gelateria* is sold either in a cone (*un cono*) or a paper cup (*una coppa*). Specify which you want and then decide how much you wish to pay: sizes of cone and cup go up in lire bands, usually starting small and ending enormous. You can choose up to two or three flavors (more in bigger tubs) and will usually be asked if you want a swirl of cream (*panna*) to round things off.

BARS BY DAY

Bar etiquette

You almost always pay a premium to sit down (inside or outside) and to enjoy the privilege of waiter service in Roman bars. If you stand— which is cheaper— the procedure is to pay for what you want first at the cash-desk (*la cassa*). You then take your receipt (*lo scontrino*) to the bar and repeat your order (a tip slapped down on the bar will work wonders in attracting the bar-person's attention). Pastry shops, cafés, and ice cream parlors often double as excellent all-around bars to be enjoyed during the day. They include Giolitti and Tre Scalini (➤ 67), and Camilloni, Sant'Eustachio, and Bernasconi (➤ 69).

ALEMAGNA
This big century-old bar has a huge and varied passing trade. Good self-service selection of hot and cold food.
➕ fl, D5 ⊠ Via del Corso 181 ☎ 678 9135 ⏰ Mon–Sat 7:30AM–11PM 🚇 Spagna 🚌 119 to Piazza Augusto Imperatore

BAR DELLA PACE
Extremely trendy, but quieter by day, when you can sit outside or enjoy the mirror-and-mahogany 19th-century interior.
➕ ell, C5 ⊠ Via della Pace 3, off Piazza Navona ☎ 686 1216 ⏰ Daily 9AM–2AM 🚌 70, 81, 87, 90, 186, 492 to Corso del Rinascimento

CANOVA
Canova is pricier and less atmospheric than Rosati, though its sunny outside tables provide a welcome pause for the feet.
➕ D4 ⊠ Piazza del Popolo 16 ☎ 361 2231 ⏰ Daily 7:30AM– 12:30AM 🚇 Flaminio or Spagna 🚌 119 to Piazza del Popolo

CASINA VALADIER
Join the chatting Roman matrons and their dogs on the terrace bar of this neoclassical folly overlooking the city.
➕ D4 ⊠ Piazzale Napoleone, Viale Valadier, Pincio ☎ 6992 0264 ⏰ Tue–Sat 10AM–noon, 8–midnight 🚇 Spagna 🚌 119 to Piazza del Popolo

CIAMPINI
You can sit here for hours facing Bernini's Fontana dei Quattro Fiumi (➤ 54), but watch the prices.
➕ ell, C5 ⊠ Piazza Navona 94–100 ☎ 686 1547

⏰ Tue–Sun 8:30AM–12:30AM 🚌 46, 62, 64 to Corso Vittorio Emanuele II or 70, 81, 87, 90, 186, 492 to Corso del Rinascimento

DONEY
Most of the bars famous in the *dolce vita* days of the 1950s are now tacky and expensive. Doney, however, is as tasteful and inviting as ever.
➕ gl, E5 ⊠ Via Vittorio Veneto 145 ☎ 482 1788 ⏰ Tue–Sat 8AM–1AM 🚇 Barberini 🚌 52, 53, 56, 58, 95 to Via Vittorio Veneto

LATTERIA DEL GALLO
Old-fashioned, with original marble tables and 1940s décor. Try the big, sticky cakes and steaming bowls of hot chocolate.
➕ dll, C6 ⊠ Vicolo del Gallo 4 ☎ 686 5091 ⏰ Thu–Tue 8:30–2, 5–midnight 🚌 46, 62, 64 to Corso Vittorio Emanuele II

ROSATI
Wonderful coffee, cocktails, cakes and pastries (from 70-year-old ovens), and a glittering 1922 art nouveau interior.
➕ D4 ⊠ Piazza del Popolo 5 ☎ 322 5859 ⏰ Nov–Mar Wed–Mon 7:30AM–midnight. Apr–Oct daily 7:30AM–midnight 🚇 Flaminio or Spagna 🚌 119 to Piazza del Popolo

TRASTÈ
This trendy tea and coffee shop in Trastevere also serves light meals. People come to chat, read newspapers, and lounge away the time.
➕ elV, C6 ⊠ Via della Lungaretta 76 ☎ 589 4430 ⏰ Daily 4PM–1AM 🚌 44, 56, 60, 75, 170, 181, 280, 717 to Piazza S. Sonnino

CAFFÈ & PASTICCERIE

ANTICO CAFFÈ BRASILE

Beans and ground coffee are sold from vast sacks; there is also a superb variety of coffees at the bar. Try the "Pope's blend": John Paul II bought his coffee here before becoming pontiff.

✚ hlll, E6 ⊠ Via dei Serpenti 23 ☎ 488 2319 ⏰ Mon–Sat 6:30AM–8:30PM 🚌 57, 64, 65, 70, 75, 81, 170 to Via Nazionale

BABINGTON'S TEA ROOMS

Only the well-heeled and tourists visit Babington's, established by a pair of English spinsters in 1896. Prices are sky-high, but the tea (although not the cakes) is the best in Rome.

✚ fl, D5 ⊠ Piazza di Spagna 23 ☎ 678 6027 ⏰ Wed–Mon 9AM–8PM Ⓜ Spagna 🚌 119 to Piazza di Spagna

BERNASCONI

Famous and central. All Rome seems to congregate here on Sunday after church to drink coffee and buy cakes for Sunday lunch.

✚ elll, D6 ⊠ Largo di Torre Argentina 15 ☎ 679 2371 ⏰ Mon–Sat 6AM–1PM 🚌 44, 46, 56, 60, 61, 64, 65, 70, 75, 81, 87, 90, 170, 492, 710 to Largo di Torre Argentina

CAFFÈ GRECO

Rome's most famous and historic (but no longer its best) coffee shop, founded in 1767. Plush and atmospheric.

✚ fl, D4 ⊠ Via Condotti 86 ☎ 678 2554 ⏰ Mon–Sat 8AM–9PM Ⓜ Spagna 🚌 119 to Piazza di Spagna, or 52, 53, 58, 61, 71, 85, 160 to Piazza San Silvestro

CAMILLONI

A long-time rival to Sant'Eustachio, with whom it shares a piazza.

✚ ell, D5 ⊠ Piazza Sant'Eustachio 54 ☎ 271 6068 ⏰ Tue–Sun 8AM–9PM 🚌 119 to Piazza della Rotonda, or 70, 81, 87, 90, 186, 492 to Corso del Rinascimento

DAGNINO

Not even the customers have changed in this superb 1950s *pasticceria*, famous for Sicilian specialties, lemon water ices, and fine ice cream.

✚ hl, E5 ⊠ Galleria Esedra, Via V. E. Orlando 75 ☎ 481 8660 ⏰ Mon–Fri, Sun 7:30AM–10:30PM Ⓜ Spagna 🚌 57, 64, 65, 75, 170, 492, 910 to Piazza della Repubblica

KRECHEL

Fine, expensive cakes and chocolates in an upscale shopping street.

✚ fl, D5 ⊠ Via Frattina 134 ☎ 678 0946 ⏰ Mon–Sat 8:30AM–8:30PM Ⓜ Spagna 🚌 119 to Piazza di Spagna

LA TAZZA D'ORO

The "Cup of Gold" sells only coffee, and probably the city's best espresso.

✚ ell, D5 ⊠ Via degli Orfani 84 ☎ 678 9792 ⏰ Mon–Sat 7AM–8PM 🚌 119 to Piazza della Rotonda, or 70, 81, 87, 90, 186, 492 to Corso del Rinascimento

SANT'EUSTACHIO

A rival of Tazza d'Oro for the best cup of coffee, and with a welcoming interior; tables outside.

✚ ell, D5 ⊠ Piazza Sant'Eustachio 82 ☎ 686 1309 ⏰ Tue–Sun 8:30AM–1AM 🚌 119 to Piazza della Rotonda, or 70, 81, 87, 90, 186, 492 to Corso del Rinascimento

Breakfast and coffee

Breakfast in Rome consists of a sweet and sometimes cream-filled croissant (*un cornetto* or *brioche*) washed down with a cappuccino or the longer and milkier *caffè latte*. At other times espresso, a short kick-start of caffeine, is the coffee of choice (Italians never drink cappuccino after lunch or dinner).

Decaffeinated coffee is *caffè Hag*, iced coffee *caffè freddo*, and American-style coffee (long and watery) *caffè Americano*. Other varieties include *caffè corretto* (with a dash of grappa or brandy) and *caffè macchiato* (espresso "stained" with a dash of milk).

SHOES

Shopping areas

Although Rome's individual neighborhoods boast their own butchers, bakers, and corner shops (*alimentari*), most of the city's quality and specialty shops are concentrated in specific areas. Via Condotti and its surrounding grid of streets (Via Frattina, Via Borgognana, and Via Bocca di Leone) contain most of the big names in men's and women's fashion, accessories, jewelry and luxury goods. In nearby Via del Babuino and Via Margutta the emphasis is on top-price antiques, paintings, sculpture, and modern glassware and lighting. Via della Croce, which runs south from Piazza di Spagna, is known for its food shops, while Via del Corso, which bisects the northern half of central Rome, is home to inexpensive mid-range clothes, shoes, and accessories stores. Similarly, inexpensive stores can be found along Via del Tritone and Via Nazionale. Nice areas to browse for antiques, even if you are not buying, include Via Giulia, Via dei Coronari, Via dell'Orso, Via dei Soldati, and Via del Governo Vecchio.

BATA

A well-known and respected chain devoted predominantly to casual footwear. It also sells children's shoes.

🚇 gl, D5 ✉ Via dei Due Macelli 45 ☎ 679 1570 🕐 Tue–Sat 9:30–7:30; Mon 3:30–7:30

BELTRAMI

One of Rome's most impressive-looking shops, Beltrami is a name fabled for its superlative shoes and leather bags.

🚇 fl, D5 ✉ Via Condotti 18–19 ☎ 679 1330 🕐 Mon–Sat 10–7:30

BRUNO MAGLI

A middle- to up-scale chain with a choice of classic styles.

🚇 fl, D5 ✉ Via Barberini 94 ☎ 486 850. 🚇 gl, E5 ✉ Via Vittorio Veneto 70a ☎ 488 4355. 🚇 C4 ✉ Via Cola di Rienzo 237 ☎ 324 1759 🕐 Tue–Sat 9:30–7:30; Mon 1–7:30

CAMPANILE

This shop, in chic Via Condotti, is dedicated to the most elegant (and expensive) shoes and styles.

🚇 fl, D5 ✉ Via Condotti 58 ☎ 678 3041 🕐 Tue–Sat 9:30–7:30; Mon 3:30–7:30

FAUSTO SANTINI

An iconoclastic designer whose witty, innovative and occasionally bizarre shoes are aimed at the young and daring.

🚇 fl, D5 ✉ Via Frattina 122 ☎ 678 4114 🕐 Tue–Sat 10–7:30; Mon 3:30–7:30

FERRAGAMO

A long-established family firm and probably Italy's best-known shoe store, though branches grace exclusive shopping streets the world over.

🚇 fl, D5 ✉ Via Condotti 73–4 ☎ 679 1565. 🚇 fl, D5 ✉ Via Condotti 66 ☎ 678 1130 🕐 Tue–Sat 10–7; Mon 3–7:30

FRATELLI ROSSETTI

This family company, founded 30 years ago by the brothers Renzo and Renato, pushes Ferragamo hard for the title of Italy's best shoe store. Classic and current styles at slightly lower prices than its rival.

🚇 fl, D5 ✉ Via Borgognona 5a ☎ 678 2676 🕐 Tue–Sat 9:30–7:30; Mon 3:30–7:30

MARIO VALENTINO

Exquisitely made shoes from this Rome-based Neapolitan designer. Also leather clothing, bags, and accessories.

🚇 fl, D5 ✉ Via Frattina 84 ☎ 679 1246 🕐 Tue–Sat 9:30–7:30; Mon 3–7:30

POLLINI

Up-to-the-minute boots and bags in lively styles for men and women.

🚇 fl, D5 ✉ Via Frattina 22–4 ☎ 678 9028 🕐 Tue–Sat 10–1, 3–7:30; Mon 3–7:30

RAPHAEL SALATO

None of Rome's cobblers comes cheap, and Salato's sublimely crafted shoes are no exception. More individual than the likes of Ferragamo.

🚇 gl, E5 ✉ Via Vittorio Veneto 149 ☎ 482 1816. 🚇 fl, D5 ✉ Piazza di Spagna 34 ☎ 679 5646 🕐 Tue–Sat 9:30–7:30; Mon 3:30–7:30

ACCESSORIES & LEATHER GOODS

BELTRAMI
Finest-quality shoes and leather goods, particularly bags, are the mainstay of this famous and decadently decorated shop in the heart of Rome's premier shopping district.

🕂 fl, D5 ⌧ Via Condotti 18–19 ☎ 679 1330 🕔 Mon–Sat 10–7:30

BORSALINO
This shop is on one of the city's less exclusive shopping streets, but is still the first port of call if you are looking to buy a hat in Rome.

🕂 gIII, D6 ⌧ Via IV Novembre 157b ☎ 679 4192 🕔 Mon–Sat 9–8

CALZA E CALZE
A cornucopia of socks, stockings, and tights in every color and style imaginable.

🕂 fl, D5 ⌧ Via della Croce 78 🕔 Tue–Sat 9:30–1, 3:30–7:30; Mon 3:30–7:30

FENDI
A famous family-run high-fashion name whose burgeoning Via Borgognana shop deals in both clothes and fine leather goods.

🕂 fl, D5 ⌧ Via Borgognona 36a–39 ☎ 679 7641 🕔 Mon–Sat 10–2, 3–7:30

GUCCI
Recovering from the turmoil of the 1980s, when tax problems and family feuds threatened to destroy the business, this famous family name is once more in the ascendant. Expensive and high-quality bags, shoes and leather goods are a feature of this elegant shop.

🕂 fl, D5 ⌧ Via Condotti 8 ☎ 678 9340 🕔 Tue–Sat 10–2, 3–7; Mon 3–7

MEROLA
Specializes in a wide range of highly priced gloves and scarves.

🕂 fl, D5 ⌧ Via del Corso 143 ☎ 679 1961 🕔 Tue–Sat 9:30–7:30; Mon 3:30–7:30

SERGIO DI CORI
Romans in search of gloves know they need look no further than this shop, which is devoted to almost nothing else.

🕂 fl, D5 ⌧ Piazza di Spagna 53 ☎ 678 4439 🕔 Tue–Sat 9:30–7:30; Mon 1–7:30

SERMONETA
Specializes in gloves, though it is not as famous as its nearby rival, Sergio di Cori.

🕂 fl, D5 ⌧ Piazza di Spagna 61 ☎ 679 1960 🕔 Tue–Sat 9:30–7:30; Mon 3:30–7:30

SIRNI
Exquisite artisan-made bags and briefcases crafted on the premises are the great attraction of this shop.

🕂 D5 ⌧ Via della Stelletta 33 ☎ 6880 5248 🕔 Tue–Sat 9:30–1:30, 3:30–7:30; Mon 3:30–7:30

VALEXTRA
This shop, close to Piazza di Spagna, sells a wide range of traditional bags, briefcases, and other leather goods.

🕂 D4 ⌧ Via del Babuino 94 ☎ 679 2323 🕔 Mon 3–7; Tue–Sat 10–2, 3–7

Jewelry
Jewelry, and lots of it, is a key part of any Roman woman's wardrobe. Gold, in particular, is popular, and is still worked in small artisan's studios in the Jewish Ghetto, around Via Giulia and Campo de' Fiori and on Via dei Coronari, Via dell'Orso, and Via del Pellegrino. For striking costume jewelry try Delettré (⌧ Via Fontanella Borghese) or Bozart (⌧ Via Bocca di Leone 4). For a more traditional look visit Massoni (⌧ Largo Carlo Goldoni 48), founded in 1790, or Petocchi (⌧ Piazza di Spagna), jewelers to Italy's former royal family from 1861 to 1946. For the purchase of a lifetime, visit the most famous of Italian jewelers, Bulgari, whose shop at Via Condotti 10 is one of the most splendid in the city.

FOOD & WINE

Local shopping

Roman supermarkets are few and far between (see panel opposite) and most shopping for food is still done in tiny neighborhood shops known as *alimentari*. Every street of every "village" or district in the city has one or more of these general stores, a source of everything from olive oil and pasta to candles and corn treatments. They are also good places to buy picnic provisions—many sell bread and wine—and most have a delicatessen counter that will make you a sandwich (*panino*) from the meats and cheeses on display. For something a little more upscale, or for food gifts to take home, visit the shops on Via della Croce, a street that is particularly renowned for its wonderful delicatessens.

AI MONASTERI
This unusual, large and rather dark old shop sells the products of seven Italian monasteries, from honeys, wines, natural preserves, and liqueurs to herbal cures and elixirs.
✚ ell, C5 ✉ Piazza Cinque Lune 76 ☎ 6880 2783 🕐 Mon–Wed, Fri, Sat 9–1, 4:40–7:30; Thu 9–1. Closed first week of Sep

CASTRONI
Castroni boasts Rome's largest selection of imported delicacies, a mouth-watering array of Italian specialties and an outstanding range of coffees.
✚ C4 ✉ Via Cola di Rienzo 196 ☎ 687 4383 🕐 Mon–Sat 8–8

CATENA
Founded in 1928 this luxury food store sells Italian hams, cheeses, coffees, regional delicacies, and vintage wines and liqueurs.
✚ F7 ✉ Via Appia Nuova 9 ☎ 7049 1664 🕐 Tue–Sat 9:30–1, 3:30–7:30; Mon 3:30–7:30

ENOTECA BUCCONE
Rome's most select and best-stocked wine shop occupies a 17th-century coach house.
✚ D4 ✉ Via di Ripetta 19–20 ☎ 361 2154 🕐 Mon–Sat 9–1:30, 4–8:30. Closed Aug

ENOTECA AL GOCCETTO
Wines from all over Italy are sold in this old bishop's palazzo, complete with original floors and wooden ceiling.
✚ dll, C5 ✉ Via dei Banchi Vecchi 14 ☎ 686 4268 🕐 Mon–Sat 10:30–1:30, 5–9

PIETRO FRANCHI
A rival to nearby Castroni for the title of Rome's "best delicatessen." Offers a selection of regional food and wines, and dishes to take out—anything from cold *antipasti* to succulent roast meats.
✚ C4 ✉ Via Cola di Rienzo 204 ☎ 686 4576 🕐 Mon–Sat 8AM–9PM

ROFFI ISABELLI
A beautiful old-fashioned shop where you can buy wine by the bottle or sip it by the glass amid trickling fountains and marble-topped tables.
✚ fl, D5 ✉ Via della Croce 76b ☎ 679 0896 🕐 Daily 11AM–midnight

SALUMERIA FOCACCI
One of the best delicatessens in a street renowned for its food shops. Other excellent outlets nearby include Fratelli Fabbi (✉ Via della Croce 27), a good all-round *alimentari*, and Fior Fiore (✉ Via della Croce 17–18), known for its pizzas, pastas, and pastries.
✚ fl, D5 ✉ Via della Croce 43 ☎ 679 1228 🕐 Mon–Wed, Fri, Sat 8:30–1:30, 4:30–7:30; Thu 8:30–1:30

VINCENZO TASCIONI
This most famous of Roman neighborhood shops sells fresh pasta in over 30 different varieties, all made on the premises.
✚ C4 ✉ Via Cola di Rienzo 211 ☎ 324 3152 🕐 Mon–Wed, Fri, Sat 8–1:30, 4:30–7:30; Thu 4:30–7:30

STREET MARKETS

CAMPO DE' FIORI

This picturesque, central market is in a pretty square. Fruit and vegetables dominate, but you can also buy fish, flowers and beans, or just watch the streetlife.
🚹 elll, c6 ⊠ Piazza Campo de' Fiori 🕐 Mon–Sat 7AM–1:30PM

MERCATO ANDREA DORIA

A large, local market which serves the neighborhood residents northwest of the Vatican. Stalls sell meat, fish, fruit, and vegetables, but there are a few with shoes and quality clothes.
🚹 B4 ⊠ Via Andrea Doria-Via Tunisi 🕐 Mon–Sat 7AM–1PM

MERCATO DEI FIORI

Not to be confused with Campo de' Fiori, this wholesale flower market in a covered hall is open to the public only on Tuesdays. Prices are extremely reasonable for all manner of cut flowers, potted plants, and exotic Mediterranean blooms.
🚹 B4 ⊠ Via Trionfale 47–9 🕐 Tue 10:30AM–1PM

MERCATO DI PIAZZA VITTORIO

Stallholders in central Rome's biggest and most colorful general market are fighting plans to restore the square to its 19th-century grandeur and move the stalls to nearby Via Giolitti.
🚹 F6 ⊠ Piazza Vittorio Emanuele II 🕐 Mon–Sat 7AM–2PM

MERCATO DELLE STAMPE

Tucked away, about a dozen stalls sell old books, magazines, and prints. Be sure to haggle.
🚹 el, D5 ⊠ Largo della Fontanella di Borghese 🕐 Mon–Sat 9–5:30

MERCATO DI VIA SANNIO

This market in the shadow of San Giovanni in Laterano sells bags, belts, shoes, toys, and cheap clothes. Stalls nearby peddle more interesting bric-a-brac and secondhand clothes.
🚹 F7 ⊠ Via Sannio 🕐 Mon–Fri 10–1:30; Sat 10–6

PIAZZA COPPELLE

This tiny, attractive local food market is an oasis among the cars and tourists. Close to the Pantheon.
🚹 ell, D5 ⊠ Piazza Coppelle 🕐 Mon–Sat 7AM–1PM

PIAZZA SAN COSIMATO

Few visitors find this mid-sized general neighborhood food market in Trastevere.
🚹 C7 ⊠ Piazza San Cosimato 🕐 Mon–Sat 7AM–1PM

PORTA PORTESE

Everything and anything is for sale in this famous flea market, though the few genuine antiques are highly priced. By mid-morning the crowds are huge, so come early and guard your belongings.
🚹 C7 ⊠ Via Porta Portese-Via Ippolito Nuevo 🕐 Sun 6:30AM–2PM

Supermarkets

At the other extreme to Rome's sprawling markets are its handful of supermarkets and department stores, both types of shop that are still rather alien to most Italians. The best department store is La Rinascente, which has a central branch at Via del Corso 189, and another in Piazza Fiume. Coin is also good, though a little less stylish, and is located close to San Giovanni in Laterano at Piazzale Appio 15. The larger Standa and Upim chains are more down-scale, and offer reasonably priced clothes and general household goods: Upim has branches at Via del Tritone 172, Via Nazionale 211 and Piazza Santa Maria Maggiore; Standa's Rome branches are at Viale Trastevere 62–4, Via Appia Nuova 181–183, and Via Cola di Rienzo 173.

BOOKS & STATIONERY

Foreign newspapers

If you need to keep in touch with what is happening at home, foreign newspapers can be bought at many newsstands (*edicole*) around the city. European editions of the *International Herald Tribune*, *Financial Times,* and the *Guardian* usually hit the stands first thing in the morning with the Italian papers. Other foreign editions arrive at around 2:30PM on the day of issue, except for Sunday editions, which are not usually available until Monday morning. The best-stocked stands, which also include a wide range of foreign magazines and periodicals, are found in Piazza Colonna on Via del Corso, at Termini train station, and at the southern end of the Via Vittorio Veneto.

ECONOMY BOOK AND VIDEO CENTER
A long-established fixture of expat life, this is the largest English-language bookstore in Italy. New and secondhand titles are available. Prices are high.
🔲 hII, E5 ✉ Via Torino 136 ☎ 474 6877 🕐 Mon–Fri 9:30–7:30; Sat 9:30–1:30

FELTRINELLI
An Italy-wide chain, with well-designed shops and shelves displaying a broad range of Italian titles, and usually a reasonable choice of French-, German-, and English-language books.
🔲 eIII, C6 ✉ Largo di Torre Argentina 5a ☎ 6880 3248. 🔲 D4 ✉ Via del Babuino 39–40 ☎ 679 7058. 🔲 hI, E5 ✉ Via Vittorio Emanuele II Orlando 84–6 ☎ 484 430 🕐 Mon–Sat 9–8; Sun 10–1:30, 4–7:30

IL SIGILLO
Close by the Pantheon, this little shop specializes in fine pens, hand-printed stationery and a wide variety of objects covered in marbled paper.
🔲 eII, D5 ✉ Via della Guglia 69 ☎ 678 9667 🕐 Mon–Fri 9:30–8; Sat 9:30–1, 4:30–8

MONDADORI
This showcase shop for one of Italy's largest publishing houses sells books, maps, and music, plus videos, posters, and greetings cards.
🔲 C4 ✉ Piazza Cola di Rienzo 81–3 ☎ 321 0323 🕐 Mon–Sat 9:30–7:30

PINEIDER
Rome's most expensive and exclusive stationers. Virtually any design can be printed onto personalized visiting or business cards.
🔲 gI, D5 ✉ Via dei Due Macelli 68 ☎ 678 9013. 🔲 fI, D5 ✉ Via della Fontanella Borghese 22 ☎ 687 8369 🕐 Tue–Sat 10–1:30, 3–7:30; Mon 3–7:30

POGGI
Vivid pigments, exquisite papers, and the softest brushes have been on sale at Poggi's since 1825.
🔲 fIII, D6 ✉ Via del Gesù 74–5 ☎ 678 4477. 🔲 fIII, D5 ✉ Via Piè di Marmo 40–1 ☎ 6830 8014 🕐 Mon–Fri 9–1, 4–7:30; Sat 9–1

RIZZOLI
Italy's largest bookstore now appears a little dated alongside some of its newer rivals, but you should be able to find virtually any book in Italian in print (and a selection in English).
🔲 fII, D5 ✉ Galleria Colonna, Largo Chigi 15 ☎ 679 6641 🕐 Mon–Sat 9–7:30; Sun 10–1:30, 4–8

VERTECCHI
The best source of stationery, napkins, wrapping paper, and all manner of boxes, obelisks, and books covered in beautiful Florentine marbled paper.
🔲 fI, D5 ✉ Via della Croce 70 ☎ 678 3110. 🔲 C4 ✉ Via dei Gracchi 179 ☎ 321 3559 🕐 Tue–Sat 9–7:30; Mon 3:30–7:30

CHINA, GLASS, & FABRIC

BISES

A breathtaking range of fabrics is housed in an elegant 17th-century palazzo in Via del Gesù. At No. 63 you can find silks and other high-fashion fabrics (wools and velvets), while at No. 91 materials more suited to home furnishing are stocked.

✚ fIII, D6 ✉ Via del Gesù 63 ☎ 678 9156. ✚ fIII, D6 ✉ Via del Gesù 91 ☎ 678 0941 ⏰ Tue–Sat 9:30–1, 3:30–7:30; Mon 3:30–7:30

CESARI

Cesari sells a wide range of outstanding linen and lingerie, but is better known for its fabrics, especially furnishing materials. The shop's setting is almost as beautiful as the products on sale.

✚ D4 ✉ Via del Babuino 16 ☎ 361 1441 ⏰ Tue–Sat 9:30–1, 3:30–7:30; Mon 3:30–7:30

CROFF CENTRO CASA

Almost a design supermarket, Croff stocks many examples of furniture, linen, and household and kitchen equipment.

✚ el, D5 ✉ Via Tomacelli 137 ☎ 6830 0022 ⏰ Tue–Sat 9:30–1:30, 3:30–7:30; Mon 3:30–7:30

GINORI

One of the top Italian names in modern and traditional glass and chinaware.

✚ C4 ✉ Via Cola di Rienzo 223 ☎ 324 3132. ✚ gl, D5 ✉ Via del Tritone 177 ☎ 679 3836 ⏰ Tue–Sat 9:30–1:30, 3:30–7:30; Mon 3:30–7:30

MAGAZZINI FORMA E MEMORIA

This high-tech showcase for the Forma e Memoria design team ranges over four floors of a converted printing works, with fine views from the top and a small bar and restaurant in the basement.

✚ cII, B5 ✉ Vicolo Sant'Onofrio 24 ☎ 6880 1088. ✚ C4 ✉ Passeggiata di Ripetta 19 ☎ 321 4768 ⏰ Tue–Sat 9:30–1:30, 3:30–7:30; Mon 3:30–7:30

MYRICAE

Bold, bright, and slightly unconventional ceramics (including regional specialties), glassware and folk art are the hallmarks of this popular, reasonably priced shop.

✚ fl, D5 ✉ Via Frattina 36 ☎ 679 5335 ⏰ Tue–Sat 9:30–1, 3:30–7:30; Mon 3:30–7:30

SPAZIO SETTE

The goods spread over three floors of the splendid Palazzo Lazzaroni comprise superbly designed objects ranging from candles to clocks and corkscrews.

✚ elII, C6 ✉ Via dei Barbieri 7 ☎ 6880 4261 ⏰ Tue–Sat 9:30–1, 3:30–7:30; Mon 3:30–7:30

STILVETRO

Italian glass and china, much of it from Tuscany, make this long-established shop a great source for authentic and inexpensive gifts.

✚ fl, D5 ✉ Via Frattina 56 ☎ 679 0258 ⏰ Tue–Sat 9:30–2, 2:30–7:30; Mon 3:30–7:30

Gifts with a twist

For a souvenir with a difference, visit the extraordinary shops on Via dei Cestari, just south of the Pantheon, which specialize in all sorts of religious clothes, candles, and vestments. Other religious souvenirs can be found in shops on Via di Porta Angelica near the Vatican. Alternatively, visit the Farmacia Santa Maria della Scala (✉ Piazza Santa Maria della Scala), an 18th-century monastic pharmacy that sells herbal remedies. For interesting toys try Città del Sole (✉ Via della Scrofa 65). For the best in old prints and engravings (at a price) investigate the 100-year-old Casali (✉ Piazza della Rotonda 81a) or the renowned Nardecchia (✉ Piazza Navona 25).

WOMEN'S FASHION

Sales and bargaining

Sales (*saldi*) in Rome are not always the bargains they can be in other major cities. This said, many shoe stores and top designers cut their prices drastically during the summer and winter sales (mid-July–mid-September and January–mid-March). Other lures to get you into a shop, notably the offer of *sconti* (discounts) and *vendite promozionali* (promotional offers), rarely save you any money in practice. While bargaining has all but died out, it can still occasionally be worth asking for a discount (*uno sconto*), particularly if you are paying cash (as opposed to using a credit card) for an expensvie item, or if you are buying several items from one shop.

FENDI
From recent beginnings, the Fendi sisters have built a powerful fashion, perfume, and accessories empire. Clothes are classic, sleek, and stylish.
fl, D5 ✉ Via Borgognona 36a–39 ☎ 679 7641 ⏰ Mon–Sat 10–2, 3–7:30

GIANFRANCO FERRÈ
One of Italy's top designers. His Rome outlet is known for its outlandish steel and black mosaic décor.
fl, D5 ✉ Via Borgognona 42c ☎ 679 0050 ⏰ Tue–Sat 9:30–1:30, 3:30–7:30; Mon 3:30–7:30

GIANNI VERSACE
Flashier and trashier than Ferrè or Armani, Versace's bright, bold color combinations need panache (and cash) to carry them off. His cheaper diffusion range, Versus, has an outlet at Via Borgognona 33–4.
fl, D5 ✉ Via Bocca di Leone 26 ☎ 678 0521 ⏰ Tue–Sat 10–7:30; Mon 3:30–7:30

GIORGIO ARMANI
King of cut and classic, understated elegance. His slightly cheaper range is at Emporio Armani (➤ 77).
fl, D5 ✉ Via Condotti 77 ☎ 699 1460 ⏰ Mon 3:30–7:30; Tue–Sat 10–7

KRIZIA
Flies less high in the international PR and fashion firmament than the likes of Armani and Versace, but boasts a high profile in Italy, especially for knitwear.

fl, D5 ✉ Piazza di Spagna 77b ☎ 679 3419 ⏰ Tue–Sat 10–7; Mon 3:30–7

LAURA BIAGIOTTI
Easy to wear, easy on the eye and less aggressively "high fashion" than the other outlets in Via Borgognona.
fl, D5 ✉ Via Borgognona 43–44 ☎ 679 1205 ⏰ Tue–Sat 10–1:30, 3:30–7:30; Mon 3:30–7:30

MAX MARA
A popular mid-range label known for reliable suits, separates, knitwear, and bags and other accessories at fair prices.
fl, D5 ✉ Via Condotti 46 ☎ 678 7946. fl, D5 ✉ Via Frattina 28 ☎ 679 3638 ⏰ Tue–Sat 10–2, 3:30–7:30; Mon 3:30–7:30

TRUSSARDI
Flagship store for another of the top names in Italian fashion.
fl, D5 ✉ Via Condotti 49 ☎ 679 2151 ⏰ Tue–Sat 10–7:30; Mon 3:30–7:30

VALENTINO
This famous designer has been dressing celebrities and the rich since the *dolce vita* days of 1959. For more affordable ready-to-wear creations visit Via Condotti and Via Bocca di Leone. The still cheaper "Oliver" diffusion range is on sale at Via del Babuino 61.
fl, D5 ✉ Piazza Mignanelli 22 ☎ 67 391. fl, D5 ✉ Via Bocca di Leone 15 ☎ 679 5862. fl, D5 ✉ Via Condotti 12 ☎ 6783 3656 ⏰ Tue–Sat 10–2, 3:30–7:30; Mon 10–2

MEN'S TAILORS & CLOTHES

BABILONIA

Famed for its garish and —by Rome standards— daring window displays, Babilonia is a favorite among young Italians looking for street-fashion essentials.

🔲 fl, D5 ✉ Via del Corso 185 ☎ 678 6641 🕐 Mon–Sat 9–8

BATTISTONI

This famous and traditional top tailoring shop has been making made-to-measure and ready-to-wear suits and shirts for over half a century.

🔲 fl, D5 ✉ Via Condotti 57 and 61a ☎ 678 6241 🕐 Tue–Sat 9:30–1:30, 3:30–7:30; Mon 3:30–7:30

CUCCI

Those members of the Roman gentry who do not shop at Battistoni probably patronize Cucci, another old-world tailor of ready-to-wear and made-to-measure clothes.

🔲 fl, D5 ✉ Via Condotti 67 ☎ 679 1882 🕐 Tue–Sat 9:30–1:30, 3:30–7:30; Mon 3:30–7:30

DAVIDE CENCI

The English (or Scottish) "country gentleman's" look—tweeds, brogues, and muted classics—is hugely popular among older Italian men. This shop, established in 1926, caters to the taste with its own versions of the look and of originals like Burberry and Aquascutum.

🔲 ell, D5 ✉ Via Campo Marzio 1–7 ☎ 699 0681 🕐 Tue–Sat 9–1, 3:30–7:30; Mon 3:30–7:30

EMPORIO ARMANI

The "cheaper" way to buy Armani.

🔲 D4 ✉ Via del Babuino 140 ☎ 678 8454 🕐 Mon–Sat 10–7

ENZO CECI

Ready-to-wear clothes with a high-fashion bias.

🔲 fl, D5 ✉ Via della Vite 52 ☎ 679 8882 🕐 Tue–Sat 9:30–1:30, 3:30–7:30; Mon 3:30–7:30

POLIDORI UOMO

Beautifully tailored and restrained tweeds and worsted in the manner of Davide Cenci (see above): ready to wear or made to measure.

🔲 fl, D5 ✉ Via Borgognona 4a ☎ 6994 1171 🕐 Tue–Sat 9:30–1:30, 3:30–7:30; Mon 3:30–7:30

TESTA

Exquisite suits cut to appeal to a younger set.

🔲 fl, D5 ✉ Via Borgognona 13 ☎ 679 6174. 🔲 fl, D5 ✉ Via Frattina 104 ☎ 679 1296 🕐 Tue–Sat 9:30–1:30, 3:30–7:30; Mon 3:30–7:30

VALENTINO UOMO

Sober and conservative clothes in the finest materials from Rome's leading tailor.

🔲 fl, D5 ✉ Via Condotti 12 ☎ 6783 3656. Oliver: 🔲 D4 ✉ Via del Babuino 61 ☎ 3600 1906 🕐 Tue–Sat 10–2, 3:30–7:30; Mon 3:30–7:30

VERSACE UOMO

Bold, sexy clothes for lounge lizards, and real or aspirant rock and film stars.

🔲 fl, D5 ✉ Via Borgognona 33–4 ☎ 678 3977 🕐 Tue–Sat 10–7:30; Mon 3:30–7:30

Top people's tailor

While the young turn to the mainstream Milanese designers like Armani, Rome's older and more traditional élite still choose Battistoni for their sartorial needs. Giorgio Battistoni started out almost half a century ago as a shirtmaker, but quickly graduated to the role of top-class tailor, dressing the city's older aristocracy and the more conservative hedonists of the late 1950s *dolce vita*. Clothes with the Battistoni label are still as prestigious as they were in the past, and just as costly—a custom-made shirt starts at around L300,000.

BARS BY NIGHT

What to drink

The cheapest way to drink beer in Italy is from the keg (*alla spina*). Measures are *piccola*, *media*, and *grande* (usually 33cl, 50cl, and a liter respectively). Foreign canned or bottled beers (*in lattina* or *in bottiglia*) are expensive. Italian brands like Peroni are a little cheaper: a Peroncino (25cl bottle) is a good thirst-quencher. Aperitifs (*aperitivi*) include popular non-alcoholic drinks like Aperol, Crodino, and San Pellegrino bitter. A glass of red or white wine is *un bicchiere di vino rosso/bianco*.

BAR DELLA PACE
(➤ 68)

BEVITORIA
Friendlier and more intimate than most large or touristy bars on Piazza Navona. Primarily a wine bar (the cellar is part of Domitian's former stadium). Becomes busy, so arrive early.
🚇 eII, C5 ✉ Piazza Navona 72 ☎ 6880 1022 🕐 Mon–Sat 2PM–1AM 🚌 46, 62, 64 to Corso Vittorio Emanuele II, or 70, 81, 87, 90 to Corso del Rinascimento

CAVOUR 313
At the Forum end of Via Cavour, this easily missed wine bar has a relaxed, student feel. Good snacks from the bar, and wine by the glass or bottle, at tables to the rear. A good alternative to tourist bars nearby.
🚇 gIII, E6 ✉ Via Cavour 313 ☎ 678 5496 🕐 Mon–Sat 10–3:30, 7:30–11:30 🚌 11, 27, 81 to Via Cavour, or 85, 87, 186 to Via dei Fori Imperiali

DRUID'S DEN
Friendly and authentic Irish pub that appeals to Romans and expats alike. Also try The Fiddler's Elbow, a popular sister pub around the corner at Via dell'Olmata 43.
🚇 E6 ✉ Via San Martino ai Monti 28 ☎ 4890 4781 🕐 Tue–Sun 8PM–midnight 🚌 Cavour 🚌 11 to Via G. Lanzi, or 27, 81 to Via Cavour, or 4, 9, 14, 16 to Piazza Santa Maria Maggiore

HEMINGWAY
Although rather languid and decadent, this atmospheric and highly priced bar has for years been the favored watering hole of the city's gilded youth.
🚇 eII, D5 ✉ Piazza Coppelle 10 ☎ 686 4490 🕐 Daily 9PM–12:30AM 🚌 70, 81, 87, 90 to Corso del Rinascimento

IL PICCOLO
This intimate and pretty little wine bar close to Piazza Navona is ideal for a romantic interlude.
🚇 dII, C5 ✉ Via del Governo Vecchio 74–5 ☎ 6880 1746 🕐 Mon–Fri 11AM–2AM; Sat, Sun 7PM–2AM 🚌 46, 62, 64 to Corso Vittorio Emanuele II

LA VINERIA REGGIO
There is no better place in Rome to see the more rough-and-ready side of night-time drinking. Fusty and old-fashioned inside, with characters to match; tables on the city's most evocative square.
🚇 eIII, C6 ✉ Campo de' Fiori 15 ☎ 6880 3268 🕐 Mon–Sat 10AM–4PM, 6PM–2AM 🚌 46, 62, 64 to Corso Vittorio Emanuele II, or 70, 81, 87, 90 to Corso del Rinascimento

TRASTÈ (➤ 68)

TRIMANI
A wine bar recently added to the city's oldest wine shop (founded 1821 and still in the same family). Away from the key nightlife areas, but well placed if you find yourself near Stazione Termini.
🚇 E5 ✉ Via Cernaia 37b ☎ 446 9661 🕐 Mon–Sat 11:30–3, 5:30–midnight 🚌 60, 61, 62 to Via Cernaia, or services to Termini and Piazza della Repubblica

CLUBS & DISCOS

ALIEN
An *Alien*-inspired refit and up-to-the-minute music policy has turned this futuristic club into one of Rome's nightspots of the moment.
➕ E4 ✉ Via Velletri 13 ☎ 841 2212 🕐 Tue–Sun 11PM–4AM 🚌 20N, 21N to Piazza Fiume 💰 Very expensive

BLACK OUT
Regaining the reputation it won over a decade ago as one of the best of the more alternative discos. Music is mainly punk, thrash, Gothic—"dark" in Roman parlance.
➕ F7/8 ✉ Via Saturnia 18 ☎ 7049 6791 🕐 Thu–Sat 10PM–4AM; Sun 4:30–7:30PM 🚇 Re di Roma 🚌 55N and 4, 87, 673 to Piazza Tuscolo 💰 Moderate

GILDA
If you like the Hemingway (▶ 78) then you will also like Gilda, whose louche atmosphere has been attracting stars, VIPs and wanna-bes for years. There is a bar, two stylish restaurants, and a glittering dance floor.
➕ f1, D5 ✉ Via Mario de' Fiori 97 ☎ 678 4838 🕐 Tue–Sun 11PM–4AM 🚌 52, 53, 58, 61, 71, 85, 160 to Piazza San Silvestro 💰 Expensive

L'ALIBI
Primarily, but not exclusively, a gay disco, L'Alibi is one of the most reliable (and also longest-established) of the clubs now mushrooming in the newly trendy Testaccio district.
➕ D8 ✉ Via Monte Testaccio 44–57 ☎ 574 3448 🕐 Tue–Sun 11PM–4AM 🚇 Piramide 🚌 11, 13, 23, 27, 30, 57, 718 to Piazza di Porta San Paolo 💰 Winter: free (depending on evening). Summer: moderate

LE STELLE
Another chic disco that has been running longer than most. Convenient to downtown, just northwest of Piazza del Popolo. Le Stelle is renowned for staying open until dawn.
➕ C4 ✉ Via Cesare Beccaria 22 ☎ 361 1240 🕐 Tue–Thu, Sun 10:30PM–3AM; Fri, Sat 10:30PM–dawn 🚇 Flaminio 🚌 119 to Piazza del Popolo, or 81, 90, 926 to Ponte Regina Margherita 💰 Very expensive

PIPER
Rome's clubs and discos fade in and out of fashion from one season to the next. Piper, which has been open since the 1960s, is among the more consistently popular, thanks partly to its program of constant updating and refurbishment.
➕ F3 ✉ Via Tagliamento 9 ☎ 855 5398 or 855 8046 🕐 Wed–Sat 10PM–5AM; Sun 3:30–7PM, 10PM–5AM 🚌 6N, 56, 57, 319 to Via Tagliamento 💰 Very expensive

RADIO LONDRA
Currently among the trendiest club-cum-discos in the city. Small and invariably full to bursting.
➕ D8 ✉ Via Monte Testaccio 67 🕐 Wed–Mon 10:30PM–5AM 🚌 13, 23, 27, 57, 95, 716 to Via Marmorata 💰 Free

Membership and admission

Many Roman clubs and discos are run as private clubs (Associazioni Culturali), usually to circumvent planning or licensing laws. In practice this generally only means you have to buy a "membership card" (*una tessera*) in addition to the usual admission fee. The latter are high for the stylish places—mainly because Romans drink modestly and so clubs make little on their bar takings (admission usually includes a free first drink).

OPERA & CLASSICAL MUSIC

Church music

Following a decree from Pope John Paul II, all concert programs in Roman churches currently have a marked religious bias. Music can range from small-scale organ recitals to full-blown choirs and orchestras. Be on the lookout for posters advertising concerts outside churches and around the city. The Coro della Cappella Giulia sings at 10:30AM and 5PM on Sundays in St. Peter's. You can hear Gregorian chant every Sunday at 11AM in Sant'Apollinare, while Sant'Ignazio di Loyola is one of the churches that regularly hosts choral concerts.

ACCADEMIA BAROCCA

Although one of the city's smaller musical associations, this Accademia's recitals reflect Rome's affinities with the baroque. Recitals, most of which are held in the Palazzo della Cancelleria on Piazza Farnese, or in the church of San Paolo entro le Mura in Via Nazionale, are not held on fixed days, so look out for flyers with details and dates of performances.

➕ elII, C5 ✉ Palazzo della Cancelleria ☎ 6641 1152.
➕ hII, C6 ✉ San Paolo entro le Mura

ACCADEMIA FILARMONICA ROMANA

Founded in 1821, the Accademia Filarmonica Romana numbered Rossini, Verdi and Donizetti among its distinguished early luminaries. Though it does not support its own choir or orchestra, it presents high-quality recitals of contemporary, choral, and symphonic music by top-name national and international performers. Concerts are held at either the Sala Casella (details as below) or the nearby Teatro Olimpico (➤ 81).

➕ C2 ✉ Via Flaminia 118
☎ 320 1752 🕓 Concerts: mid-Oct–mid-May Thu, occasionally Tue. Box office: daily 9AM–1PM, 6–7PM. Information: daily 3–7PM
🚌 225, 910 to Piazza Antonio Mancini

ACCADEMIA NAZIONALE DI SANTA CECILIA

In existence since the 16th century, Rome's main classical music body stages concerts by its own orchestra and choir, and organizes recitals and concerts by visiting choirs and orchestras. Most events are held at the Auditorio Pio, also known as the Auditorio di Santa Cecilia (➤ 81). Outdoor recitals and ballet performances are held in July at the Villa Giulia (➤ 35).

➕ fI, D4 ✉ Via Vittoria 6
☎ 678 0742. Villa Giulia:
☎ 678 6428; 678 0742/3/4/5 for information

ASSOCIAZIONE GIOVANILE MUSICA (AGIMUS)

Agimus is a well-respected and predominantly choral body that also organizes piano and other recitals. Concert performances are usually held in the Sala Accademica (see below for details) or the Aula del Pontificio Istituto di Musica Sacra (➤ 81).

➕ D5 ✉ Sala Accademica, Via dei Greci 18 ☎ 678 9258
🕓 Concerts: mid-Oct–mid-Jun
🚌 119 to Via del Corso-Via Condotti

AUDITORIO DEL FORO ITALICO

Rome's premier state-owned auditorium is part of the Mussolini-era sports city in the northwest. It is home to the orchestra of RAI, the national radio and television company.

🔲 B2 ⊠ Piazzale Lauro De Bossis ☎ 3686 5625 🎔 Concerts: Nov–Jun Fri 6:30PM. Oct Fri 6:30PM; Sat 9PM. Box office: Thu–Sat 10–1, 4–7 🚋 32, 186, 280, 291, 391 to Lungotevere Maresciallo Cadorna

AUDITORIO PIO (AUDITORIO DI SANTA CECILIA)

🔲 cII, B5 ⊠ Via della Conciliazione 4 ☎ 6880 1044 🎔 Concerts: Oct–Jun Thu–Tue 8:30 🚋 64 to Piazza San Pietro, or 23, 34, 41, 46, 62, 65, 98, 280, 881 to Ponte Vittorio Emanuele II

AULA DEL PONTIFICIO ISTITUTO DI MUSICA SACRA

🔲 eII, C5 ⊠ Piazza Sant'Agostino 20a ☎ 678 9258 🚋 119 to Piazza Cinque Lune, or 70, 81, 87, 90, 186, 492 to Corso del Rinascimento

AULA MAGNA DELL'UNIVERSITÀ LA SAPIENZA

🔲 G5 ⊠ Piazzale Aldo Moro ☎ 361 0052 🎔 Concerts: Oct–May Tue 8:30PM; Sat 5:30PM 🚋 9, 310 to Viale dell'Università

IL GONFALONE

The Gonfalone is a small but prestigious company that hosts chamber music and other small-scale recitals at its own Oratorio.

🔲 dIII, C6 ⊠ Oratorio del Gonfalone, Via del Gonfalone 32a. Information: Vicolo della Scimmia 1b ☎ 4770 4664 or 687 5952 🎔 Concerts: Oct–Jun Thu 9PM. Box office: Mon–Fri 9AM–1PM; day of concert 9AM–9PM 🚋 46, 62, 64 to Corso Vittorio Emanuele II, or 23, 41, 65, 280 to Lungotevere di Sangallo

ISTITUTO UNIVERSITARIO DEI CONCERTI (IUC)

The IUC's student bias ensures exciting and eclectic music. Concert cycles are currently devoted to the music and composers of a different country each year. Most recitals are held in the university's Aula Magna just east of Stazione Termini.

🔲 B2 ⊠ Lungotevere Flaminio 50 ☎ 361 0051/2 🎔 Box office: Mon–Fri 10AM–1PM, 3–6PM; Sat 10AM–1PM 🚋 225, 910 to Piazza Mancini

TEATRO DELL'OPERA

Rome's opera house is enduring lean times. Crippled by mismanagement and dwindling finances, the reputation of its orchestra and choir and the quality and range of performances has diminished. Austerity has forced a concentration on the mainstream repertoire. Between mid-June and mid-August operas are staged outdoors at the Piazza di Siena in the Villa Borghese.

🔲 hIII, E5 ⊠ Box office: Via Firenze 72 ☎ 481 601 🎔 Opera: Dec–May, mid-Jun–mid-Aug. Recitals: Nov–Jun 🚇 Termini 🚋 57, 64, 65, 70, 71, 75, 170 to Via Nazionale, or services to Termini

TEATRO OLIMPICO

🔲 C2 ⊠ Piazza Gentile da Fabriano ☎ 323 4890 🚋 225, 910 to Piazza Mancini

Music outdoors

Alfresco recitals often take place in the cloisters of Santa Maria della Pace in July (part of the "Serenate in Chiostro" season); in the Villa Doria Pamphili in July (as part of the the "Festival Villa Pamphili"); in the grounds of the Villa Giulia in the summer (as part of the "Stagione Estivi dell'Orchestra dell'Accademia di Santa Cecilia"); and in the Area Archeologica del Teatro di Marcello from July to September (as part of the "Estate al Tempietto," also known as the "Concerti del Tempietto").

LIVE MUSIC SPOTS

Listings and tickets

For details of upcoming events, consult the free *Trovaroma* listings supplement published with the Thursday edition of *La Repubblica*. Otherwise, see the daily listings of *Il Messaggero*. Tickets for events can bought at the door, from the fashion shop Babilonia (➤ 77), or from the following ticket agencies:

Orbis: ✉ Piazza Esquilino 37 ☎ 482 7403 🕐 Mon–Fri 9:30–1, 4–7:30.

Box Office: ✉ Via Giulio Cesare 88 ☎ 372 0215 or 372 0216. ✉ Via del Corso 506 ☎ 361 2682 🕐 Mon 3:30–7; Tue–Sat 10–7.

Note that credit cards are not accepted at either agency. As with clubs and discos (see panel ➤ 79), you may need to buy an annual membership card (*una tessara*) on top of a ticket. Virtually all clubs close between late July and early September.

ALEXANDERPLATZ

A restaurant and cocktail bar north of St. Peter's with live jazz.

✚ B4 ✉ Via Ostia 9 ☎ 372 9398 🕐 Sep–Jun Mon–Sat 9PM–1:30AM 🚇 Ottaviano 🚌 29N, 30N, 99N, and 23, 70, 291, 490, 913, 991, 994, 999 to Largo Trionfale-Viale delle Milizie 🎫 Four-month membership (expensive); free to tourists on production of passport

BIG MAMA

Rome's best blues club, though Big Mama also hosts rock and jazz gigs.

✚ C4 ✉ Vicolo San Francesco a Ripa 18 ☎ 581 2551 🕐 Oct–Jun daily 9PM–1:30AM 🚌 13, 44, 75, 170, 181, 280, 717 to Viale di Trastevere 🎫 One-year membership (very expensive) plus entry fee for some concerts

CAFFÈ LATINO

Longest established of the Testaccio clubs, devoted to eating, drinking and live music. Mostly jazz, though rap, blues and other genres are represented; discos follow bands.

✚ D8 ✉ Via Monte Testaccio 96 ☎ 574 4020 🕐 Sep–Jul Tue–Thu, Sun 10:30PM– 2:30AM; Fri, Sat 10:30PM–4:30AM 🚇 Piramide 🚌 13, 23, 27, 57, 95 to Via Marmorata 🎫 Annual membership (expensive)

FOLKSTUDIO

This laid-back folk and blues venue opened in the 1960s. Presents top Italian and international names.

✚ hIII, E6 ✉ Via Frangipane 42 ☎ 487 1063 🕐 Mid-Sep–early Jun daily 9:30PM–12 🚌 N20, N21 and 11, 27, 81, 85, 87, 186 to Via dei Fori Imperiali 🚇 Colosseo

🎫 One-year membership fee (moderate) plus entry (expensive)

FONCLEA

An established mixture of bar, restaurant and club (north of St. Peter's) devoted mainly to jazz.

✚ B/C5 ✉ Via Crescenzio 82a ☎ 689 6302 🕐 Mon–Thu, Sun 8PM–2AM; Fri, Sat 9PM–3AM 🚇 Ottaviano 🚌 29N, 30N and 23, 34, 49, 492, 990 to Via Crescenzio 🎫 Free until 9PM, then entry (expensive)

MELVYN'S

A glorified bar in the heart of Trastevere that plays host mainly to local rock and R&B bands.

✚ dIV, C6 ✉ Via del Politeama 8 ☎ 580 3077 🕐 Mon, Thu–Sun 9PM–2AM ; Tue, Wed 10PM–2AM 🚌 20N, 30N and 23, 717, 774, 780 to Ponte Garibaldi-Lungotevere Sanzio 🎫 Entry by open membership (expensive)

ST. LOUIS MUSIC CITY

Popular modern jazz and fusion club in an underground dive between Via Cavour and Colosseum.

✚ hIV, E6 ✉ Via del Cardello 13a ☎ 474 5076 🕐 Mon–Sat 8:30PM–2AM 🚇 Colosseo or Cavour 🚌 20N, 21N and 11, 27, 81, 85, 87, 186 to Via Cavour-Via dei Fori Imperiali 🎫 Three-month membership (expensive)

YES BRAZIL

Tiny, lively, and busy Brazilian bar. Authentic drinks, Portuguese-speaking staff, and three hours of live music nightly from 10:30PM.

✚ C5 ✉ Via San Francesco a Ripa 103 ☎ 581 6267 🕐 Mon–Sat 6PM–2AM 🚌 13, 44, 75, 170, 181, 280, 717 to Viale di Trastevere 🎫 Free

SPORTS

ACQUA ACETOSA
Heavily oversubscribed public sports facilities also used for rugby games and swimming tournaments.
🏠 E1 ✉ Via dei Campi Sportivi 48 ☎ 36 851 🕐 Daily 9AM–7:30PM 🚇 Acqua Acetosa or Campi Sportivi 🚌 4, 391

ALDROVANDI PALACE (SWIMMING)
Public swimming pools in Rome are either some way from the center or not terribly pleasant. Your best option is to use a hotel pool; many open to nonresidents on payment of a daily tariff.
🏠 E3 ✉ Via Aldrovandi 15, Pariali (north of Zoo and Villa Borghese) ☎ 322 4288 🕐 Jun–Sep daily 10–6 🚌 19, 30 to Via Aldrovandi

FORO ITALICO (TENNIS, ATHLETICS)
One of the world's finest sports complexes when built in the 1930s, the Foro Italico is today best known for the Italian open tennis tournament held each May.
🏠 B2 ✉ Lungotevere Maresciallo Diaz-Viale dei Gladiatori 31 ☎ 36851 🚌 32, 186, 280, 291, 391 to Lungotevere Maresciallo Cadorna

IPPODROMO DELLE CAPANNELLE (HORSE RACING)
Flat racing, steeple-chasing, and trotting can all be seen at Rome's main race course.
✉ Via Appia Nuova 1255 ☎ 718 3143 🕐 Races: Sep–Jun Mon, Wed, Fri, Sun 1:30–7:30PM 🚌 650, 671 to Via Appia Nuova

PALAZZO DELLO SPORT
Part of the EUR complex built for the 1960 Olympics, this stadium is now used for a range of indoor sports, most notably basketball (games are played on Sunday at 5:30PM).
🏠 C13 ✉ Via dell'Umanesimo ☎ 592 5006 or 592 6809 🚇 EUR Palasport

PALAZZETTO DELLO SPORT
Another stadium built for the 1960 Olympic Games. Hosts spectator sports such as boxing, fencing, tennis, and wrestling.
🏠 C2 ✉ Piazza Apollodoro-Via Flaminia 🕐 Daily 7AM–8PM 🚇 Flaminio 🚌 225, 910 to Piazza Apolladoro

STADIO OLIMPICO (SOCCER)
Rome's two big soccer teams, AS Roma and Lazio, play their home games here on alternate Sundays.
🏠 B1 ✉ Viale dei Gladiatori ☎ 3685 7520. Ticket office: 323 7333. Information: (AS Roma) 506 0200; (Lazio) 3685 7566 or 323 7465 🕐 Ticket office: daily 9–1:30, 2:30–6 🚌 32, 186, 280, 291, 391 to Lungotevere Maresciallo Cadorna

TRE FONTANE
Part of the extensive EUR sports facilities. Hosts different indoor spectator sports on most days of the week.
🏠 C13 ✉ Via delle Tre Fontane 🕐 Tue–Sun 7:30AM–8PM; Mon 4–8PM 🚇 Magliana 🚌 671, 707, 714, 717, 764, 771, 791 to Via delle Tre Fontane

Local rivalry
Rivalry between Rome's two *Serie A* (first division) soccer teams is intense. Lazio, a traditional underachiever, is currently doing as well as AS Roma, once among Italy's soccer élite (its last championship, or *scudetto*, was in 1982–1983). AS Roma is known as the *i giallorossi* (after the team's red and yellow uniform), while the blue-and-white-shirted Lazio players sport the nickname *i biancocelesti*. AS Roma's symbol is the Roman wolf-cub, while Lazio's is an eagle (both often seen among the city's graffiti).

LUXURY HOTELS

A double room in one of Rome's most luxurious hotels costs about L300,000 (although a few may cost considerably more).

Booking

Rome's peak season runs from Easter to October, but the city's hotels (in all categories) are almost invariably busy. Telephone, write, or fax well in advance to book a room (most receptionists speak some English, French, or German). Leave a credit card number or send an international money order for the first night's stay to be certain of the booking. Reconfirm bookings a few days before your trip. If you arrive without a reservation, get to a hotel early in the morning; by afternoon most of the vacated rooms will have been snapped up. Don't accept rooms from touts at Stazione Termini.

ALBERGO DEL SOLE AL PANTHEON

A hotel since 1467; chic and the location opposite the Pantheon—if you can stand the crowds—is one of Rome's best.
✚ ell, D5 ✉ Piazza della Rotonda 63 ☎ 678 0441 🚌 119 to Piazza della Rotonda, or 70, 81, 87, 90 to Corso del Rinascimento

AMBASCIATORI PALACE

One of the more venerable and stately of the Via Veneto's large luxury hotels, with a traditional feel and opulent appearance.
✚ gl, E5 ✉ Via Vittorio Veneto 62 ☎ 47 493 🚇 Barberini 🚌 52, 53, 56, 58, 95 to Via Vittorio Veneto

EXCELSIOR

One of the largest and grandest of Rome's luxury hotels. Everything here is on an enormous scale, from the vast silk rugs to the palatial bedrooms.
✚ gl, E5 ✉ Via Vittorio Veneto 125 ☎ 4708 🚇 Barberini 🚌 52, 53, 56, 58, 95 to Via Vittorio Veneto

HASSLER-VILLA MEDICI

Magnificently situated and famous hotel just above the Spanish Steps, long the haunt of VIPs and the jet-set.
✚ fl, D5 ✉ Piazza Trinità dei Monti 6 ☎ 678 2651 🚇 Spagna 🚌 119 to Piazza di Spagna

HOLIDAY INN CROWNE PLAZA MINERVA ROME

A new and well-designed five-star chain hotel in the shadow of the Pantheon and Santa Maria sopra Minerva.
✚ flll, D5 ✉ Piazza della Minerva 69 ☎ 6994 1888 🚌 119 to Piazza della Rotonda, 70, 81, 87, 90 to Corso del Rinascimento

INGHILTERRA

Founded in 1850, and host to such guests as Liszt and Hemingway, this clublike hotel is near the best shopping streets.
✚ flll, D5 ✉ Via Bocca di Leone 14 ☎ 69981 🚇 Spagna 🚌 119 to Piazza di Spagna, or 52, 53, 58, 61, 71, 85, 160 to Piazza San Silvestro

LE GRAND HOTEL

Not in the most salubrious location, but an immensely opulent hotel that is often rated the most luxurious in the city.
✚ hl, E5 ✉ Via Vittorio Emanuele Orlando 3 ☎ 474709 🚇 Repubblica 🚌 57, 64, 65, 75, 170, 492, 910 to Piazza della Repubblica

LORD BYRON

A small, extremely chic and refined five-star hotel away from the center in leafy Parioli. Particularly noted for its excellent restaurant.
✚ D3 ✉ Via G. de Notaris 5 ☎ 361 3041 🚇 Flaminio 🚌 52, 926 to Via Buozzi

RAPHAEL

An intimate, charming, ivy-covered hotel hidden away and yet close to Piazza Navona. Rooms are perhaps a little small, but renovations mean furniture and fittings are immaculate. Book ahead.
✚ ell, C5 ✉ Largo Febo 2 ☎ 683 8881 or 682 831 🚌 70, 81, 87, 90 to Corso del Rinascimento

MID-PRICE HOTELS

CAMPO DE' FIORI
Good value, close to Campo de' Fiori. Rooms are small but pretty, and there is a roof garden.

🏠 elII, C6 ✉ Via del Biscione 6 ☎ 6880 6865 🚌 46, 62, 64 to Corso Vittorio Emanuele II

CESARI
A thoroughly reliable, friendly and no-frills hotel with a loyal clientele. Perfectly located for the area midway between the Corso and the Pantheon.

🏠 fII, D5 ✉ Via di Pietra 89a ☎ 679 2386 🚌 56, 60, 62, 85, 90, 160 to Via del Corso

COLUMBUS
A converted monastery just a minute's walk away from St. Peter's. A favorite with visiting cardinals.

🏠 elII, B5 ✉ Via della Conciliazione 33 ☎ 686 5435 🚌 23, 24 to Via della Conciliazione or 64 to Piazza San Pietro

DUE TORRI
Hidden in a tiny alley between Piazza Navona and the Tiber. Rooms are all adequate, but vary from the stylish to the plain.

🏠 elI, C5 ✉ Vicolo del Leonetto 23–5 ☎ 6880 6956 🚌 70, 81, 87, 90, 186 to Corso del Rinascimento or Lungotevere Marzio

HOTEL PORTOGHESI
Well-known if slightly fading hotel with roof terrace. Situated in a cobbled street just north of Sant'Agostino and Piazza Navona.

🏠 elI, C5 ✉ Via dei Portoghesi 1 ☎ 686 4231 🚌 70, 81, 87, 90 to Corso del Rinascimento

LA RESIDENZA
A good choice: near the Via Vittorio Veneto and reasonably priced. Stylish public spaces, rooms spacious and comfy. Terrace and roof garden.

🏠 E4 ✉ Via Emilia 22–4 ☎ 488 0789 🚇 Barberini 🚌 52, 53, 56, 58, 95 to Via Vittorio Veneto

LOCARNO
In a quietish side street close to Piazza del Popolo. Much genuine 1920s art nouveau décor.

🏠 C4 ✉ Via della Penna 22 ☎ 361 0841 🚇 Flaminio 🚌 90, 119, 926 to Via di Ripetta, or 81 to Lungotevere in Augusta

MARGUTTA
Quaint hotel near Piazza del Popolo. Public areas a little spartan, but the redecorated rooms are bright and comfortable.

🏠 D4 ✉ Via Laurina 34 ☎ 679 8440 🚇 Spagna 🚌 119 to Piazza di Spagna

SCALINATA DI SPAGNA
An old-fashioned pension loved by generations of romantics, this tiny hotel is located at the top of the Spanish Steps.

🏠 D4 ✉ Piazza Trinita dei Monti 17 ☎ 679 3006 🚇 Spagna 🚌 119 to Piazza di Spagna

SISTINA
Small, reliable, and efficient hotel close to the Piazza di Spagna. Lovely terrace for drinks and summer breakfasts.

🏠 gI, D5 ✉ Via Sistina 136 ☎ 4890 0316 🚇 Spagna or Barberini 🚌 119 to Piazza di Spagna, or 52, 53, 56, 58, 60, 61, 62 to Piazza Barberini

Expect to pay L125,000–300,000 per night for a double room in a mid-price hotel.

Prices
Italy's hotels are classified into five categories from one star (basic) to five stars (luxury). The prices each can charge are set by law and must be displayed in the room (usually on the door). Prices within a hotel, however, can vary for different rooms (and some hotels have low- and high-season rates). Therefore if a room is too expensive, do not be afraid to inquire whether there is anything cheaper. Look out for extras like air-conditioning or obligatory breakfasts. Single rooms cost about two-thirds the price of doubles, and to have an extra bed in a room adds 35 percent to the bill.

BUDGET ACCOMMODATIONS

Budget accommodations can cost anything up to L125,000 per night for a double room.

Noise

Noise is a fact of life in almost any Roman hotel (in whatever price category). Surveys have shown Rome to be the noisiest city in Europe. You will never escape the cacophony entirely (unless the hotel is air-conditioned and double-glazed), but to lessen the potential racket you should avoid main thoroughfares and the area around Termini in favor of hotels near parks or in more obscure back streets. Also try asking for rooms away from the front of the hotel or facing on to a central courtyard (cortile).

ABRUZZI

Twenty-five large, basic rooms (and eight shared bathrooms), some with a view of the Pantheon (noisy); rooms at the rear are quieter.
⊞ ell, D5 ⊠ Piazza della Rotonda 69 ☎ 679 2021 🚌 119 to Piazza della Rotonda, or 44, 46, 75, 87, 94, 170 to Largo di Torre Argentina

FIORELLA

Eight bright, airy, and spotless rooms (two shared bathrooms) in a part of town with few budget-priced hotels. 1AM curfew.
⊞ D4 ⊠ Via del Babuino 196 ☎ 361 0597 🚇 Spagna 🚌 119 to Piazza di Spagna

KATTY

The Katty is less grim than most of the countless cheap hotels in the unsavory area near Rome's main train station, and its 11 rooms are always well booked.
⊞ F5 ⊠ Via Palestro 5 ☎ 444 1216 🚇 Termini 🚌 27, 64, 65, 170 and all other services to Termini

NAVONA

Simple rooms, friendly owners, and a superb central location (just west of Piazza Sant'Eustacchio) mean it is essential to book well in advance to secure one of the 26 rooms.
⊞ elll, C5 ⊠ Via dei Sediari 8 ☎ 686 4203 🚌 70, 81, 87, 90, 186, 492 to Corso del Rinascimento

PERUGIA

Little-known hotel, quiet and well located, between Via Cavour and the Colosseum. All eight doubles have private bathrooms.
⊞ hIV, E6 ⊠ Via del Colosseo 7 ☎ 679 7200 🚌 11, 27, 81 to Via Cavour, or 85, 87, 186 to the Colosseum

PICCOLO

Another fine little hotel close to Campo de' Fiori. Only half of the 16 rooms have private bathrooms.
⊞ C6 ⊠ Via dei Chiavari 32 ☎ 6880 2560 or 689 2330 🚌 46, 62, 64 to Corso Vittorio Emanuele II, or 44, 56, 60, 65, 75, 170 to Via Arenula

POMEZIA

The 22 rooms are small (11 have private bathrooms), but the location is central and close to Campo de' Fiori. Roof terrace and small bar.
⊞ elll, C6 ⊠ Via dei Chiavari 12 ☎ 686 1371 🚌 46, 62, 64 to Corso Vittorio Emanuele II, or 44, 56, 60, 65, 75, 170 to Via Arenula

SMERALDO

Plain, clean, and straightforward hotel located in a back street a couple of minutes' walk from the central Campo de' Fiori.
⊞ elll, C6 ⊠ Vicolo dei Chiodaroli 11 ☎ 687 5929 🚌 46, 62, 64 to Corso Vittorio Emanuele II, or 44, 56, 60, 65, 75, 170 to Via Arenula

SOLE

A popular budget choice, on the edge of Campo de' Fiori. There are 62 rooms, but booking is essential. Small garden terrace.
⊞ elll, C6 ⊠ Via del Biscione 76 ☎ 6880 6873 or 6880 5258 🚌 46, 62, 64 to Corso Vittorio Emanuele II, or 44, 56, 60, 65, 75, 170 to Via Arenula

ROME
travel facts

ARRIVING & DEPARTING

Before you go
- All visitors to Italy require a valid passport.
- Visas are not required for US, Canadian, UK, Irish, Australian, or New Zealand citizens, or for other EU nationals staying under three months.
- Vaccinations are not required unless you are coming from a known infected area.

When to go
- April to early June and mid-September to October are the best periods.
- July and August are uncomfortably hot, and many restaurants and businesses close for a month's holiday in August.
- Holy Week (Easter) is especially busy.
- January and February are the quietest months.

Climate
- Winters are short and cold.
- Spring begins in March, but April and May can be muggy and rainy.
- Summers are hot and dry, though sudden thunderstorms are common.
- Weather in autumn is mixed, but can produce days of crisp temperatures and clear skies.

Arriving by air
- Scheduled flights arrive at Leonardo da Vinci airport, better known as Fiumicino.
- Fiumicino information: ☎ 65 951, 6595 3640 or 6595 3088. Alitalia information: ☎ 65 601, 46 881 or 65 643.
- Shuttle trains link Fiumicino to Stazione Termini in the city center. Information: ☎ 4775.
- Taxis are slow and expensive.

Take only licensed (yellow) cabs or a pre-paid "car with driver" available from the SOCAT desk in the International Arrivals hall.
- Charter flights use Ciampino, a military airport south of Rome. Information: ☎ 794 941.
- From Ciampino go by COTRAL bus to Anagnina or Subaugusta, and then by Metro line A to Stazione Termini.

Arriving by train
- Most trains arrive and depart from Stazione Termini, which is well placed for most of central Rome.
- Taxis and buses leave from the station forecourt, Piazza dei Cinquecento.

Customs regulations
- EU nationals do not have to declare goods imported for their personal use.
- Limits for non-EU visitors are: 400 cigarettes or 200 small cigars or 500g of tobacco; 1 liter of spirits (over 22 percent alcohol) or 2 liters of fortified wine (over 22 percent alcohol); 50g of perfume.

ESSENTIAL FACTS

Travel insurance
- It is vital to take out full health and travel insurance before traveling to Italy.

Tourist information
- Ente Provinciale per il Turismo di Roma ✉ Via Parigi 11 ☎ 488 991 🕐 Mon–Sat 8:15AM–7:15PM.

Opening hours
- Stores: Tue–Sat 8AM–1PM, 4–8PM; Mon 4–8PM (with slight seasonal variations). Food shops open on Monday mornings but usually close on Thursday afternoons.

- Restaurants: daily 12:30–3PM, 7:30–10:30PM. Many close on Sunday evenings and Monday lunchtimes. Bars and restaurants also have a statutory closing day (*riposo settimanale*) and many close for much of August.
- Churches: daily 7AM–noon, 4:30–7PM.
- Museums and galleries: vary considerably; usually close on Monday (see individual entries).
- Banks: Mon–Fri 8:30AM–1:30PM. Major branches may also open 3–4PM.
- Post offices: Mon–Fri 8:15AM–2PM; Sat 8:15AM–noon. The main post office in Piazza San Silvestro opens Mon–Fri 8AM–9PM; Sat 8AM–noon.

Public holidays

- January 1; January 6; Easter Monday; April 25; May 1; June 29; August 15 ; November 1; December 8; December 25; December 26.

Money matters

- The Italian currency is the lira, abbreviated to "L."
- Notes: L1,000, L2,000, L5,000, L10,000, L50,000, and L100,000.
- Coins: L5 and L10 (both rare), L50, L100, L200, and L500, plus a L200 telephone token (*gettone*) which can be used as a coin.
- Most major traveler's checks can be changed at banks, though lines can be long.
- Credit cards (*carte di credito*) are slowly gaining in popularity, but cash is preferred.

Women travelers

- Women can expect some (rarely threatening) hassle from Italian men.
- At night avoid the parks and the area around Termini.

Time differences

- Italy is six hours ahead of New York and nine hours ahead of Los Angeles.

Electricity

- Current is 220 volts AC, 50 cycles; plugs are the two-round-pin type.

Etiquette

- Do not wear shorts, short skirts, or skimpy tops in churches.
- Avoid entering churches while services are in progress.
- Many churches and galleries forbid flash photography, or ban photography altogether.
- Smoking is common in bars and restaurants, but is banned on public transport.
- Public drunkenness is rare and frowned upon.

PUBLIC TRANSPORTATION

Buses and trams

- Rome's orange buses and trams, run by ATAC, have cheap and frequent services.
- Blue regional and suburban buses are run by COTRAL.
- Buses are often crowded and the city's traffic-clogged streets can make travel slow.
- Information: ⊞ F5 ✉ ATAC Information, Piazza dei Cinquecento ☎ 4695 4444 ⊙ Daily 7:30AM–7PM ⊙ Termini. Tickets and information can also be found at Piazza del Risorgimento (⊞ bI, B5), Piazza San Silvestro (⊞ fII, D5), and at automatic machines dotted around the city.
- Tickets must be bought before boarding the bus and can be obtained from automatic machines, shops and newsstands displaying an ATAC sticker, and tobacconists

(indicated by signs showing a white "T" on a blue background).

- Tickets must be stamped at the rear of each bus or tram. They are valid for any number of bus rides and one Metro ride within a 75-minute time period. Remember to enter buses by back doors, and to leave by center doors (if you have a pass or validated ticket with unexpired time you can also use the front doors).
- Buy several tickets at once as some outlets close early.
- There are L50,000 fines if you are caught without a ticket.
- Daytime services: buses run 5:30AM–11:30PM, depending on the route. Bus stops (*fermate*) list numbers and routes of the buses that serve them. Note that one-way systems mean buses often have slightly different return routes.
- Night buses: 30 night buses (*servizio notturno*) run on key routes from about midnight to 5:30AM. Unlike day buses they have a conductor who sells tickets.
- Useful services:
  23 Piazza del Risorgimento (for the Vatican Museums)–Trastevere–Piramide.
  27 Termini–Roman Forum–Colosseum–Piramide.
  46 Piazza Venezia–Vatican.
  56, **60** and **75** Piazza Venezia–Trastevere.
  64 Stazione Termini–Piazza Venezia–Corso Vittorio Emanuele II–St. Peter's.
  81 Piazza del Risorgimento (Vatican Museums)–Via Nazionale–Roman Forum–Colosseum–San Giovanni in Laterano.
  119 Circular minibus service in the historic center: Piazza Augusto Imperatore–Piazza della Rotonda (Pantheon)–Via del Corso–Piazza di Spagna.

Metro

- Rome's subway system (*la Metropolitana*, or *Metro*) has just two lines—named A and B—which intersect at Stazione Termini. Primarily a commuter service, it is of only limited use in the city center. It is good, however, for quick trans-city rides.
- Stations at Colosseo, Spagna, Barberini, Repubblica, Termini, and San Giovanni are convenient to major sights.
- Station entrances are marked by a large, red M, and each has a map of the network.
- Tickets are valid for one ride and can be bought from tobacconists (*tabacchi*), bars, and shops displaying ATAC or COTRAL stickers, and—if they are working—from machines at stations (exact money only). Day passes are also available.
- Services: Line A daily 5:30AM–11:30PM. Line B Mon–Fri 5:30AM–9:30PM; Sat and Sun 5:30AM–11:30PM.

Passes

- An integrated ticket, the *Biglietto Integrato* (BIG) is available from the sources listed above and is valid for a day's unlimited travel on ATAC buses, the Metro, COTRAL buses and the suburban FS rail network (except Fiumicino airport).
- Weekly passes (*Carta Integrata Settimanale*) are valid for a week on buses and Metro only.

Taxis

- Licensed taxis: official Rome taxis are yellow (and occasionally white), with a "Taxi" sign on the roof. Use only these and refuse offers from touts at Fiumicino, Termini, and elsewhere.

- Calling a cab: the cab firm will give you a taxi code name, a number and the time it will take to get to you. The meter starts running as soon as they are called. Firms include Cosmos Radio Taxis (☎ 88 177), Autoradio Taxi (☎ 3570), and Capitale Radio (☎ 4994).
- When hailing a cab make sure the meter is set at zero. The minimum fare is valid for 3km or the first 9 minutes of a ride. Surcharges are levied between 10PM and 7AM, all day Sunday, on public holidays, for airport trips, and for each piece of luggage in the trunk.
- Drivers are not supposed to stop on the streets (though some do), and it is therefore difficult to hail a passing cab. Taxis congregate at stands, indicated by blue signs with *Taxi* written on them in white. Stands can be found downtown at Termini, Piazza Venezia, Largo Argentina, Piazza S. Sonnino, Pantheon, Piazza di Spagna, and Piazza San Silvestro.

MEDIA & COMMUNICATIONS

Telephones

- Public telephones are indicated by a red or yellow sign showing a telephone dial and receiver. They are found on the street, in bars and restaurants, and in special offices (*Centri Telefoni*) equipped with banks of phones and (occasionally) staff.
- A few *Centri Telefoni* have phones that allow you to speak first and pay later, but most phones at booths require prepayment.
- Phones accept L100, L200, and L500 coins, L200 tokens known as *gettoni*, and—increasingly—

phone cards, or *schede telefoniche* (available from post offices, tobacconists, and some bars in L5,000 and L10,000 denominations). Remember to break off the card's small marked corner before use.
- Cheap rate for calls is Mon–Sat 10PM–8AM and all day Sunday.

Postal service

- Stamps (*francobolli*) can be bought from post offices and most tobacconists.
- Post boxes are red and have two slots, one for Rome (marked *Per La Città*) and one for other destinations (*Per Tutte Le Altre Destinazioni*).
- The Vatican postal service is quicker (though tariffs are the same), but stamps can be bought only at the post offices in the Vatican Museums (◉ Mon–Fri 8:30AM–7PM) and in Piazza San Pietro (☎ 6982 ◉ Mon–Fri 8:30AM–7PM; Sat 8:30AM–6PM). Vatican mail can only be posted in the Vatican's blue *Poste Vaticane* mail boxes.
- Most post offices (*Posta* or *Ufficio Postale*) open Mon–Fri 8:15AM–2:30PM; Sat and the last day of each month 8:15AM–noon. The main post office, the *Ufficio Postale Centrale*, is located at Piazza San Silvestro 18–20 (☎ 6771) and opens Mon–Fri 8:30AM–7:40PM; Sat 8:30AM–noon.

Newspapers and magazines

- Most Romans read the Rome-based *Il Messaggero*, the mainstream and authoritative *Corriere della Sera*, or the center-left and popularist *La Repubblica* (it has a special Rome edition). Sports papers and news magazines (like *Panorama* and *L'Espresso)* are also popular.

- Foreign newspapers can usually be bought after about 2:30PM on the day of issue from booths (*edicole*) in and near Termini, Piazza Colonna, Largo di Torre Argentina, Piazza Navona, Via Vittoria Veneto, and close to several other tourist sights. European editions of the *International Herald Tribune* and *Financial Times* are also available.

Radio and television

- Italian television is divided between the three channels of the state network RAI, the three private channels founded by Silvio Berlusconi (Canale 5, Rete 4, and Italia 1), and a host of smaller commercial stations.
- RAI also runs a public radio service, although the airwaves are dominated by dozens of smaller (mainly FM) stations.

EMERGENCIES

Safety

- Carry all valuables in a belt or pouch—never in a pocket.
- Hold bags across your front, never over one shoulder, where they can be grabbed or rifled.
- Wear your camera—never put it down on a café table.
- Leave valuables and jewelry (especially chains and earrings) in the hotel safe.
- Beware the persistent small gangs of street children. If approached, hang on to everything, raise your voice and—if necessary—push them away.
- Never leave luggage or other possessions in parked cars.
- Beware pickpockets, especially in buses (the 64 bus to St. Peter's is notorious), crowded tourist areas and busy shopping streets.

- Avoid parks and the back streets around Termini late at night.

Lost property

- To make an insurance claim on lost or stolen property report the loss to a police station, which will issue you a signed declaration (*una denuncia*) for your insurance company. The central police station is the Questura ✉ Via San Vitale 15 (off Via Nazionale) ☎ 4686 Ⓜ Repubblica.
- Main lost property offices: ATAC (bus or tram network): ✉ Via Nicola Bettoni 1 ☎ 581 6040 Ⓒ Daily 9AM–noon. Metro Line A: ✉ Furio Camillo Metro Station ☎ 5753 3620 Ⓒ Mon, Tue, Fri 9AM–noon. COTRAL (suburban buses): inquire at the origin (*capolinea*) of individual routes or ☎ 57 531 or 591 5551. Trains: ✉ Stazione Termini, Via Giovanni Giolitti 24 (near Platform 22) ☎ 4730 6682 Ⓒ Mon–Fri 7AM–10PM.

Medical and dental treatment

- For urgent medical treatment go to the casualty department (*Pronto Soccorso*) of the Ospedale Fatebenefratelli ✉ Isola Tiberina ☎ 58 731; or Policlinico Umberto I ✉ Viale Policlinico ☎ 446 2341.
- The American-run George Eastman Clinic provides a 24-hour emergency dentist service: ✉ Viale Regina Elena 287 ☎ 445 4851. 24-hour line: 491 949. No credit cards.
- Pharmacies are indicated by a large green cross. Opening times are usually Mon–Sat 8:30AM–1PM, 4–8PM, but a rotating schedule (displayed on pharmacy doors) ensures at least one pharmacy is open 24 hours a day, seven days a week. The most central

English-speaking pharmacist is
Internazionale ✉ Piazza Barberini
49 ☎ 482 5456.

Key telephone numbers

- Police, Fire and Ambulance
  (General SOS) ☎ 113
- Ambulance (Red Cross) ☎ 5510
- Police (Carabinieri) ☎ 112
- Central Police Station ☎ 4686
- ACI Auto Assistance (car
  breakdowns) ☎ 116
- US Embassy ☎ 46741
- Samaritans ☎ 7045 4444
- Operator ☎ 12
- International Operator (Europe)
  ☎ 15
- International Operator (rest of
  the world) ☎ 170

LANGUAGE

- Italians respond well to foreigners
  who make an effort to speak their
  language (however badly). Many
  Italians speak some English, and
  most upscale hotels and restaurants have multilingual staff.
- All Italian words are pronounced as
  written, with each vowel and
  consonant sounded. The letter c is
  hard, as in English "cat" except
  when followed by i or e, when it
  becomes the soft ch of "children."
  The same applies to g: soft (as in
  the English "giant") when
  followed by i or e—*giardino*; otherwise hard (as in "gate")—*gatto*.
  Words ending in o are almost
  always masculine in gender
  (plural— i); those ending in a are
  feminine (plural—e).
- Use the polite second person (*lei*)
  to speak to strangers, and the
  informal second person (*tu*) to
  friends or children.

Courtesies

good morning	buon giorno
good afternoon/ good evening	buona sera
good night	buona notte
hello/goodbye (informal)	ciao
hello (answering the telephone)	pronto
goodbye	arrivederci
please	per favore
thank you (very much)	grazie (mille)
you're welcome	prego
how are you? (polite/informal)	come sta/stai?
I'm fine	sto bene
I'm sorry	mi dispiace
excuse me/ I beg your pardon	mi scusi
excuse me (in a crowd)	permesso

Basic vocabulary

yes/no	sí/no
I do not understand	non ho capito
left/right	sinistra/destra
entrance/exit	entrata/uscita
open/closed	aperto/chiuso
good/bad	buono/cattivo
big/small	grande/piccolo
with/without	con/senza
more/less	più/meno
near/far	vicino/lontano
hot/cold	caldo/freddo
early/late	presto/ritardo
here/there	qui/là
now/later	adesso/più tardi
today/tomorrow	oggi/domani
yesterday	ieri
how much is it?	quant'è?
when?/do you have?	quando?/avete?

Emergencies

help!	aiuto!
where is the nearest telephone?	dov'è il telefono più vicino
there has been an accident.	c'è stato un incidente.
call the police.	chiamate la polizia.
call a doctor/ an ambulance.	chiamate un medico/ un'ambulanza.
first aid	pronto soccorso
where is the nearest hospital?	dov'è l'ospedale più vicino?

INDEX

Citypack
Rome

While every care has been taken to ensure the accuracy of the information in this guide, time brings change, and consequently the publisher cannot accept responsibility for errors that may occur. Prudent travelers will therefore want to call ahead to verify prices and other "perishable" information.

Published in the United States by Fodor's Travel Publications, Inc.
Published in the United Kingdom by AA Publishing

Fodor's is a registered trademark of Fodor's Travel Publications, Inc.

ISBN 0–679–00004–6
Second Edition

FODOR'S CITYPACK ROME

           AUTHOR *Tim Jepson*
           CARTOGRAPHY *The Automobile Association*
                            RV Reise- und Verkehrsverlag
           COVER DESIGN *Tigist Getachew, Fabrizio La Rocca*
           COPY EDITOR *Moira Johnston*
           VERIFIER *Kerry Fisher*
           INDEXER *Marie Lorimer*
           SECOND EDITION UPDATED BY *OutHouse Publishing Services*

Acknowledgments

The Automobile Association would like to thank the following photographers, libraries and associations for their assistance in the preparation of this book: © NIPPON TELEVISION NETWORK CORPORATION TOYKO 1991 1; SPECTRUM COLOUR LIBRARY 33b. The remaining pictures are held in the Association's own library (AA PHOTO LIBRARY) with contributions from: M ADLEMAN 87a; J HOLMES 5a, 7, 17, 18, 19, 24a, 25, 26, 29a, 29b, 32, 33a, 37a, 38a, 39, 41b, 44, 46a, 46b, 48b, 54, 55, 57, 60; D MITIDIERI 5b, 12, 13a, 16, 23, 28, 31, 34a, 34b, 35, 38b, 43, 45a, 47, 49a, 49b, 50, 53, 58, 59a, 59b; C SAWYER 2, 6, 20, 27a, 27b, 30a, 40, 41a; A SOUTER 13b, 21; P WILSON 9, 24b, 30b, 36, 37b, 42a, 42b, 45b, 48a, 51, 52, 56, 61, 87b.

Special sales

Fodor's Travel Publications are available at special discounts for bulk purchases (100 copies or more) for sales promotions or premiums. Special editions, including personalized covers, excerpts of existing guides, and corporate imprints, can be created in large quantities for special needs. For more information write to Special Marketing, Fodor's Travel Publications, 201 East 50th St., New York NY 10022.

Color separation by Daylight Colour Art Pte Ltd, Singapore
Manufactured by Dai Nippon Printing Co. (Hong Kong) Ltd
10 9 8 7 6 5 4 3 2

Titles in the Citypack series

- Amsterdam • Atlanta • Berlin • Boston • Chicago • Florence • Hong Kong •
- London • Los Angeles • Miami • Montréal • New York • Paris • Prague •
- Rome • San Francisco • Tokyo • Toronto • Venice • Washington, D.C. •